REBOOTED

REBOOTED

AN UNCOMMON GUIDE TO
RADICAL SUCCESS AND
FAIRNESS IN THE NEW WORLD
OF LIFE, DEATH, AND TECH

ARNOBIO MORELIX

NEW DEGREE PRESS

REBOOTED

An Uncommon Guide to Radical Success and Fairness in the New World of Life, Death, and Tech

ISBN   978-1-63676-313-2   *Paperback*

978-1-63676-314-9   *Kindle Ebook*

978-1-63676-315-6   *Ebook*

To family and the Muse.

CONTENTS

———

WELCOME TO THE
GREAT REBOOT

———

Elena and Ryan were stranded at sea.

After spending twenty-five days crossing the Atlantic from the Canary Islands en route to the Caribbean, they were told they could not come on land. Borders were closed. Not just to them but for pretty much all foreigners.

Unknown to Elena and Ryan, a deadly virus was spreading around the world while they were isolated in their sailboat. It was the start of the global COVID-19 pandemic. The couple had heard whispers of a virus spreading in China before, but they figured things would be under control by the time they landed in mid-March 2020.

It was not the arrival they had hoped for after quitting their jobs, buying a boat, and taking to the seas to pursue their dreams a couple of years before.[1]

After finding closed borders in one of the French islands in the Caribbean and still not fully understanding what was happening, they got back to the boat and headed for Grenada. Once they got a strong enough 4G signal, they were able to talk with a friend on the island of Saint Vincent. They learned much of the world was on lockdown because of the novel coronavirus. To make matters worse, Lombardy, Italy—where Elena is originally from and where her family lives—was one of the world's most affected places.

"Ryan and I hadn't realized how it had affected our families until we docked and I managed to call my dad," Elena told the BBC. Speaking at the time, she added, "It's a very macabre picture at home; there are no more coffins, no more cemetery space, or room in the crematorium. My family is thankfully safe at home and have been in lockdown for over six weeks, but people we've known for years have died."[2]

The couple was eventually able to dock in Saint Vincent. Authorities were hesitant to let them in because Elena is an Italian citizen, and Italy was one of the most affected countries at the time. But they proved they had been out at sea

---

1   Elena Manighetti and Ryan Osbourne, "The Route," *Sailing Kittiwake* (blog), accessed June 25, 2020

2   Jessica Sherwood, "'Nobody Told Us about the Coronavirus Pandemic'," *BBC News*, April 21, 2020.

for twenty-five days by showing their GPS data and were allowed to come on dry land. They had been social distancing, after all.

THE POST-PANDEMIC ECONOMY

Over the course of Elena and Ryan's almost month-long excursion, the coronavirus went from being seemingly contained to China to rapidly spreading across the globe, infecting over ninety thousand people and killing more than three thousand.[3] As of this writing, global cases are in the dozens of millions, and deaths from the virus are at more than one million. (I gave up updating precise figures for this in the draft because they change too fast.)

But the pandemic's public health impact is just one of the dimensions affected by the novel coronavirus. COVID-19 has triggered a global economic recession, expected to be the worst the world has seen since the Great Depression of 1929.[4] [5] Even if you are among the lucky ones not catching the virus in your family, the virus's downstream effects have probably affected your business, market, or industry.

Global labor income is estimated to have dropped by $3.5 trillion in the first three quarters of 2020 (10.7 percent decline

---

3   Derrick Bryson Taylor, "A Timeline of the Coronavirus Pandemic," *The New York Times*, February 13, 2020.

4   Szu Ping Chan, "Coronavirus: Worst Economic Crisis since 1930s Depression, IMF Says," *BBC News*, April 9, 2020.

5   Though at this stage, nobody is sure how deep the recession will go until some time has passed.

compared to the previous year), with the largest drop in lower-middle-income countries.[6]

Within the first month of the pandemic in the US (where I live), more than twenty-six million Americans filed for unemployment (especially people working in industries that can be digitized and automated relatively quickly like retail and entertainment). Over one hundred thousand small businesses permanently shut their doors. American GDP dropped steeply by 4.5 percent in the second quarter of 2020.[7] [8] The details across countries vary, but the general story globally is one of significant contraction.

Moreover, inequality in our society has been laid bare. Pre-pandemic, the wealthiest 5 percent of people already owned almost two-thirds of the country's combined wealth, compared to the bottom 90 percent who owned a little over one-fifth of it.[9] If previous pandemics are a guide, inequality will worsen, with the low-income population being the most affected.[10] [11]

6   "COVID-19 Leads to Massive Labour Income Losses Worldwide," *International Labour Organization*, September 23, 2020.

7   Jeffry Bartash, "Jobless Claims Jump Another 4.4 Million—26 Million Americans Have Lost Their Jobs to the Coronavirus," *MarketWatch*, April 23, 2020.

8   Joseph Guzman, "More than 100,000 Small Businesses Have Permanently Closed Due to Coronavirus, Study Estimates," *TheHill*, May 13, 2020.

9   Edward Wolff, "Household Wealth Trends in the United States, 1962 to 2016: Has Middle Class Wealth Recovered?" *NBER Working Paper Series*, No. 24085 (2017).

10   Davide Furceri, Prakash Loungani, Jonathan D. Ostry, and Pietro Pizzuto, "COVID-19 Will Raise Inequality If Past Pandemics Are a Guide," *VOX, CEPR Policy Portal*, May 8, 2020.

11   "How the COVID-19 Pandemic Is Deepening Economic Inequality in the US," *NPR*, August 16, 2020.

We also see flashes of hope: 3D printing created medical equipment that was previously imported and hard to access. Tech companies like Google, Facebook, and Amazon deployed support and grant programs to help small businesses, health care, and frontline workers. We have seen a renewed interest in assisting people in learning technology skills.[12][13][14]

As society scrambles to move much of our lives from analog to digital, there are also some clear winners. Video conferencing apps like Zoom and people management platforms like Lattice thrive as work goes remote, while an interior design marketplace in Brazil booms as people's desire for more beautiful homes grows.[15][16] Similarly, digital pharmacy Alto, tech-enabled healthcare provider Carbon Health, and at-home fitness startup P.volve grew through people's increasing at-home wellness needs. LinkedIn's Top 50 Startups 2020 list was dominated by businesses able to leverage the current pandemic (the industries of enterprise software and health care by themselves comprised nearly half of the top startups on the list).[17]

---

12 Iman Ghosh, "What Is Big Tech Contributing to Help Fight COVID-19?" *Visual Capitalist*, April 14, 2020.

13 Steve Lohr, "Remember the MOOCs? After Near-Death, They're Booming," *The New York Times*, May 26, 2020.

14 Dhawal Shah, "By the Numbers: MOOCs During the Pandemic," *The Report by Class Central*, August 31, 2020.

15 Dain Alex Evans, "How Zoom Became So Popular during Social Distancing," *CNBC*, April 4, 2020.

16 Ingrid Lunden, "Lattice, a People Management Platform, Picks up $45M at a $400M Valuation," *TechCrunch*, July 14, 2020.

17 Jessi Hempel, "LinkedIn Top Startups 2020: The 50 US Companies on the Rise," *LinkedIn*, September 22, 2020.

Just like in every crisis, chaos also creates opportunities. As my friend Dane Stangler writes, over half of the Fortune 500 were founded during recession years, such as Hewlett-Packard (HP) after the Great Depression of 1929 and Uber after the Great Recession of 2007.[18] [19] The COVID-19-triggered crisis will be no different.

The move from analog to digital with all its facets (e.g., automation, remote work, e-commerce) was already brewing pre-crisis long before patient zero got infected. The same is true for the underlying inequalities along racial, educational, and socioeconomic lines. But the economic shutdown combined with social distancing has dramatically accelerated trends previously lurking beneath the surface. Changes many of us expected to unfold over ten years happened in ten weeks.

We rebooted.

A NEW OPERATING SYSTEM

For the first time in one hundred years, the economy literally shut down to start again—not just in one or two countries, but everywhere. However, the systems that come back to life will not be like the ones we knew before. Like a rebooting

---

18 Dane Stangler, "The Economic Future Just Happened," *The Ewing Marion Kauffman Foundation*, June 9, 2009.

19 Matthew Wilson, "14 Successful Companies That Started during US Recessions," *Business Insider*, April 20, 2020.

computer with a new operating system, our society will function in fundamentally different ways.[20]

Every major crisis (like hurricanes) gets a name: the Great Depression, the Great Recession, the Dot-Com Bust. I believe this one will become known as the Great Reboot, as already has begun to be the case. Since I started this project in March 2020 (including a website and publishing about it in my columns with *Inc. Magazine*), the concept has been used widely in places ranging from a Tom Hanks commencement speech to an all-new editorial vertical by Thomson Reuters titled "Great Reboot."[21] [22]

This book is about how you can navigate this Great Reboot and the years post-pandemic in a way that is intentional, deliberate, and proactive, rather than reactive. But before we get to that, it pays off to imagine the kind of situations we as entrepreneurs and tech creators are up against.

***

THE TECH CREATOR'S CONUNDRUM

Imagine yourself waking up to your phone buzzing with alerts. Email, social media, text, phone calls—it feels like everybody is trying to talk with you at the same time. You

---

20 Arnobio Morelix, "The Post-Pandemic Economy: The Great Reboot," *Inc.*, April 28, 2020.

21 "Tom Hanks Delivers Powerful Graduation Speech to Class of 2020: 'You've Been Chosen'," *NBC Bay Area*, May 4, 2020.

22 "Reuters Launches 'The Great Reboot,' a Section Dedicated to the Future of the Workplace," *Thomson Reuters*, September 29, 2020.

soon learn the reason why. After years of hard work on your product (or company), you find out you are on the front page of a major newspaper.

But this is not a dream. It is a nightmare. You are in the headline for all the wrong reasons.

Perhaps the news article does not fully understand how your product works, and you think the coverage is unfair. But that turned out to be beside the point. The damage is already done.

The specifics of the nightmare will depend on the kind of product and company you work on. But it could be, among other things:

- some out-of-left-field group of users is misusing what you created (e.g., to spread hate speech)
- an unknown bug was exploited by malicious actors
- your app was engaging users to a fault, and people are accusing it of being addictive

While the above is a hypothetical scenario, it has happened in some flavor to numerous companies—both big corporates and startups. Consider these examples, for instance:

Twitter taught Microsoft's AI chatbot to be a racist asshole in less than a day[23]

---

23   James Vincent, "Twitter Taught Microsoft's AI Chatbot to Be a Racist Asshole in Less than a Day," *The Verge*, March 24, 2016.

How to avoid a dystopian future of facial recognition in law enforcement[24]

The secretive company that might end privacy as we know it[25]

Digital assistants like Siri and Alexa entrench gender biases, says UN[26]

You do not know exactly what went wrong, but you think back to your experience before this problem hit the fan and realize you had a vague idea something like this was possible:

- You had some worry your product could have serious unintended consequences, but you did not know *what* to do differently or *how*.
- You had some idea of what you wanted to change to build more responsibly, but you could not convince your colleagues—perhaps you were missing the language and tools to talk about this complicated topic.
- Changing course was expensive, and the incentives to change just were not there (or at least you or your colleagues thought so at the time).
- You thought your hazy unease was not warranted since things seemed to be going fine as you built the technology.

24 Ghaffary, Shirin. "How to Avoid a Dystopian Future of Facial Recognition in Law Enforcement," *Vox*, December 10, 2019.

25 Kashmir Hill, "The Secretive Company That Might End Privacy as We Know It," *The New York Times*, January 18, 2020.

26 Kevin Rawlinson, "Digital Assistants like Siri and Alexa Entrench Gender Biases, Says UN," *The Guardian*, May 21, 2019.

You and your team had the best of intentions, but it turned out that was not enough.

***

The nightmare above is a reality for many companies. But in a way, the tech industry is living a dream.

Tech founders often talk about "putting a dent in the universe." Collectively, that has happened. The tech ecosystem has changed the world with many extraordinary gains for society. One example is it provided the basic digital infrastructure that kept life going even in the strictest of lockdowns (through remote working tools, e-commerce, food delivery, etc.). Impressively, this digital infrastructure performed well even while a significant part of other societal infrastructures failed—public health and political systems, for instance.

These positive gains also come with financial rewards. While 2020 saw the worst economic crisis in decades, you would not necessarily know if you only looked at tech companies' performance. Many hit record revenue numbers and have market caps higher than they had pre-crisis, even in the middle of the 2020 lockdowns. Consider the headlines below:

> *Dell beats revenue estimates as remote working lifts workstation demand*[27]

---

27 Neha Malara, "Dell Beats Revenue Estimates as Remote Working Lifts Workstation Demand," *Thomson Reuters*, May 28, 2020.

Adobe stock rises as coronavirus work-from-home shift boosts subscription revenue[28]

UberEats demand soars due to COVID-19 crisis[29]

Hopin raises $40M Series A as its virtual events business accelerates[30]

When it comes to building tech responsibly, there are companies and people are doing exceptionally well and already reaping the rewards from it, pre- and post-crisis:

- Upstart's endeavor to develop fair lending algorithms earned it the praise of the Consumer Financial Protection Bureau, the regulatory watchdog.[31]
- PayPal has earned praise and growth by creating accessible products for small business, from tools to facilitate online sales in a lockdown context to access to capital during the pandemic.
- Companies like Salesforce, Dataiku, and Fiddler gained ground while bringing in boards and executives focused on ethics and humane usage of technology.

---

28 Wallace Witkowski, "Adobe Stock Rises as Coronavirus Work-from-Home Shift Boosts Subscription Revenue," *MarketWatch*, June 11, 2020.

29 Marco Chiappetta, "Uber Eats Demand Soars Due to COVID-19 Crisis," *Forbes Magazine*, March 25, 2020.

30 Alex Wilhelm, "Hopin Raises $40M Series A as Its Virtual Events Business Accelerates," *TechCrunch*, June 25, 2020.

31 Patrice Alexander Ficklin and Paul Watkins, "An Update on Credit Access and the Bureau's First No-Action Letter," *Consumer Financial Protection Bureau*, August 6, 2019.

Tech companies have gone from guys and gals in a garage to the major economic force of the world—a shift accelerated in the Great Reboot. This change carries tremendous opportunity but also increased responsibility and scrutiny.

These tensions between growth and risk set the context for the Tech Creator's Conundrum: **how can we build responsibly in a world where tech is more central to life than ever?** How do we, as a community, pick up the mantle of responsibility that comes with all the new opportunities?

To help address this conundrum, we created this book. But it was a windy journey to get here, with much help along the way.

THE STRANGEST EMAIL

On February 2, 2020, I received the strangest message from a business contact in China.

My colleagues and I had a trip to Beijing scheduled ten days later to discuss a business partnership. But before we left, our hosts sent a two-sentence email saying something to the effect of "do not come to Beijing now due to the coronavirus situation, and we urge you to reconsider your trip to Seoul." South Korea was our stop before China. The dates all blur in our minds today, but on February 2, there were fewer than two hundred reported COVID-19 cases in the world outside of China. The United States, the country with most cases at the time of this writing, had fewer than ten confirmed COVID-19 cases in total versus the millions it has today.[32] [33]

The shifting ground around all of us got me on the path of digging deep into the topic. I started this Great Reboot Project, along with a website and early writing, in March 2020.

Rebooted is the fruit of the collective wisdom of founders, tech executives, academics, investors, policymakers, and technologists from every continent of the world. While writing this book, I have talked with hundreds of leaders worldwide and conducted dozens of in-depth interviews with people currently or formerly at places like Google, Facebook, Amazon, Netflix, Stanford University, Singularity University, unicorn startups, and many others. I am also thrilled to include in this book external contributions from:

- Vint Cerf (father of the internet and chief internet evangelist at Google) and David Nordfors (founder of Innovation4Jobs, together with Vint, and senior data researcher at BOLD)
- Frances West (author of the book *Authentic Inclusion* and former C-suite executive at IBM)
- Krishna Gade (founder and CEO of Fiddler, a human-centered AI startup, formerly at Facebook and Pinterest) and Anusha Sethuraman (head of marketing at Fiddler)
- Cosmin Gheorghe, MD (psychology professor and therapist to tech founders)

---

32 "Ninth Case of Fast-Moving Coronavirus Confirmed in the US," *Thomson Reuters*, February 3, 2020.

33 "Coronavirus: US Passes Six Million Covid-19 Cases," *BBC News*, August 31, 2020.

- JF Gauthier (founder and CEO of Startup Genome, an innovation policy firm, where I served as CIO)
- Martin Cooper (inventor of the mobile phone) and Dane Stangler (senior advisor at the Global Entrepreneurship Network)
- Keyur Desai (Silicon Valley executive, former Managing Director and Chief Data Officer at TD Ameritrade)

Between the nine months from idea and early writing (March) to finishing the book (December), *Rebooted* is the result of an intense quest with weird and wonderful (and terrifying) steps along the way. Gratefully, we have come through more or less unscathed. I imagine your journey has also been wild in 2020, and you might recognize some of the events below from your own life:

- Family and friends contracting and recovering from COVID-19
- Babies at home and daycares closed with both parents working (at least the baby loved having mom and dad home all day every day)
- Bets with family members about lockdown dates (the stakes: baking cookies)[34]

---

34 Honorable mention for the optimism of my wife, who works as a social worker at a school and in mid-March bet schools would "never" close in California until summer 2020. They closed the following week.

- Scrambling to switch focus with our products and team, as well as moving major events from in-person to online[35] [36]
- Wildfires in California turning the sky outside my house a pleasant, post-apocalyptic hue (as a friend said, "I missed it when it was just the pandemic.")
- Professional ups and downs, sometimes even a lucky break[37]

A HANDBOOK FOR THE DECADES AFTER THE PANDEMIC

We might not have been literally drifting on water like Elena and Ryan, but sometimes it feels that way.

What you have in your hands is a guide for sailing in a sea of change at the complex intersection of society, the economy, and technology in a world we do not fully understand.[38] This

---

35 I led the global research and data science team at Startup Genome (where I served as CIO). We and our clients (governments and ecosystem leaders in over thirty-five countries) were glad to have been able to create in just nine weeks an all-new product (tracking COVID-19 impact on innovation ecosystem in real-time); publish six research reports; and articles for *The Next Web* and *The World Economic Forum* (where I am part of the Expert Network).

36 We were fortunate to have a great event, co-hosted by us at Startup Genome with the *Financial Times* and *The Next Web* (the lead organizer). It turned out that removing travel constraints allowed us to reach probably the most global attendance we have had. Speakers included government ministers, tech executives (e.g., from Google and Amazon), founders, city leaders (e.g., deputy mayors of Seoul and London), and executives from Startup Genome, including myself.

37 I was fortunate to have one related to this project. Part III of *Rebooted* builds upon ideas I had already been working on for a while. I gladly incorporated those into the book.

38 As Nassim Taleb has convincingly demonstrated in his *Incerto* series, complexity and connectedness make the world more unpredictable but

book explains the specific ways tech companies and creators can navigate the post-pandemic economy with examples, tools, and actionable insights—for both the opportunities and the risks.

If you are a founder, technology creator, or leader in the technology industry (or are interested in these worlds) and you deeply care about the broader impact of technology on society, this book is for you—no matter if you are in a start-up or a big corporation.

PART I: TWO ECONOMIES

Provides an economic framework for understanding the impact of the pandemic on markets (and your business or job) and how trends will unfold in years to come, including:

- The (surprisingly) simple economics of pandemics and how they will affect you
- The three waves of the Great Reboot, and the shifts that characterize each one of them[39]
- Why we are in for a Roaring 2020s decade
- Ten years in ten weeks: how a global pandemic triggered the fastest recession on record and the most dramatic shift from analog to digital in history
- Why asking if the economic recovery will be V-shaped, L-shaped, or W-shaped is the wrong question

---

not unnavigable.

39 Something I previewed in my columns for *Inc. Magazine*, where I serve as Chief Data Scientist

PART II: CIRCLES OF IMPACT

Discusses the macro context we will all operate in during the coming decades and the Great Reboot impact on the spheres of the home, work, city, and world. Historical events have historical consequences, and this section is about those, including insights surrounding:

- The two I's of loneliness, and how they will be affected by machine-intermediated socialization
- The strangest story of the interaction of social media, elections, and inequality (if you think Russian bots are the worst, you have not heard about what is happening in the developing world)
- What the modern Holy Trinity of Despair is and how it is changing society (with lessons from a Nobel Prize winner)
- The vicious cycle of cities, and why it matters
- What the many people predicting a version of "the end of cities" get wrong
- Why the future of work is probably less remote than you think

PART III: NEW OPERATING SYSTEM TOOLKIT

Explores actionable insights and tools to navigate the post-pandemic world. Covers both the positive and negative unintended consequences of technology so we can build more responsibly. The toolkit includes lessons on:

- Why the creator of the world wide web thinks the internet is broken and what he is doing to fix it

- How the shadow twin of technical debt affects society, and why you should learn about it[40]
- The tech butterfly effect, and why the same things making tech beautiful can also make it ugly
- Understanding the puzzle of why good people create bad technology (and why Silicon Valley, one of the most liberal clusters of people in the US, help make the tools that helped bring about the right-wing presidency of Donald Trump)
- The all-new framework of the Four Quadrants of Unintended Consequences of tech (Flywheel, Hijack, Black Box, and Uncharted Zone)—with actionable tools on how to use it to build tech more responsibly
- The threats of unequal digital access, the six E's of inclusion, and how to build more inclusive companies and products
- Why innovation policy is the new industrial policy, and takeaways for policymakers to act in the new world of life, death, and tech
- The three critical opportunities for traditional companies to adapt to the new economy

∗∗∗

Now that we covered what the book is about, it is also worth mentioning what it is not about:

---

40 A topic I covered in my contribution to the book edited by Bill Franks, *97 Things about Ethics Everyone in Data Science Should Know: Collective Wisdom from the Experts* (Newton, MA: O'Reilly Media, Inc., 2020).

IT IS NOT ABOUT FORECASTING, BUT RATHER FIRST-PRINCIPLES THINKING.

While we make some predictions here, the book's focus is on identifying fundamental changes and first principles, something we find a lot more useful for making decisions than point-in-time forecasts.

IT IS NOT ABOUT BASHING TECHNOLOGY COMPANIES, NOR PUTTING THEM ON A PEDESTAL.

Much criticism to tech companies in popular media and even academia misses crucial points on both context and technical aspects. In a memorable headline, a major newspaper wrote "How YouTube Radicalized Brazil," based on an academic paper.[41] [42] They were referring to the 2018 election of Jair Bolsonaro, a controversial right-wing politician, for the presidency.

While it's plausible, far-right online content and recommendation algorithms played some role, pinning the responsibility of political radicalization on an app overlooks the context.

---

41   When we talk about technology and tech companies in this book, we are primarily using the popular language we see today in Silicon Valley and startup ecosystems. In this definition, "tech" encompasses software, hardware, and life sciences (and within those, other products and services which are primarily electronics or digitally based). The word "technology" itself is borrowed from Ancient Greek (*tékhnē*), and in a way, the story of unintended consequences of technology is as old as Prometheus and Pandora's Box. Nonetheless, the speed and scale of modern "tech" in the Silicon Valley sense set it apart from previous technological revolutions, so we focus on more recent technological developments for case studies (though not exclusively).

42   Which I prefer not to name here—this book is not about bashing the media either.

The main opposing party—which was the party of the previous two Brazilian presidents-elect—had one of those former presidents in jail and the other impeached (with the country being ruled by her VP at the time). Besides, Brazil was going through one of its worst recessions in recent history.

As a Brazilian whose family was contentiously split during the election (something you might relate to if you are in one of the many countries heavily polarized now), it is off-putting to read something that ignores so much of the real issues that preceded polarization.

Similarly, it is not about lionizing founders, technology creators, or tech companies. Instead, it is about taking a hard look at both the good and bad of the double-edged sword of technology. It is easy to forget, but before the so-called "techlash," this lionization was a prevalent trope in the early 2010s.[43] For instance, as late as 2017, you could find passionate arguments proposing Mark Zuckerberg should run for president of the United States, and many people expressed fondness toward the idea.[44] [45] [46] [47] Whether or not that is a good proposal (I am partial to younger leaders

---

43   Colin Tomkins Bergh,"A Reflection of Entrepreneurs in Pop Culture: The Celebritization of Entrepreneurs," *The Ewing Marion Kauffman Foundation*, February 26, 2015.

44   Eric Levitz, "Mark Zuckerberg Should Run for President as Nominee of the 'Innovation Party,' Argues Brilliant Political Journalist," *Intelligencer*, April 26, 2016.

45   Jim VandeHei, "Bring on a Third-Party Candidate," *The Wall Street Journal*, April 25, 2016.

46   Abby Ohlheiser, "Even Mark Zuckerberg Can't Stop the Meme That He Is Running for President," *The Washington Post*, August 3, 2017.

47   Abby Ohlheiser, "A Year Ago, You Probably Thought Mark Zuckerberg Was Running for President," *The Washington Post*, April 10, 2018.

who build things), you will not find newspapers making that case today.

IT IS NOT ABOUT PUBLIC HEALTH NOR THE PANDEMIC ITSELF.
The book is about the long-run consequences of this strange global event and how to navigate them in the decades to come. It is not about the immediate public health disaster. Other people are covering that better. Incidentally, as the world becomes: a) increasingly interdependent, b) more reliant on complex technology that nobody, not even the creators, fully understand (more on this in Chapter 1), and c) more globally connected, we are likely to have even stranger events happening, including future reboots.

A pandemic triggered this particular reboot, and we might well have other pandemics in the future. But with the growing uncertainty around topics ranging from political unrest to economic inequality to climate change, we can expect the world to be growing weirder.

* * *

I cannot promise you this book has everything you need to build tech responsibly and navigate the opportunities and threats of the Great Reboot. The world is too strange for anybody to make that promise. But I can promise if you do not take the time to think intentionally and deliberately about how you act and run your business in this new world, you are at serious risk of trouble.

In this book, we assembled collective wisdom from founders, scientists, experts, makers, and investors from all around the world. Altogether, what you have in your hands is what I think the most comprehensive guide to not only survive but thrive in the economy of the Great Reboot (and future reboots to come).

But before we get into all of that, we need to understand the (surprisingly) simple economics of pandemics. Here we go.

PART I

TWO ECONOMIES

CHAPTER 1

ECONOMICS OF
PANDEMICS

Consider these two economic scenarios:

1. The economy shrinks at a nearly unprecedented rate, comparable to wartime economic contractions, and the unemployment rate is the highest it has been in decades.[48]
2. Companies report record revenues, announce new hirings, and (for those not hitting record performance) smash the expectations of analysts on Wall Street.

As you might imagine, these two scenarios were happening at the same time, exemplified by the two top headlines in my newsfeed in late July 2020:

1. *Economic contracts at record pace*[49]
2. *Big tech smashes expectations*[50]

---

48 "Unemployment Rate," *Current Employment Statistics*, US Bureau of Labor Statistics, accessed September 28, 2020.
49 Cate Chapman, "Economy Contracts at Record Pace," *LinkedIn*, August 1, 2020.
50 Alexandra Scaggs, "Big Tech Smashes Expectations," *LinkedIn*, August 24, 2020.

We do not always realize it, but we are living in two economies. This chapter is about how to understand and navigate them.

BITS AND ATOMS

The two economies we are living in are analog and digital. They work closely together but are ultimately different. While they are obviously interwoven, thinking of them as two economies (even if just as an analogy) helps us understand the shift we are going through in the Great Reboot. Incidentally, this analogy is the same as the online payments giant Stripe uses when it talks, for example, about "increasing the GDP of the internet."[51] In other words, it wants to grow how much economic value the internet produces.

These two economies are moving at different paces; the analog economy is slowing down while the digital economy is accelerating. While we use the digital versus analog terminology here, these economies approximately map to other concepts, listed below:

Analog	Digital
Atoms	Bits
Tangible	Intangible
Hardware	Software

Companies and countries on the right side of the Digital Divide will perform better (directly or indirectly), even across industries that can look the same from a traditional markets point of view. For example:

---

51   Robert Siegel and Ryan Kissick, "Stripe: Increasing the GDP of the Internet," Faculty & Research, *Stanford Graduate School of Business*, 2016.

	Analog	Digital
Fitness[52] [53 54 55]	24-Hour Fitness and Gold's Gym file for bankruptcy	Peloton (the connected bike and online fitness class company) nearly triples its revenue and cannot keep up with demand
Retail[56] [57 58 59]	J.C. Penney, Men's Wearhouse, and Neiman Marcus contract heavily	Despite apparel purchases going down across the board, online clothing retailers Boohoo and StichFix posted growth (Q2 2020 saw a 44.4% increase in online retail sales in the US year-over-year)
Gaming[60] [61 62 63 64]	GameStop plans to close up to 450 stores worldwide	Steam (the online gaming platform) experiences record usage throughout the pandemic with more than twenty million concurrent players

52 Jordan Valinsky, "24 Hour Fitness Files for Bankruptcy and Closes 100 Gyms," *CNN*, June 15, 2020.

53 Peter Martinez, "Gold's Gym Files for Bankruptcy after Blow from Coronavirus Pandemic," *CBS News*, September 2, 2020.

54 Kimberly Chin, "Peloton Posts First-Ever Profit as Pandemic Speeds Sales," *The Wall Street Journal*, September 10, 2020.

55 Jessica Hartogs, "Peloton Can't Keep up with Demand," *LinkedIn*, September 15, 2020.

56 Adam K. Raymond, "Household-Name Companies That Have Filed for Bankruptcy Because of Coronavirus," *Intelligencer*, August 3, 2020.

57 Fareeha Ali, "Ecommerce Trends amid Coronavirus Pandemic in Charts," *Digital Commerce 360*, August 26, 2020.

58 Mary Hanbury, "Fast-Fashion Giant Boohoo Reports Blockbuster Sales Growth during the Lockdown and Acquires Oasis and Warehouse," *Business Insider*, June 17, 2020.

59 Demitri Kalogeropoulos, "Stitch Fix Isn't Nearly Done Growing," *The Motley Fool*, September 27, 2020.

60 Nicolette Accardi, "GameStop to Close up to 450 Stores Worldwide," *NJ.com*, September 16, 2020.

61 Thomas Bardwell, "23 Million Gamers on Global Pandemic Lockdown Shatter Steam Records," *CCN.com*, September 23, 2020.

62 "Steam—Lifetime concurrent players on Steam chart," Steam Database, accessed October 5, 2020.

63 Lakshay Kumar, "Gaming Becomes Top Activity Online During Coronavirus Lockdown," *TheQuint*, March 21, 2020.

64 "Verizon CEO Hans Vestberg: Gaming Traffic Up 75% Since Virus (Video)," *Bloomberg*, March 18, 2020.

Notice even in categories where overall demand dropped (e.g., clothing sales), the companies on the right side of the Digital Divide are doing better.

Traditional Industry Classifications

Thinking about analog and digital classifications makes sense, particularly when considering the limitations of traditional industry classifications governments and researchers typically use to study economic activity. After years of working with governments and academics in over thirty-five countries with Startup Genome and the Kauffman Foundation (including leading a public-private partnership, from the private side, with the US Census Bureau to survey over two hundred thousand entrepreneurs), I realized that typical industry classifications are largely outdated. This is hardly a controversial statement when you consider social media and web content companies (e.g., Google) are typically classified under "information and cultural industries," which includes magazines and TV, and Netflix is classified under "video tape and disc rental," along with cable companies.[65] [66]

While the traditional industry classification systems like NAICS (North American Industry Classification System) codes capture valuable information, they are not well-suited

---

65 "51—Information and cultural industries—Sector," *North American Industry Classification System (NAICS) Canada 2012*, Statistics Canada, March 23, 2018.

66 "Video-on-Demand Research Guide: Industry Classification—NAICS and SIC," LibGuides, last updated September 29, 2020.

for understanding the future of the digital and analog economies.[67]

The examples I present above are pretty clean-cut versions of "mostly analog" versus "mostly digital" companies. In these particular cases, digital companies are relatively young upstarts while analog companies are primarily traditional incumbents.

But that divide is not always so tidy. Consider the following companies (average age: eighty-five years) that experienced over 90 percent growth in their online sales in the second quarter of 2020:[68]

	Year-over-year online sales growth (Q2 2020)	Company age during pandemic[69]
Best Buy	242%	54
Target	195%	118
Dick's Sporting Goods	194%	72
Lowe's	135%	99
Tiffany & Co	123%	183
Home Depot	100%	42
Walmart	97%	58
Gap	95%	51

---

67 *North American Industry Classification System* (Suitland, MD: United States Census Bureau, 2017).

68 Lauren Thomas, "Retailers Are Reporting Record Online Sales during the Pandemic. But It Won't Last Forever," *CNBC*, August 30, 2020.

69 Author's compilation.

Even then, the figures above are for the *digital* component of more traditional companies. How do we make sense of decidedly *analog* businesses like FedEx (no longer working with Amazon) and UPS being among the top twenty performing stocks in the S&P 500 in the first 150 days of the pandemic?[70] [71]

To understand that and future developments in the analog and digital economies, we first need to understand the simple economics of pandemics.

THE (SURPRISINGLY) SIMPLE ECONOMICS OF PANDEMICS

SUBSTITUTES AND COMPLEMENTS

In economic terms, you could describe the Great Reboot simply. The pandemic has made the costs of moving people and goods in the *analog* world skyrocket, both explicitly in monetary terms and implicitly through higher risks and restricted movement. For example, the simple act of getting onto an airplane costs more than pre-pandemic times, as you're taking the chance of getting sick by taking that flight.

When the cost of an input rises, economic analysis suggests two main effects. First, the demand for substitutes for that

---

70 Thomas Black, "FedEx Surges as Ecommerce Demand Sends Profit Climbing," *Bloomberg*, September 16, 2020.

71 Philip van Doorn, "After 150 Days of the COVID-19 Pandemic, Here Are the Best- and Worst-Performing Stocks," *MarketWatch*, August 11, 2020.

input also rises. If you cannot get chicken because it became too expensive, you might substitute it for fish. Second, complements—the goods and services that go together with the substitutes rising in demand—also have their demand grow. For example, you might end up consuming more chips now that you are eating more fish.[72] This straightforward economic framework can also be used for other business problems.

We can use this basic framework for analyzing the shifts happening in the economy—and the ones still to come. During the COVID-19 pandemic, a single category of inputs rose in cost dramatically: the *analog* movement of people and goods. The main substitute for that is the *digital* movement of people and goods. Since you can't hang out with friends like you once did in person, there is more demand to hang out with them in digital spaces such as Zoom video chats. As meeting to sign documents (or even mailing them) becomes a bigger hassle, we use tools like DocuSign to get contracts completed digitally.[73]

This shift from analog to digital is why asking whether the recovery will be V-shaped, W-shaped, L-shaped, or whatever other shape misses the point. What is important is that the *composition* of the economy will be dramatically different

---

72 Arnobio Morelix, "The Post-Pandemic Economy: The Great Reboot," *Inc. com*, April 28, 2020. I previewed some of these insights in an article for *Inc. Magazine*.

73 This economic framework of complements and substitutes can also be used for countless other business problems, as is used by Ajay Agrawal, Joshua Gans, and Avi Goldfarb. "The Simple Economics of Machine Intelligence," *Harvard Business Review*, February 17, 2017.

after the recovery, no matter how you measure it (e.g., products, jobs, stock performance) and regardless of shape.[74]

HOW LONG WILL THE EFFECTS OF THE PANDEMIC LAST?

Recent research from the Federal Reserve Bank of San Francisco suggests that pandemics' aftereffects have lasted for forty years historically, depressing at least one key economic indicator for decades.[75] [76] Major recessions (which mostly happen without pandemics) tend to have an impact for five to ten years.

Even the smallest of these figures, five years, is a long time. Nonetheless, these estimates are: a) historical, and perhaps this pandemic will have a different timeline, and b) expected to vary by sector (different industries will be affected differently) and by companies within sectors (better management leads to better performance, even for companies in the same business and geography). In addition, our policy responses can make the years post-pandemic better or worse—whether the aftereffects last five, ten, or forty years.

---

74 I have previously published an article about this in *The World Economic Forum*, together with Srikar Reddy (CEO of Bangalore-based Sonata Software). Srikar Reddy and Arnobio Morelix, "Companies Now Face an Urgent Choice: Go Digital, or Go Bust," World Economic Forum, October 19, 2020.

75 Rate of return on assets—which we can roughly think of as the investment returns the economy is producing on average.

76 Òscar Jordà, Sanjay Singh, and Alan Taylor, "Longer-Run Economic Consequences of Pandemics," *Federal Reserve Bank of San Francisco Working Paper* (September 2020).

In other words, while the figures sound depressing, they are not destiny. We can take action to navigate them.

HOW TO NAVIGATE UNFOLDING ECONOMICS SHIFTS

The discussion of navigating the post-pandemic economy brings up two crucial points:

First, the defining characteristic of companies that will succeed in the decades after the Great Reboot is not their *size* or *age.* The string of household names going bankrupt, as well as the number of older companies succeeding (along with startups), points to that. Their defining characteristics instead are their *digital proficiency* and speed proficiency. Digital proficiency is about how well-equipped companies are to navigate the Digital Divide—as either digital natives or complements of digital economic activity. *Speed proficiency* is about how fast companies can make decisions and act on them in a fast-moving market.[77]

Second, no matter how long the aftereffects will last, they will unfold very differently over time. The following chapter about the three waves of the Great Reboot is about helping you understand and prepare for shifts over time, starting from the core observations around complements and substitutes.

---

77   Tyler Cowen, "The Speed Premium in an Exponentially Growing Pandemic World," *Marginal Revolution* (blog), March 24, 2020. I am grateful to, along with other observations, Tyler Cowen, who pointed out early in the pandemic the growing importance of speed.

CHAPTER 2

THREE WAVES OF THE GREAT REBOOT

The pandemic-triggered economic crisis affects different industries, in different ways, at different times. This chapter is about the three waves of the Great Reboot and how they will shape the economy.[78] [79]

FIRST WAVE: SHOCK AND SUBSTITUTES
Trigger of the First Wave: Widespread Lockdowns

The First Wave of the Great Reboot is the shock wave and the responses to the sharp increase in the costs of analog movement—for people more than goods. Lockdowns happened in a widespread fashion, and the cost of moving people

---

78 I previewed some of the insights covered in this chapter in two articles for *Inc. Magazine*. Arnobio Morelix, "The Post-Pandemic Economy: The Great Reboot," *Inc.com*, April 28, 2020.

79 Arnobio Morelix, "What the Lower Unemployment Rate Really Means for the Economy," *Inc.com*, June 9, 2020.

rose so much the demand for most things involving analog movement dropped. Only the most essential analog services remained in operation, such as hospitals, doctors' offices, grocery stores, pharmacies, and utility providers.

SHORT-TERM SUBSTITUTION

Moving people became prohibitively expensive or risky, so every product that could substitute analog movement of people for the digital substitute (or for no movement at all) became popular. The demand for alternatives grew dramatically, and this first happened in the industries where it was fast, even if not easy, to substitute.

In-home meals, fast food delivery, and sourdough bread starters became substitutes for traditional restaurant dining. Much in-person office work and many work-related social interactions were replaced with video calling apps like Zoom (which had its share price more than quadrupled since the beginning of the year) and chat apps for remote work like Slack. Live entertainment and movie theaters were substituted with Netflix, in-house drinking, and crafts like painting and knitting.

Graph: Zoom App Store Ratings Surged After the Pandemic
Total app store ratings (in thousands). App store ratings are a proxy for usage

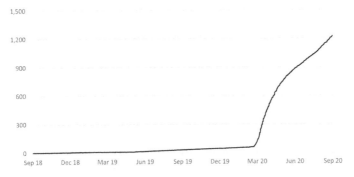

Source: Thinknum, retrieved September 30, 2020; Great Reboot
Project analysis (www.greatreboot.com)

For small business owners, we see a similar trend in the data from the *Inc. Magazine* Entrepreneurship Index (a project I lead with *Inc. Magazine*). The first industries hit were the ones in the "fast-to-substitute" categories.

Industry	Small Business Job Growth 3-Month Change, as of March 2020
Leisure and Hospitality	-0.4%
Professional and Business Services	-0.1%
Manufacturing	-0.1%
Other Services (except Public Administration)	0.0%
Education and Health Services	0.1%
Trade, Transportation, and Utilities	0.2%
Construction	0.3%
Financial Activities	0.4%

Source: Inc. Entrepreneurship Index, via Paychex

We saw this First Wave of shock and substitutes around the world. For example, MAX.ng, an e-hailing startup from Nigeria, started as a courier platform in 2015 before venturing into a bike-hailing service in 2017. It has been one of the beneficiaries of the coronavirus-induced lockdowns in Nigeria. Due to the virus, most of the people in Nigeria were stuck at home and unable to move, which helped the startup expand its operations and drive growth. "We expect that we'll be in a position to grow the size of our network to more than 5,000 drivers within the next 12 to 18 months," said Max Nigeria's chief financial officer Guy-Bertrand Njoya.[80]

The first wave of ten million people losing their jobs in March 2020 in the United States overwhelmingly came from industries affected by the First Wave—the restaurants, live entertainment, and gyms.[81] [82] Most of the nonessential workers sadly had their products and services substituted by other things.

THE FASTEST RECESSION ON RECORD AND TEN YEARS IN TEN WEEKS

One of the remarkable features of the Great Reboot is its speed of change. In fact, in terms of unemployment, this is the fastest recession on record. While it took twenty-two months from the onset of the Great Recession for the US

80 Mary-Ann Russon, "Coronavirus: How Africa's Supply Chains Are Evolving," *BBC News*, June 25, 2020.

81 Thomas Franck, "Hardest-Hit Industries: Nearly Half the Leisure and Hospitality Jobs Were Lost in April," *CNBC*, May 8, 2020.

82 Rakesh Kochhar and Amanda Barroso, "Young Workers Likely to Be Hard Hit as COVID-19 Strikes a Blow to Restaurants and Other Service Sector Jobs," *Pew Research Center*, August 26, 2020.

economy to hit a 10 percent unemployment rate, we surpassed that number in the first full month of lockdowns in the Great Reboot.[83] [84]

In the digital economy, interactions that used to be physical and based on human-to-human are going online. Some of this shift is temporary; people will still crave experiences like live concerts and eating out. But some will be permanent.

With this speed, changes we expected to take ten years to materialize happened in ten weeks. For instance:

- Curbside pickup service for sales, which started as early as 1921, was available for only 6.9 percent of retailers pre-pandemic. Now, 43.7 percent of top retailers offer it.[85] [86]
- Governments and traditional businesses that never accepted remote work had to adapt and create capabilities for it. This is similar for schools and e-learning.
- It took ten years for the share of e-commerce in the US to go from 0.8 percent (2000) to 4.2 percent (2010), and another decade for it to reach 11.8 percent (Q1 2020). But it took only one quarter of the Great Reboot for it to reach 16.1 percent (Q2 2020).[87] China's figure is a whopping 41.2

83 "US Business Cycle Expansions and Contractions," National Bureau of Economic Research, accessed September 28, 2020.

84 "Unemployment Rate," *Current Employment Statistics*, US Bureau of Labor Statistics, accessed September 28, 2020.

85 "What Is Curbside Pick Up?" *Parcel Pending* (blog), September 6, 2019.

86 Fareeha Ali, "Ecommerce Trends amid Coronavirus Pandemic in Charts," *Digital Commerce 360*, August 26, 2020.

87 US Census Bureau, "2Q 2020 E-commerce, Quarterly Data." Accessed November 1, 2020. Author's calculations from data.

percent—the world will be trending in that direction (the current global average is about 16 percent, though worldwide figures are harder to estimate).[88] [89] [90]

Graph: COVID-19 Dramatically Accelerated the Growth of E-Commerce
E-commerce as a % of total retail sales in the U.S.

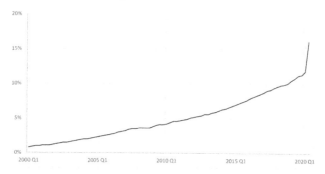

United States Census Bureau, retrieved September 30, 2020; Great Reboot Project analysis (www.greatreboot.com)

The point is not that all these figures and changes will stay the same after the pandemic because they won't. But to understand changes likely to stick around and ones likely to fade away, we need to better understand the Second and Third Waves.

88   Ethan Cramer-Flood , "Global Ecommerce 2020," *eMarketer,* June 22, 2020.

89   Matteo Ceurvels, "Latin America Ecommerce 2020," *eMarketer,* June 17, 2020.

90   Ethan Cramer-Flood, "China Ecommerce 2020," *eMarketer,* June 10, 2020.

SECOND WAVE: THE RISE OF COMPLEMENTS
Trigger of the Second Wave: Uneasy Reopenings (with Potential Back-and-Forths of Reopening and Closing Again)

In the Second Wave of the Great Reboot, costs for the analog movement of people and goods remain high. Even as the curve was "flattened" and we implemented policies like contract tracing and exposure notifications, it was still more costly and riskier to move people and goods in the analog world than it was pre-COVID-19.

In the analog economy, products and services such as concerts, movie theaters, restaurants, and travel will eventually return, but we'll likely have less of these to choose from. This comes from a mix of continued physical distancing norms and consumer caution. A meaningful portion of the new hires in May 2020 was for industries such as these, but they reopened with much less traffic.[91] Las Vegas casinos, for instance, reopened with the allowance of 50 percent capacity and far fewer people were interested in Vegas generally because of the risks associated with large crowds.[92]

The economy then started substituting things that were not so easy to substitute as the things in the First Wave. Canceling global travel and scheduling a video conference for a sales call is relatively easy. Changing your supply chain so it relies less on fragile global pipelines and more on local resources is

---

91   "Many in US Won't Return to Gym or Dining out, New Poll Shows," *Los Angeles Times*, May 23, 2020.

92   Dawn Gilbertson, "Same Old Vegas? Here's What Coronavirus Has and Hasn't Changed about Sin City," *USA Today*, June 10, 2020.

hard. Similarly, it is easy to make office work digital but not factory work. Increasing opportunities to substitute things is not easy to change out, such as factory-floor robots.

The Second Wave has been dominated by two effects throughout 2020. First, the substitute for things that were not easy to substitute. This included accelerated automation in manufacturing, drone deliveries to facilitate logistics, 3D printing as a substitute for overcomplicated supply chains, and more. We've already begun to see innovators printing medical parts when conventional versions are in shortage. These are all things that were trending before and are now accelerated.

Second, we are seeing the complements of the digital movement of people and goods rise in demand and value. This includes anything from internet and cell phone infrastructure (e.g., 5G) to teams and people who can perform well without co-location (e.g., digital nomads and companies like Automattic, the maker of WordPress, which have been remote-only for years).[93]

THIRD WAVE: A FRAGILE RETURN

Trigger of the Third Wave: Widespread Vaccine Adoption, Herd Immunity, and/or Highly Effective and Widespread Containment Systems (e.g., frequent testing, contact tracing)

Once we have the COVID-19 pandemic reasonably under control with vaccines and effective treatments, the Third

---

93 "Work with Us," Automattic, September 30, 2020.

Wave will be characterized by two main drivers: a whiplash effect and downstream consequences dominated by changes in preferences and capabilities.

THE ROARING 2020S

In the Third Wave, we can expect the costs of moving in the analog world will be low again. With this, we will see a whiplash effect as the world returns in droves to behavior and consumption patterns from the pre-COVID-19 times. People will flock back to restaurants, live entertainment, global travel, and in-person offices for camaraderie's sake.

Part of the whiplash effect is economic. It is not prohibitively expensive or risky to move in the analog world anymore, so we engage in more of it. I suspect part of it will be emotional. We will have been more or less cooped up for so long many of us will crave human interaction and engagement again.

After all, after the Spanish Flu devastated the world one hundred years ago came the glitz and exuberance of the Roaring Twenties (1920s): a global phenomenon, especially in the Western world (e.g., it was called *Années folles* in France and the *Golden Twenties* in Germany. In my home of Brazil, 1919 hosted the "End of the World Carnaval," often called the greatest and craziest carnival of all time).[94] [95] [96] [97]

---

94 Staff, "Paris Années Folles," *ParisVoice*, March 19, 2017.

95 "Ball Fever—Berlin Celebrates the 'Golden Twenties'—Arts.21," *Deutsche Welle*, January 6, 2008.

96 "O inesquecível carnaval de 1919," *Folha de S.Paulo*, May 27, 2020.

97 Thiago Gomide, "O Mais Louco Carnaval De Todos Os Tempos," *O Dia— Coisas do Rio*, January 27, 2020.

We might just have the "Roaring 2020s" ahead of us after the pandemic is in our rearview mirror.

PREFERENCES, CAPABILITIES, AND DOWNSTREAM CONSEQUENCES

At the same time, we will see a rebound of in-person activity (specifically around things associated with human desire for interaction) and the levels of moving goods and people will almost come back to pre-crisis figures, but not quite.

There are two reasons for this "not quite back" to pre-pandemic activity: a change in preferences and a change in capabilities.

First, our preferences will change. For instance, people and companies that never worked remotely will realize they like it. Maybe they will not wholly change to remote work like what was required during lockdowns, but they will not exclude remote work like they had before either. Similarly, people who used to do much international travel might cut back. Some of these choices might be due to having revealed preferences during COVID-19 that already existed but had not been tested yet.

Second, our capabilities will change. Digital infrastructure will improve (e.g., 5G connectivity), and new tools will be developed (e.g., AR/VR for work, as Facebook is developing now) and adopted (e.g., retailers that implemented self-checkout machines and curbside pickup will not destroy those capabilities even if we are done with social distancing).[98]

We will realize some digital alternatives to the analog world are just as good or better (in some ways) than their analog counterparts. This new normal will have several downstream effects:

- automation of manufacturing and agriculture will continue to grow
- human-less logistics will remain
- local-first supply chains (e.g., helped by 3D printing) will gain strength in contrast to global-first chains
- returns to exciting, expensive cities like San Francisco, New York, or London will decline somewhat, and people will be more inclined to live in less expensive places
- automation and "touchless" retail activity and services will remain

Sadly, this will mean many of the jobs lost during the First and Second Waves will have disappeared and will not come back. Like in the Great Recession of 2007–09, many workers will be kept on the sideline even in the recovery. The labor force participation in the US never quite got back up to previous levels after 2009.

---

98   Nick Statt, "Facebook Teases a Vision of Remote Work Using Augmented and Virtual Reality," *The Verge*, May 21, 2020.

At this point, the new operating system for the economy with Great Reboot will be completed. It will define the next several decades of our world.[99]

THE NO NORMAL

"We are seeing the end of an era during which the human brain has been the main shaper of the future. And as we hand over that future to non-human minds, the future might be really, really weird."

—JAAN TALLINN, A PROGRAMMER AND FOUNDING
ENGINEER OF SKYPE AND KAZAA

As the three waves unfold, our society becomes more reliant on computer software and hardware in all its manifestations. This brings tremendous productivity, wealth, and efficiency gains for society.

But it comes with a hidden cost. As our technology systems grow more prevalent and complex, they also grow more unpredictable, not just for governments and laypeople, but for tech creators themselves.

As Sam Arbesman—scientist in residence at Lux Capital, a venture capital firm, and my colleague in our past roles at

---

99   Arnobio Morelix, "The Post-Pandemic Economy: The Great Reboot," *Inc. com*, April 28, 2020.

the Kauffman Foundation—argues in his book *Overcomplicated*, our technology systems are so complex nobody fully understands them.

"Why did the New York Stock Exchange suspend trading without warning on July 8, 2015? Why did certain Toyota vehicles accelerate uncontrollably against the will of their drivers? Why does the programming inside our airplanes occasionally surprise its creators? After a thorough analysis by the top experts, the answers still elude us.

You don't understand the software running your car or your iPhone. But here's a secret: neither do the geniuses at Apple or the Ph.D.'s at Toyota—not perfectly, anyway."[100]

Combined with our global interconnectedness of businesses, people, and governments, this will lead to an increasingly weird world. The fact Arbesman published his book in 2016, a very strange year, and the world has gotten stranger since then, bolster the claim.

After the Third Wave of the Great Reboot, new preferences and capabilities will settle in. But this will not mean a return to normal, nor even a new normal. We will arrive at a No Normal.

Although we cannot fully predict how the No Normal will look, we do not need to walk blindly toward it. The following section of this book identifies the impact of the Great Reboot

---

100 Samuel Arbesman, *Overcomplicated: Technology at the Limits of Comprehension* (New York: Portfolio/Penguin, 2017).

on the spheres of the home, work, city, and world. It will help us understand—reasoning from underlying principles—the macro context post-pandemic we will all live in.

"We think we can manage risk by predicting extreme events. This is the worst error we make…It's more effective to focus on the consequences—that is, to evaluate the possible impact of extreme events. Realizing this, energy companies have finally shifted from predicting when accidents in nuclear plants might happen to preparing for the eventualities. In the same way, try to gauge how your company will be affected, compared with competitors, by dramatic changes in the environment."

—NASSIM N. TALEB, DANIEL G. GOLDSTEIN,

AND MARK W. SPITZNAGEL

PART II

CIRCLES OF IMPACT

CHAPTER 3

FOUR CIRCLES OF IMPACT OF THE GREAT REBOOT

___

"Crises usually accelerate real trends in society and technology; they don't create or refute them."

—GARY KASPAROV, CHESS GRANDMASTER

"This virus has been, both literally and metaphorically, a disease of modernity. Why? Because It attacks via the vectors of modernity: trade linkages, obesity, diabetes, air travel, mass transportation, urban density, social media, etc. Understanding long-run change requires understanding where modernity itself is under threat, and whether those threats will lead to meaningful and investable change."

—PAUL KEDROSKY, INVESTOR AND RESEARCHER

The post-pandemic economy will function in very different ways from the world pre-pandemic. But that does not mean the COVID-19 pandemic caused these shifts. Rather, it accelerated existing trends and triggered changes society was already susceptible to.

Marina Gorbis, the executive director of the Institute for the Future (ITFT), shares this analogy: viruses and harmful bacteria are around us all the time, but you are in danger only when your immune system is susceptible to it. Much like an immune system, our society was vulnerable to shocks, and the pandemic exposed fragilities which were already in place.

The Great Reboot is influencing society in many ways, but some changes—especially the day-to-day and month-to-month shifts tracked nearly 24/7 in the news—will be largely temporary. In many ways, observers significantly overestimate the impact of the Great Reboot, like a machine learning algorithm over-indexing recent data. Remote work will grow, but it will not be the death of the office. Superstar urban areas will face pressure and cool down in terms of activity, but it will not be the death of cities. People will spend more time with digital entertainment, but they will come back with a vengeance to live concerts and parties.

Strangely, some observers also significantly underestimate how different the world will be. The frequent discussions about what the shape of the economic recovery will be like—V-shaped, L-shaped, W-shaped, or something else—is one such example. As I have written with Bangalore-based CEO Srikar Reddy of Sonata Software for *The World Economic Forum,* focusing on the shape of the recovery misses

the crucial shifts happening.[101] The reality is regardless of
the shape of the recovery, the composition of the post-pandemic economy—whether you measure it in jobs, products, or stock prices—will be dramatically different from
pre-pandemic.

The approach we take here to identify long-term impacts
is to reason from first principles (e.g., the substitutes and
complements happening in the digital and analog economy),
decode the collective wisdom of founders, tech executives,
investors, policymakers, and scientists from every continent
of the world, and analyze accelerated preexisting trends. In
the following pages, we include external contributions from
tech luminaries like Vint Cerf, the father of the internet, and
insights from people at Google, Amazon, Netflix, and Stanford University, amongst many others.

THE POST-PANDEMIC AFTERMATH

As a founder, executive, or technology creator, the second
part of *Rebooted* covers the macro-scenario that will serve
as context for your business and decision-making. Historical events have historical consequences, and we will feel the
shockwaves of the Great Reboot in the decades to come. To
ignore the changing landscape your business and technology
will be operating in would be like driving without looking
around the car.

---

101 Srikar Reddy and Arnobio Morelix, "Companies Now Face an Urgent
    Choice: Go Digital, or Go Bust," *World Economic Forum*, October 19,
    2020.

We break down how the Great Reboot will affect our lives in four circles of impact:

Circles of Impact of the Great Reboot

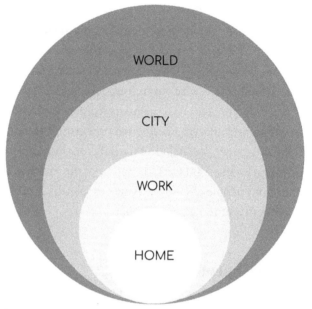

In the following chapters, we explore in detail each of these spheres.

CHAPTER 4

HOME: THE LONELIER FUTURE OF OUR SOCIAL LIVES

THE LONELIER FUTURE OF OUR SOCIAL LIVES

Kara works part-time as a customer care representative at a Fintech company. She lives alone in a one-bedroom apartment in a building without a doorman. On a recent Sunday morning, which is not a weekend day for her, she woke up to The Velvet Underground and Nico singing "Sunday Morning" thanks to a feature on her Amazon Echo. She completed her morning chores while listening to the *Up First* podcast on NPR.

She realizes stores will close early since it's Sunday and decides to make a quick trip to the grocery store before starting work at 10:00 a.m. She leaves her house and goes to the Amazon Go store, where there are no checkout kiosks so you can be in and out fast. After making the purchases, she realizes her checkout bags are too heavy and she needs a cab to go back home. She books an Uber and reaches her apartment complex.

It's almost time for Kara's work to start. Her work focuses on resolving customer questions through an online chat, which cannot be answered by chatbots. At the end of her workday, she spends time watching the latest season of *The Chef Show* on Netflix before switching off the lights. She thinks to herself how she will try a featured recipe from the show on her next day off. In the same moment, lying in her bed, she realizes the only words she spoke directly to a human that day were "Hello" and "Thank you" to her Uber driver when he dropped her off after the grocery store visit.

* * *

Overwhelmingly, we are substituting away in-person, analog interactions for human-machine-human interactions and even just human-machine ones. The downstream consequences are scary.

Kara's fictional story is not an unusual one. We are living in the middle of what many have described as a loneliness epidemic—even pre-pandemic—with the UK even introducing a Minister for Loneliness to address the problem.[102] [103]

---

102 I am grateful to my friend Lais de Oliveira (author of the book *Hacking Communities)* for pointing out the UK Minister for Loneliness story to me.

103 Peter Walker, "May Appoints Minister to Tackle Loneliness Issues Raised by Jo Cox," *The Guardian*, January 16, 2018.

Our social lives are becoming lonelier, and our social interactions are increasingly intermediated by digital interfaces. Those shifts are accelerated by COVID-19-related social distancing, and some of these measures and communication tools (e.g., the human-less stores, the growing reliance on apps to avoid leaving the house) are likely to stick around well past the pandemic.

In the UK, the Office of National Statistics showed in a study 50 percent of the people in the age group sixteen to twenty-four years old felt lonely, owing to the pandemic lockdown. This was more than twice what those ages fifty-five to sixty-nine experienced. In the US, a YouGov survey showed loneliness increased for Americans of all age groups.[104] Furthermore, one-fourth felt their overall mental health has worsened during the coronavirus outbreak while more than half of the respondents felt their mental health did not improve or worsened during the outbreak.[105] Suicides rates have been increasing in the US for the last two decades.[106] Cases of depression among the general population are expected to deepen and widen due to stress, anxiety, and loneliness and are expected to increase the already rising rates of suicides.[107]

---

104 Jamie Ballard, "Amid COVID-19, Millennials Are (Still) the Loneliest Generation," *YouGov*, May 1, 2020.

105 Ibid.

106 H. Hedegaard, Curtin SC, Warner M. "Suicide mortality in the United States, 1999-2017," *NCHS Data Brief* (2018).

107 Leo Sher, "The Impact of the COVID-19 Pandemic on Suicide Rates," *QJM: An International Journal of Medicine* 113, no. 10, pp. 707–712 (2020).

TWO "I"S OF EMOTIONAL DISTANCING: ISOLATION AND INTERMEDIATION

The emotional distance we increasingly experience in our society grows primarily from "two Is": isolation and intermediation. Both of them became more prevalent with the social distancing measures arising from the pandemic and its aftereffects.

In modest amounts, isolation and intermediation are not necessarily bad. At their current levels, they are associated with widespread depression, political polarization (as anthropologist Jared Diamond argues in his work), and erosion of public trust in institutions (as former CIA global media analyst Martin Gurri convincingly shows in his book *The Revolt of the Public*).[108] [109]

---

108 Nathan Gardels and Nicolas Berggruen, "Jared Diamond: Why Nations Fail or Succeed When Facing a Crisis," *Berggruen Institute*, July 31, 2020.

109 Martin Gurri, *The Revolt of the Public and the Crisis of Authority in the New Millennium* (San Francisco: Stripe Press, 2018).

ISOLATION

"We had then (in the 90s and early 2000s) already entered a period of sharp decline in face-to-face communication in the United States more than in any other country and before any other country."

—PROFESSOR JARED DIAMOND, UCLA, AUTHOR OF
THE BESTSELLER *GUNS, GERMS, AND STEEL*

Isolation is defined by a sparsity of person-to-person interaction, and our social lives are increasingly dominated by this. Face-to-face interactions have decreased, young people report higher levels of loneliness than previous generations, and previous community stalwarts of society—churches, clubs, and the like—have declined.

We can see evidence of this increasing isolation in many statistics:

- Young US adults are having less sex on average. A study found sexual inactivity increased in young men and women (aged twenty-five to thirty-four) from 2000 to 2018. Between 2016 and 2018, 14 percent of men and 13 percent of women reported no sexual activity during the time frame, compared to 7 percent of men and 7 percent of women who did not report any sexual activity between 2000 and 2002.[110]

---

110 Peter Ueda, Catherine H. Mercer, Cyrus Ghaznavi, and Debby Herbenick, "Trends in Frequency of Sex and Number of Sexual Partners

- US church membership has decreased from 70 percent of Americans in 1998 to 50 percent of Americans in 2018.[111] Similarly, the majority of the US social clubs have witnessed a decrease in membership and popularity.[112] [113]
- iGeners (people born between 1995 and 2012) are less likely to go out and have in-person interactions according to a study of eight million Americans examined over the time frame between 1976 and 2017. Other research found 2016 college bound seniors spent four hours and twenty-two minutes less each week in social in-person interactions with friends compared to 1987 college bound seniors. In addition, almost 19 percent of twelfth graders in 2017 were less likely to go out less than once a week compared to 8 percent of Boomers.[114] [115]

Some of this decline comes from communications technology, but it's not only that. Professor Jared Diamond at UCLA reports growing isolation coming from a drop in person-to-person interactions going back to the 1990s for

Among US Adults Aged 18 to 44 Years," *JAMA Network Open* 3, no. 6, June 12, 2020.

111 Jeffrey M Jones, "US Church Membership Down Sharply in Past Two Decades," *Gallup*, April 8, 2020.

112 Taya Flores, "Fraternal, Service Groups Battle Declining Membership," *Journal and Courier*, October 11, 2014.

113 Michael Brand, "Why Our Service Organizations Are Dying (and 6 Ways to Fix Them)," *LinkedIn*, June 21, 2016.

114 The Baby Boomers generation is defined as people born between 1946 and 1964.

115 Jean M. Twenge, Brian H. Spitzberg, and W. Keith Campbell, "Less in-Person Social Interaction with Peers among US Adolescents in the 21st Century and Links to Loneliness," *Journal of Social and Personal Relationships* 36, no. 6: 1892–1913 (2019).

the United States.[116] This decline comes from three main driving factors:

1. People move far away from their original communities to places where they have fewer social connections, typically for economic reasons.[117]
2. Growing inequality leads to, within a given place, people having more segregated social interactions along lines of educational and socioeconomic backgrounds. This is a trend economists like Tyler Cowen have described as the "self-segregation" of communities, where people only socialize within their own economic strata.[118]

This shows up in the rates at which people across different social classes get married. For example, in the case of Organisation for Economic Co-operation and Development (OECD) member countries, the proportion of partners belonging to the same or neighboring income bracket increased from 33 percent to 40 percent over a two-decade period.[119]

1. We see the hollowing out of entire communities, both inner cities and rural areas, as is seen in the US Rust Belt. The basic pattern here is defined by the fact that once more traditional jobs in factories, agriculture, and the like leave (resulting from a mix of automation and globalization), people also leave and the community begins

116 Nathan Gardels and Nicolas Berggruen, "Jared Diamond: Why Nations Fail or Succeed When Facing a Crisis," *Berggruen Institute*, July 31, 2020.
117 Ibid.
118 Heidi Glenn, "America's 'Complacent Class': How Self-Segregation Is Leading to Stagnation," *NPR*, March 2, 2017.
119 Katrin Bennhold, "Equality and the End of Marrying Up," *The New York Times*, June 12, 2012.

to crumble, as noted by author Chris Arnade in his ethnographic-inspired book *Dignity*.[120]

This is a global phenomenon—not just in the US or the developed Western world. Both Japan and South Korea have their share of loneliness tragedies. The proportion of single-person households has almost doubled in Japan from 17 percent in 1960 to 35 percent in 2015. Kazuhisa Arakawa, a leading commentator and researcher on the growing shift to "single life," predicted by 2040, 50 percent of the population age fifteen or older will be living solo.[121] In my own home state of Brazil—Minas Gerais, traditionally heavily reliant on mining and metalworking industries—we have begun to see small towns becoming less dynamic with hollowed-out communities.

INTERMEDIATION

The second "I" driving loneliness is intermediation, defined by human interactions being done indirectly through machines as opposed to being human-to-human. These intermediating machine interfaces can be screens, apps, audio, and video streams.

Think back on the last ten people you interacted with for personal or professional reasons (e.g., a colleague or someone you bought something from). Odds are a large share of these interactions happened through a digital

---

120 Chris Arnade, *Dignity: Seeking Respect in Back Row America* (New York: Sentinel, 2019).

121 Bryan Lufkin, "The Rise of Japan's 'Super Solo' Culture," *BBC Worklife*, January 15, 2020.

interface—many of them asynchronous, rather than real-time. By 2030, accelerated by the shifts triggered in the COVID-19 crisis, digital interfaces will mostly dominate human social interaction.

If the medium is the message, in many ways the interface is the interaction.

"The internet is disastrous for large-scale cohesion and amazing for small-scale community. I always thought that was a good trade but now I don't."

—SAM ALTMAN, CEO OF OPENAI AND FORMER
PRESIDENT OF Y COMBINATOR

Technology-driven loneliness is something we acknowledge as a society as suggested by the stereotype of the loner playing video games. Nonetheless, there is some absurdity in knowing we are also working on robots and AI assistants to tackle this loneliness. Take Pepper for example, an emotional robot developed by SoftBank Mobile and Aldebaran Robotics whose purpose is to "help people grow" and "enhance relationships" and has been tried in both the UK and Japan to reduce the loneliness of elderly people.[122] [123]

---

122 "Pepper the Humanoid and Programmable Robot: SoftBank Robotics," SoftBank Robotics, accessed September 19, 2020.

123 Robert Booth, "Robots to Be Used in UK Care Homes to Help Reduce Loneliness," *The Guardian*, September 7, 2020.

The intermediated interactions are unfolding and will continue to unfold in two key ways:

Human-Machine-Human Interactions

The time we spend on social media daily is consistently increasing. According to a survey by Global Web Index, 63 percent of global internet users in 2019 said they are constantly connected (up from 56 percent in 2015).[124] Additionally, average time spent daily on social media has increased from one hour and thirty minutes in 2012 to two hours and twenty-four minutes in 2019.[125] For people sixteen to twenty-four years old, the average is three hours per day. For all groups, the number one reason for using social media is keeping in touch with friends.[126]

Even for the deepest social relationships, like those of romantic partners, we see increased machine-intermediated connections.

For instance, in the US four out of every ten couples met online—the most popular meeting mode for couples as of 2013—as research from Stanford University shows.[127] In fact, meeting online is more common for couples today than meeting through friends, family, and co-workers *combined*.

---

124 Global Web Index, *2019 Social Media User Trends Report*, (London: Global Web Index, 2019).

125 Ibid.

126 Ibid.

127 Michael J. Rosenfeld, Reuben J. Thomas, and Sonia Hausen. "Disintermediating Your Friends: How Online Dating in the United States Displaces Other Ways of Meeting," Proceedings of the National Academy of Sciences 116, no. 36: 17753–58, (2019).

While at face value there is nothing wrong with meeting online, the decline in using in-person social networks for meeting (family, friends, neighbors, church, school, and work) suggests a weakening of (or at least a lesser reliance on) the deep social ties on which communities rely.

Internet Has Become a Key Way of How Couples Meet

How Couple Met	1995	2017
Online	2%	39%
In a bar/restaurant	19%	27%
Through Friends	33%	20%
Through or as co-workers	19%	11%
In School or College	19%	9%
Through Family	15%	7%
In Church	7%	4%
Through or as neighbors	8%	3%

Source: How Couples Met and Stay Together, 2009 and 2017

Notice the statistics mentioned above are all pre-pandemic. The social distancing associated with the Great Reboot has only increased the prevalence of human-machine-human interactions.[128]

Human-Machine Interactions

Imagine the last interaction you had on a video call with a vendor, pen pal across the world, or customer service representative at your bank. Now imagine there is no human

---

128 Global Web Index, *2020 Social Media User Trends Report* (London: Global Web Index, 2020).

at all on the other side—a plausible scenario given the digital interface. These kinds of human-machine interactions will form a growing share of social interactions in society.

The human-machine interactions we have today are overwhelmingly focused on commercial transactions, like a chatbot for customer service when you reach out to your bank. But they are inexorably becoming just plain social also, although it might still be in fringe ways. Pornography, an industry that has always adopted new technologies early (e.g., video streaming and chat, online ads, AR, and VR), already offers interactive virtual reality experiences and sex robots.

"Among modern first-world people, within the last decade or two decades, most communication is not face-to-face, it's indirect [...], it's by digital media. We don't learn to read other people [...]".

—UCLA PROFESSOR JARED DIAMOND, AUTHOR OF
THE BESTSELLER *GUNS, GERMS, AND STEEL*

Finding Meaning in the Great Reboot: Individuality and Togetherness

By Cosmin Gheorghe, MD, MFT

No matter who we are and where we live on earth, to emerge as healthy, secure, and fulfilled individuals we all have to follow two basic human needs: individuality and belonging. We need our personal space and individual freedom, yet they have little to no value if no one reflects back on our gestures, words, emotions, and desires. Yet again, what would be the point of togetherness if we didn't have time and space to reflect, in solitude, upon our interactions with others?

It seems like a very straightforward deal, right? Take some individual time, combine it with some togetherness, and ta-taaaam! You have a new successful, blissfully happy person. Well, if that was the case my coaching and counseling practice would be out of business at this point. In reality, there are so many variables and so many ways in which this process of becoming a healthy grownup can go wrong, that it's a miracle we are alive and functional at all.

For most of us, at some point, too much individuality becomes burdening aloneness and then alienating loneliness. Spending time on our own has the advantage of not needing to satisfy anyone else's needs and wants. However, sooner or later anxiety kicks in, and for whatever reason we lack the ability to get the togetherness we need. In turn, we end up developing all sorts of coping mechanisms, some more destructive than others, like excessive busyness (also known as workaholism), substance use to sustain or ignore a certain mood, as well as many other impulsive and compulsive activities like shopping, overeating or not eating at all, exercising to the point of injuring ourselves, and the list can go on. After all, there is a reason incarceration is considered a punishment. Being together with our fellow humans is absolutely necessary for our well-being and mental health.

Togetherness, however, only goes so far. Constantly having to take into consideration someone else's needs and wants eventually becomes tiring for most healthy individuals, no matter how much love is involved in that particular relationship. If there is no possibility to retreat in the intimacy of one's own individual space, it leads again to stress and anxiety. Oftentimes, similar unhelpful coping mechanisms may be used to create a virtual personal space and prevent one's identity from being completely engulfed by togetherness.

Indeed, building a healthy identity is a complex matter and the exponential development of technology seems to have thrown in another unexpected set of variables. How are the basic needs of togetherness and individuality addressed in the era of instantaneous audio and video interaction? What is the definition of isolation, loneliness, and intermediation when we can be together virtually in seconds?

One would say that humanity is now more connected than it has ever been. At the same time, a click or tap gives us unprecedented control over when to go back into our individual space to the point we cannot distinguish between the need for personal time and the act of suddenly disappearing from friends and family (also known as "ghosting"). Are we happier, healthier, and more fulfilled than before?

That depends very much on who you ask and what research you choose to read. One thing is clear though: technology has been influencing our basic human needs on a daily basis.

It is the reason Arnobio and I decided to test the impact of technology on social relationships and human behavior. Building on a previous workshop sold out twice at the South by Southwest festival (which Arnobio hosted with Colin Tomkins-Bergh), we created an online workshop to explore how entrepreneurs' mental fitness was holding up during the times of the COVID-19 pandemic. There were many interesting insights, but for the purpose of this article, I am going to talk about those related to the basic needs of individuality and togetherness.

As expected, entrepreneurs participating were affected by COVID-19 isolation. For some, however, it took many weeks until they felt the true burden of it. Many were able to simply work from home, and some were too busy to notice the severe lack of their social lives. Others, who were drawing a good portion of their energy and creativity from physical social interactions, reported feeling a dreadful sense of disconnection. Everyone, of course, used technology to reach out to friends and family. However, some participants reported feeling technology was a decent replacement for in-person encounters, while others reported virtual interactions made their togetherness much less satisfying. Indeed, being around others in person satisfies the need for human togetherness only if the connection is a meaningful one.

Socialization improves and maintains our well-being and mental health only if we can attribute meaning to those social interactions. It appears that the way technology is perceived and situated in context is what matters. Some entrepreneurs automatically focused on what they perceived to be missing (no direct communication with humans who are present in the same physical space). Others saw technology as just another form of communication, preferred in times of uncertainty, and they managed to make new friends and online buddies in order to support each other throughout the lockdown.

We indeed live in some fascinating times, which reminds me of the words of famous American biologist E. O. Wilson. He said, "Destroying rainforest for economic gain is like burning a Renaissance painting to cook a meal." We still have some paintings left and many meals to cook. However, this is our chance for a Great Reboot, a world where using technology to create meaning is not optional, and where individuality and togetherness complete—rather than compete with—each other.

Cosmin Gheorghe, MD, MFT is a psychology professor, culture specialist, and licensed clinician. His recent work is at the intersection of psychology, culture, and technology. His latest podcast series is called Crisis & Opportunities.

* * *

Loneliness, Elections, and the Holy Trinity of Despair

Take a step back in time with me. It's 2018 and we are in the thick of Brazil's most contentious presidential election in recent history since the end of a military dictatorship in 1985.

One of the leading presidential candidates, a right-wing populist named Jair Bolsonaro (along the lines of President Donald Trump), was stabbed by an online conspiracy theorist during a rally. If you thought Russian bots in the US were the worst of it, wait until you see the hellscape of tech and politics in the developing world.

The confessed assailant is a man who often posted online conspiracies about the Illuminati and 9/11. He had been isolated from his family for the past three to four years, and family says he's basically been a "bum" without steady work. In addition to conspiracies, there is a clear incel—"involuntary celibate"—tone underlying his online postings.

For instance, in one of his posts on Facebook commenting about the presidential election he questions what the presidential candidates will propose to do about single people who cannot or will not get married because of economic reasons.

Sadly, the confessed stabber is afflicted by all three elements of the modern Holy Trinity of Despair:[129]

- loneliness
- economic exclusion
- online engagement in extreme views or communities

---

129 Dal Bo et al. "Economic and Social Outsiders but Political Insiders: Sweden's Radical Right," Working Paper, *Department of Political Science, UC Berkeley.* (March 2020).

This episode encapsulates and foreshadows the hellscape of politics, society, and tech we see all over the world. Ethnic cleansing in Myanmar, the lynching of low-caste Hindus and Muslims in India, and rightward populism in Europe all come to mind as other examples.

It would be close to outrageous to suggest tech is the only cause for Bolsonaro's rise and the attack on him (as some surprisingly did). In this case, the whole context has a Brazilian flavor. Former president, presidential hopeful, and the most mythical political figure in the country, Lula, is in jail on corruption charges. After presiding over the Brazilian Boom of the 2000s, his popularity, especially with the poorer segments of the population, soared. Yet, at the same time many were lifted out of poverty his allies were embroiled in ever-suspicious financial deals. Lula's anointed successor and president after him, Dilma Rousseff, is impeached.

Nonetheless, despite the specific Brazilian circumstances of this event, the context crunching of crazy online views combined with real-world disaster (e.g., lynching in India coordinated via web messaging) is a global phenomenon.

It is tempting to focus on individuals in these stories, like the fact that the stabber seems mentally deranged. But the more important lesson is societal.

Part of the societal problem is directly associated with tech. Social media has allowed for ubiquitous access to extreme online communities. The scale to which this allows for coordination and radicalization of someone's views is unique to the social media age. It is enabled by the nearly frictionless possibility of interacting with extreme communities without the tricky costs of actually having to physically go somewhere (and risk recognition, among other things).

But most of the problem comes from sources which have little to do with tech, or in which tech is just one of many factors. The rise in loneliness (and increasingly worse mental health) is associated with social media but precedes it and is accompanied by things like the crumbling of community institutions.[130] [131] For economic exclusion, tech is just one of many other factors leading up to it.

Sadly the trends coming from the Holy Trinity of Despair are not just isolated anecdotes. American economist Anne Case and British-American economist and Nobel Prize Laureate Angus Deaton have documented how the lack of community and economic inclusion are related to "deaths of despair" in the US—those caused by suicide, alcohol, or drugs.[132] Research shows how the excluded are more likely to go radical and join the politically extreme.[133]

---

130 Nathan Gardels and Nicolas Berggruen, "Jared Diamond: Why Nations Fail or Succeed When Facing a Crisis," *Berggruen Institute*, July 31, 2020.

131 J. Haidt and & J. Twenge, *Social media use and mental health: A review.* Unpublished manuscript, New York University, 2019.

132 Jim Zarroli, "'Deaths of Despair' Examines the Steady Erosion of US Working-Class Life," *NPR*, March 18, 2020.

133 E Dal Bo et al. "Economic and Social Outsiders but Political Insiders: Sweden's Radical Right," Working Paper, *Department of Political Science, UC Berkeley.* (March 2020).

* * *

UNEQUAL REALITIES AND EVERY MAN A BUBBLE

"Twenty years ago I would have been optimistic that we were moving away from mass communication (radio, TV) so that anybody can publish. As a technologist, we all thought we were bringing this thing that would help democracy. At the moment, it feels like it has allowed people to separate into their own bubble."

—BILL GATES, CO-FOUNDER AND
FORMER CEO OF MICROSOFT

The impact of the Great Reboot in the sphere of the home is about our literal places of living—as we see in Kara's story at the beginning of the chapter—but also our metaphorical home: our family, friends, community, and emotional well-being.

The changes post-pandemic on levels of loneliness and social isolation will vary across countries and cultures. But as we can see in the many examples in this chapter from places like Japan, Brazil, the US, and the UK, the shifts in the home sphere are widespread. As loneliness and social isolation are conditions that spread along the vectors of modernity—geographical mobility away from family and original communities, erosion of social-cohesion institutions, and rise of tech-enabled pale substitutes for social interactions—it is likely to continue to grow unless we change something dramatically.

The combination of the two isolation and intermediation has a serious side effect of leading to a situation where people process reality itself unequally—forming beliefs and opinions that vary dramatically across social bubbles.

The debacles around the refusal of mask-wearing in the United States and Brazil are good examples of unequal realities being experienced—where one side sees a fundamental threat to the health of the whole society and the other sees a minor crisis being overblown and being used to curtail freedom. In a conversation between Jared Diamond and Bill Gates (who rates Diamond's *Guns, Germs, and Steel* as one of the best things he has ever read), Diamond suggests the two fundamental reasons for political polarization in the United States are the decline in face-to-face communication and the weak social ties among people in the United States.[134]

Maybe no man is an island, but unless we change course we might instead be heading toward a state where every man is a bubble.

---

134 Bill Gates, "How to Handle a National Crisis," *gatesnotes.com*, May 20, 2019.

CHAPTER 5

WORK: THE CHAOTIC TRANSITION TO THE FUTURE OF JOBS

THE LONG SHADOW OF THE GREAT REBOOT

Like in every major crisis, the Great Recession of 2007–2009 had an impact on employment numbers in the US, with peak unemployment (which happened twenty-two months after the onset of the recession) going to 10 percent and only recovering to pre-recession levels toward the end of 2016.[135] Unlike previous crises, however, many of these jobs never came back. In fact, in one key metric—labor force participation—the job market never recovered.

Even at the time of this writing, in 2020 a large portion of people who used to be in the labor force never came back to the market—a drop of 6.5 percent, equivalent to about eleven

---

135 United States Bureau of Labor Statistics, "Civilian unemployment rate," The Employment Situation, accessed November 16, 2020.

million people.[136] [137] In other words, for some people, the jobs they lost never came back, and neither came the workers who used to do them. People who were left without jobs for a long time experienced skill erosion and discouragement and, as it happened in the Great Recession, temporary unemployment spells turn permanent.

Graph: The Labor Market Never Fully Recovered from the Great Recession
Civilian labor force participation rate, seasonally adjusted

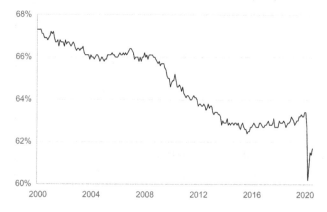

Source: U.S. Bureau of Labor Statistics; Great Reboot Project
analysis (www.greatreboot.com)

The Great Recession of 2007–2009 had a long shadow on jobs. The Great Reboot's shadow will stretch even further.

The long-term impact of the Great Reboot on the sphere of work has four main drivers: automation, a jobs divide, the unbundling of the firm, and the rise of hybrid and distributed teams. We cover each in turn below.

---

136 Decline in labor force between November 2007 and October 2020.
137 United States Bureau of Labor Statistics, "Civilian labor force participation rate," The Employment Situation, accessed July 24, 2020.

1. AUTOMATION

"Within 30 years half of humanity won't have a job."

—ANTONIO GARCÍA MARTÍNEZ, AUTHOR OF *CHAOS MONKEYS: INSIDE THE SILICON VALLEY MONEY MACHINE*

A JOBS EXTINCTION EVENT

The three most common jobs in the United States employ about ten million people and most of them will soon be gone or changed dramatically due to automation. These jobs—retail salespeople (4.3 million), fast-food and counter workers (4 million), and cashiers (3.6 million)—are under serious pressure to be replaced by technological advances that are already here.[138] This pressure is accelerating with social distancing and the COVID-19 pandemic.

For example, companies such as Amazon Go, Jack & Jones, and others are working on stores with no retail salespersons and cashiers, while fast-food chains like McDonald's, Taco Bell, Wendy's, KFC, and others are implementing more self-ordering kiosks to reduce costs.[139] [140] [141]

---

138 Arnobio Morelix, "What the Lower Unemployment Rate Really Means for the Economy," *Inc.com*, June 9, 2020.

139 Rebecca Crook, "In Pictures: Six Trendsetting Checkout-Free Stores from around the Globe," *Retail Week*, August 13, 2020.

140 "Quick-Service Restaurants Rush to Introduce Self-Ordering Kiosks," *Retail Technology Review*, February 19, 2020.

141 Alicia Kelso, "Self-Order Kiosks Are Finally Having a Moment in the Fast Food Space," *Forbes Magazine*, July 30, 2019.

Many of the jobs disappearing during the Great Reboot will not come back.

* * *

The impact of automation on jobs has been in debate for centuries, and strongly at least since the Industrial Revolution. In more recent years, artificial intelligence and information technology have been at the core of the discussions around work automation.

Over the next ten to twenty years, estimates on the number of workers likely to be impacted by computerization and automation range from the low end of 9 percent by researchers like Melanie Arntz, Terry Gregory, and Ulrich Zierahn from the Center for European Economic Research (ZEW) to a shocking 47 percent by Oxford academics Carl Benedikt Frey and Michael Osborne.[142] [143] In between these two figures, there are estimates from Brookings Institute and McKinsey Global Institute pegging the impact at around 25 percent and 20 percent, respectively.[144] [145] [146]

---

142 Melanie Arntz, Terry Gregory, and Ulrich Zierahn. "Revisiting the Risk of Automation," *Economics Letters* 159 (2017).

143 Carl Benedikt Frey and Michael A. Osborne, "The Future of Employment: How Susceptible Are Jobs to Computerisation?" *Technological Forecasting and Social Change* 114 (2017).

144 Robert Maxim and Mark Muro. "Automation and AI Will Disrupt the American Labor Force. Here's How We Can Protect Workers," *Brookings* (blog), February 25, 2019.

145 "Robot Automation Will 'Take 800 Million Jobs by 2030'—Report," *BBC News*, November 29, 2017.

146 James Manyika et al., "Jobs Lost, Jobs Gained: What the Future of Work Will Mean for Jobs, Skills, and Wages," *McKinsey & Company*, May 11, 2019.

But what none of these estimates took into account is the speed at which the automation would have happened, triggered by the COVID-19 pandemic.

The examples of automation are numerous, and the first rounds of jobs automated typically come from tasks where the technology for automation already existed but had not been implemented yet due to a mix of costs and inertia. For example, in the Bay Area where I live all toll booths were quickly automated with social distancing norms in 2020 using license plate recognition technology to send the bills by mail. Even though the technology existed for years, it took the shock of the pandemic for these changes to be implemented—and similarly for a lot of businesses to implement cashier-less checkouts, online sales, and the like. Even after the social distancing requirement goes away, businesses will continue to use these new capabilities. Many of the jobs will not return.

Eric Schmidt, formerly the CEO of Google and executive chairman of Alphabet Inc., has said pre-pandemic the acceleration of innovation—in particular technological advances that threaten to wipe out jobs previously thought to be beyond the reach of computers—are one of the biggest problems for society in the next twenty to thirty years.[147] Speaking on the topic, he said, "There is quite a bit of research that middle-class jobs that are relatively highly skilled are being automated out," using robots in the auto industry as an example.[148]

---

147 Richard Waters, "Google Chief Warns of IT Threat," *Financial Times*, January 23, 2014.
148 Ibid.

But how will the jobs that remain, and those yet to be created, play out? Those driving the jobs divide and the unbundling of the firm will overwhelmingly shape these.

2. API DIVIDE

As machine learning improves and software eats the world (and many jobs with it), the work remaining is largely defined by their relationship with technology. Venkatesh Rao, author of cult blog *ribbonfarm*, talks about this as an "API divide," referring to the application programming interfaces different apps use to communicate with one another. The divide leads to a stark gap between "below the API" jobs and "above the API" jobs.[149] [150]

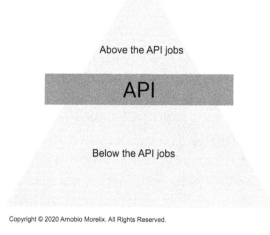

Above the API jobs

API

Below the API jobs

149 Venkatesh Rao, "The Premium Mediocre Life of Maya Millennial," *ribbonfarm* (blog), September 10, 2017.

150 Anthony Wing Kosner, "Google Cabs and Uber Bots Will Challenge Jobs 'Below the API'," *Forbes Magazine*, February 4, 2015.

"Below the API" are the jobs where the computer tells the human what to do and directs their work. Here, think about the jobs like on-demand drivers, gig grocery deliverers, warehouse workers (increasingly measured, punished, and rewarded by software directly), and computer-intermediated customer service roles (e.g., call centers). "Above the API" are the jobs where the human tells the computer what to do such as developers, designers, and executives.

Of course, many jobs interact little with computers the way the "API divides" suggest, and many of those will remain; health care is one example. But even then, there is no guarantee these kinds of jobs will not also eventually be touched by an API divide. Even quintessentially human domains like psychotherapy are being affected, with new gig-economy-style apps that match customers and therapists (and then rating and rewarding those therapists) in ways inspired by the way rideshare companies engage with drivers.

Part of the challenge of the "below the API" jobs is that, although robots might not have come to destroy the jobs, they destroy the paychecks. When the human-side of jobs gets reduced to an ever-smaller set of well-defined tasks that can be measured and monitored by computers (even if not done by them with current tech), the earnings for these jobs can fall.[151] [152]

---

151 Jeffrey Sparshott, "The Robots Are Coming for Your Paycheck," *The Wall Street Journal*, February 17, 2015.

152 David Autor and Anna Salomons, "Is Automation Labor-Displacing? Productivity Growth, Employment, and the Labor Share," *National Bureau of Economic Research* (July 2018).

"The COVID-19 crisis has forced businesses in industries previously impervious to remote working to reengineer their work processes and bolster their technology support systems...COVID-19 epidemic could well prove to be a pivotal point in the gig-ification of knowledge work."[153]

Contributing in some ways to the job divide is the unbundling of companies, which increasingly rely on freelancers or outsourced teams instead of full-time employees.

3. UNBUNDLING OF THE COMPANY

In 1937, British economist Ronald Coase set out to answer why companies exist at all if markets are supposedly so good at directing resources. His insights, which largely led to him winning the Nobel Prize in economics later, rest on the simple-but-powerful idea of *exchange costs*.[154] [155] [156]

Exchange costs are basically the direct and indirect costs associated with swapping products, services, or information among people or teams. When the exchange costs are low, each party interacts directly with each other in the market. But when exchange costs are high, parties organize into companies that bundle the transactions needed along the value chain to produce more efficiently.

---

153 Sameer Hasija, V. Padmanabhan, Prashant Rampal, "Will the Pandemic Push Knowledge Work into the Gig Economy?" *Harvard Business Review*, June 1, 2020.

154 Coase, R.H., "The Nature of the Firm," *Economica*, 4, 16 (1937).

155 "Coase's Theory of the Firm," *The Economist*, July 29, 2017.

156 Sometimes also called interaction or transaction costs.

For example, if you need organic food for your home, it is easy to go to a farmer's market to buy directly. It is also relatively easy for the farmer to go there to sell it. In other words, exchange costs are low.

But if you want to manufacture computer microchips, the steps along the way are complex and numerous, making the exchange costs high. It makes sense to bundle activities into companies. These companies in turn hire people, purchase or create key assets, and take care of the production process.

Work, through employment contracts, is a prime example of a situation where exchange costs are typically high. If you need a business analyst, a marketing executive, or an engineering leader, it is hard to go on the market and contract the service piecemeal. It is easier to bundle a team together and have one company own important assets including customer relationship, intellectual property, and office space.

But as Gary Bolles, chair for the Future of Work at Singularity University, shared in a conversation, work is being unbundled. With tasks being increasingly distributed, atomized, and measured, what previously required a co-located team (often within a single company) can be unbundled into nodes of freelancers or smaller teams who coordinate to get the job done.

"Traditional wisdom is that you have to have everybody co-resident for as long as possible. The COVID-19 crisis has proven that rhetoric wrong," he said, adding, "I don't think we will ever go back to the mothership headquarters again."

The unbundling of the company is not a new phenomenon. In the late 1990s, John Hagel III and Marc Singer wrote for *Harvard Business Review* about the unbundling of the corporation they were observing. At the time, vertically integrated businesses like IBM and Digital Equipment (which dominated the computer industry in the 1970s) had lost ground to more specialized players like Apple, Microsoft, and Adobe (which often rely on fully outsourced functions and a network of external suppliers for key inputs).[157]

But the growing digitization of the economy—including API-coordinated activities and the beginnings of decentralized protocols on the blockchain—is taking the unbundling of the company to a new level, which has been accelerated by the Great Reboot.

Singularity University's Gary Bolles expects the unbundling of the company to trigger "node-based" future of work. In this scenario, you have "nodes" that work co-located based on functions (e.g., design, engineering, sales) or products. They are not typically working inside the headquarters but can go there as needed relatively easily. For instance, a company headquartered in San Francisco might have a "sales node" in Sacramento, a "design node" in Napa, and an "engineering node" in Tahoe. This "node-based" model of work relates closely to the fourth main driver of the future of work: the rise of hybrid and distributed teams.

---

157 John Hagel III and Marc Singer, "Unbundling the Corporation," *Harvard Business Review*, August 1, 2014.

4. HYBRID FUTURE OF WORK

Remote work went from being an unusual arrangement for a minority of people pre-pandemic at about 2.1 percent of workers to standard for many. In fact, 42.9 percent of workers shifted to remote in the middle of lockdowns in the US.[158] [159]

These figures combined with the fact companies like Twitter, Slack, and Stripe announced permanent work from home (WFH) policies that led many observers to claim "telecommuting" would dominate work-life post-coronavirus. They also suggested this shift would even lead to the "death of the city," a claim we look at in more detail in the next chapter.[160]

While it is the case that distributed work will be higher post-pandemic, the story is more nuanced than the "death of cities" claim. In fact, the future of work will be a lot more hybrid than remote.

After social distancing goes away, there are three main variables that will define whether people can work remotely, or they need to be co-located and how much. These variables are:

Worker Preference. While in the middle of the pandemic, enthusiasm for remote work was high, even then the majority

---

158 "Table 6. Employed persons working at home, workplace, and time spent working at each location by full- and part-time status and sex, jobholding status, and educational attainment, 2019 annual averages," Current Employment Statistics, US Bureau of Labor Statistics, accessed October 28, 2020.

159 S.R. Baker, N. Bloom, S.J. Davis, S.J. Terry, "COVID-Induced Economic Uncertainty (No. 26983)," *National Bureau of Economic Research* (2020).

160 Aitor Hernández-Morales, Kalina Oroschakoff, and Jacopo Barigazzi, "The Death of the City," *POLITICO*, August 3, 2020.

of workers stated they did not want to work from home full-time after the pandemic ends. Research from Nick Bloom at Stanford University in May 2020 (a peak for lockdowns in the US) showed 24.2 percent of workers wanted to work from home full-time post-COVID-19.[161]

One in four workers having a preference for full-time remote work is a sizable minority, but Bloom suggests it is also likely to be an overestimation. Reflecting on a previous experiment on WFH he conducted where he followed employees switching to WFH over nine months, he talked about how over time the challenges of isolation and loneliness began to show up. "For the first three months employees were happy—it was the euphoric honeymoon period," Blooms said. "But by the time the experiment had run its full length, two-thirds of the employees requested to return to the office. They needed human company." He adds, "Currently, we are in a similar honeymoon phase of full-time WFH. But as with any relationship, things can get rocky and I see increasing numbers of firms and employees turning against this practice."

Company Preference. In addition to employees being up for remote work, companies need to also be in favor for these arrangements to work. A recent Gartner's survey of chief financial officers shows about 74 percent of these executives plan to have some percentage of the workforce permanently remote post-pandemic.[162]

---

161 S.R. Baker, N. Bloom, S.J. Davis, S.J. Terry, "COVID-Induced Economic Uncertainty (No. 26983)," *National Bureau of Economic Research* (2020).
162 "Gartner CFO Survey Reveals 74% Intend to Shift Some Employees to Remote Work Permanently," Gartner, April 3, 2020.

Ability. While most workers can to some extent do their jobs from home in the US, the share of those who say they can do it with complete efficiency is about 33.4 percent, as research from Bloom shows.[163] While the coronavirus triggered the forced experiment of remote work and will lead to a lot of companies to welcome remote work in ways they did not before, it is clear for most people remote work is not as productive as co-located work.

There is no doubt remote work technology will improve over time. Facebook has some impressive development with virtual reality for work environments, for example.[164] But there is still a lot of human communication we have not identified yet how to do remotely, let alone asynchronously, which is an important form of communication if people are in different time zones. The archetypal innovation that comes from spontaneous water-cooler talk or serendipitous connections are examples of this. Speaking on the topic, Bloom mentions, "It is hard to be creative at a distance, it is hard to be inspired and motivated at home, and employee loyalty is strained without social interaction."[165]

* * *

Taken together, these variables will lead to three main configurations for teams:

---

163 S.R. Baker, N. Bloom, S.J. Davis, S.J. Terry, "COVID-Induced Economic Uncertainty (No. 26983)," *National Bureau of Economic Research* (2020).

164 Joel Khalili, "Remote Workers Rejoice—Facebook's New Enterprise Virtual Reality Platform Is Here," *TechRadar*, May 22, 2020.

165 S.R. Baker, N. Bloom, S.J. Davis, S.J. Terry, "COVID-Induced Economic Uncertainty (No. 26983)," *National Bureau of Economic Research* (2020).

A) New Wave of Distributed Teams

As companies and people who never seriously considered full-time remote work try it out and discover it works for them, we will experience a new wave of distributed companies and teams—as we've already begun to see.

Bloom analyzed data on 2,500 workers looking at their preferences and abilities for remote work and suggests roughly 12 percent of them will work remotely full-time after the pandemic in the US.[166] Global Workforce Analytics (GWA) estimates 11 percent of white-collar workers globally will work remotely full-time, while Gartner expects it to be 19 percent of all workers.[167] [168]

I believe the current constraint for this wave of distributed teams is technology—once we have better technology (for example, innovations in AR and VR), we might go beyond roughly one in ten people working remotely full-time to one in five or more. Over time, I believe the main constraint on this number will be human—people craving in-person interactions.

After we get past the Third Wave of the Great Reboot through a mix of vaccine availability and herd immunity, most people will reduce their time working from home and crave at least some in-person interactions professionally. While some

---

166 Ibid.

167 "Work from Home Experience Survey Results," *Global Workplace Analytics*, August 25, 2020.

168 "The Executive's Guide to Returning to the Workplace Post COVID 19," Gartner, accessed November 20, 2020.

people thrive working from home and will continue to do so, the majority of people either prefer or have to spend time in an office or co-working space some of the time.

This "going back to the workplace" is certainly what we see in countries that have more or less controlled the COVID-19 crisis. Analysis of smartphone GPS data at the end of 2020 shows people are physically back in the workplace in New Zealand and Taiwan, the only two sizable places with control of the outbreak as of the time of this writing (and which were studied for their success for a research article in the medical journal *The Lancet*).[169] [170]

While both of these places saw drops in the time spent in the workplace at the beginning of the pandemic, as of November 2020 people were spending about as much in the workplace as they did pre-pandemic, as mobility data aggregated by Google shows.[171] [172] For comparison, places with ongoing outbreaks like the United States, the United Kingdom, Germany, France, and India were seeing people spend between

---

169 To analyze this, we used data aggregated by the Our World in Data initiative at the University of Oxford, looking at locations with at least three million people, which had an outbreak of at least five hundred cases and had controlled outbreaks (three or fewer new cases, rolling average of seven days) as of November 11, 2020.

170 J Summers et al., "Potential lessons from the Taiwan and New Zealand health responses to the COVID-19 pandemic," *The Lancet Regional Health—Western Pacific* (2020).

171 "Taiwan," COVID-19 Community Mobility Report, Google, November 6, 2020.

172 "New Zealand," COVID-19 Community Mobility Report, Google, November 6, 2020.

15 percent and 34 percent less time in their workplaces than they were pre-pandemic.[173] [174] [175] [176] [177]

These numbers, of course, will fluctuate, and there is no guarantee outbreaks will stay controlled. But the general story is most people get tired of working from home 100 percent of the time and want some level of in-person interaction with other workers. I certainly see this with my own team and business partners. Many are desperately ready to go back to the office.

B) Rise of Hybrid Teams

The hybrid office-plus-home-work experience will grow dramatically, being much more common than remote work. Estimates from Bloom, Gartner, and GWA put the number of people working in a hybrid way between 28 percent and 43 percent after the COVID-19 crisis ends.[178] [179] [180]

---

173 "United States," COVID-19 Community Mobility Report, Google, November 15, 2020.
174 "United Kingdom," COVID-19 Community Mobility Report, Google, November 15, 2020.
175 "Germany," COVID-19 Community Mobility Report, Google, November 15, 2020.
176 "France," COVID-19 Community Mobility Report, Google, November 15, 2020.
177 "India," COVID-19 Community Mobility Report, Google, November 15, 2020.
178 S.R. Baker, N. Bloom, S.J. Davis, S.J. Terry, "COVID-Induced Economic Uncertainty (No. 26983)," *National Bureau of Economic Research* (2020).
179 "Work from Home Experience Survey Results," Global Workplace Analytics, August 25, 2020.
180 "The Executive's Guide to Returning to the Workplace Post COVID 19," Gartner, accessed November 20, 2020.

Hybrid work arrangements will be a bit of a sweet spot between the benefits of fully in-person and fully remote work. As people experiment with distributed work arrangements, most find they do not want to work remotely full-time but only 20.3 percent want to go back to a scenario of never working remotely. Another 19.1 percent want to work remotely only rarely.[181]

C) Stable In-Person Core

For about half of the workers, professional life will still be in-person (between 46 percent and 59 percent according to estimates from Bloom, Gartner, and GWA).[182] This of course includes all the jobs that need in-person interactions to happen (e.g., most restaurants), but it also includes a significant portion of white-collar workers.

Even for white-collar workers, the share will be high: 46 percent according to GWA, the source that investigated this worker category specifically.[183]

* * *

---

181 S.R. Baker, N. Bloom, S.J. Davis, S.J. Terry, "COVID-Induced Economic Uncertainty (No. 26983)," *National Bureau of Economic Research* (2020).

182 S.R. Baker, N. Bloom, S.J. Davis, S.J. Terry, "COVID-Induced Economic Uncertainty (No. 26983)," *National Bureau of Economic Research* (2020); "Work from Home Experience Survey Results," Global Workplace Analytics, August 25, 2020; "The Executive's Guide to Returning to the Workplace Post COVID 19," Gartner, accessed November 20, 2020.

183 "The Executive's Guide to Returning to the Workplace Post COVID 19," Gartner, accessed November 20, 2020.

The four main drivers listed above all contribute to how work is being and will be reshaped. However, the following contribution by David Nordfors (co-founder of i4j Innovation for Jobs and senior data researcher at BOLD) and Vint Cerf (co-founder of i4j Innovation for Jobs, co-inventor of the internet, and chief internet evangelist at Google) takes these ideas and expounds on them in a radical new direction—the people-centered economy.

∗∗∗

PEOPLE-CENTERED ECONOMY AND THE FUTURE OF WORK

By David Nordfors (co-founder of i4j Innovation for Jobs and senior data researcher at BOLD) and Vint Cerf (co-founder of i4j Innovation for Jobs, co-inventor of the internet, and chief internet evangelist at Google)

> *Purpose of innovation:*
> *to create a sustainable economy,*
> *where we work with people we like,*
> *are valued by people we do not know,*
> *and provide for the people we love*

Today, the future of work is a serious concern, and artificial intelligence (AI) and machine learning are seen as ominous threats. This concern is based on the assumption that AI will kill more jobs than it creates, and the new jobs will be of a lower quality than the old ones. We believe this assumption is a result of focusing on tasks instead of the potential of people.

From the "task-centered" perspective, new technology threatens jobs because it can perform many tasks cheaper and better than humans can and will therefore replace humans and kill jobs. The dystopian discussion on the future of work follows as a result.

The "people-centered" perspective focuses instead on how technology can create new and better ways for people to be valuable for each other including augmenting people's capacity to do existing or new work better. The "people-centered economy" (PCE) therefore offers a solution to the future of work, and the economy as a whole, by focusing on solutions instead of on problems. In the PCE, new and better jobs are innovated at the same (or higher) rate than jobs are destroyed. Furthermore, the PCE makes a natural distinction between people and things, where things serve the purpose of making people see value in each other.

In the PCE, income and expenditure are put on the same footing; switching jobs and switching products (like phones) follow the same pattern, where people get new models and the old ones go away. The PCE thereby simplifies the understanding of the economy by reducing the levels of abstraction and placing the value of people at the center. Tasks will come and go while people will stay in the picture.

New technologies have wreaked havoc before, and even if AI and machine learning are unlike anything we have previously experienced, the pattern is the same. We can learn from history and how technological job destruction has been solved previously. We can see how analogous the patterns are by substituting only four words in excerpts from *The Communist Manifesto*, written by Karl Marx and Friedrich Engels at the dawn of the industrial revolution.

The substitutions are: *"Bourgeoisie"* with *"Internet Entrepreneurs,"* *"Proletariat"* with *"On-Demand Workers,"* *"Civilization"* with *"Digital Economy,"* and *"Revolution"* with *"Disruption."*

The result is a clear-sighted analysis from 1848 on the internet economy and the future of work today:

> *"Internet entrepreneurship cannot exist without constant disruption of markets, bringing uninterrupted disturbance of all social conditions. The need of a constantly expanding market chases Internet entrepreneurship over the whole surface of the globe, giving a digital character to production and consumption in every country. Established industries are pushed aside and the rapid improvement of all markets and cheap prices compel all nations to introduce the digital economy and become Internet*

entrepreneurs themselves. Internet entrepreneurship has merged markets and concentrated ownership into a few hands. It is like the sorcerer, who is no longer able to control the powers of the demons whom he has called up by his spells. The periodically returning market bubbles create great destruction. When these bubbles burst, society regresses; industry and commerce seem to be destroyed; and why? Because there is too much digital economy, too many ways of doing business.

Internet entrepreneurship has created the modern working class—the on-demand workers, who must sell themselves in bits and pieces. They have become a commodity, exposed to the whims of the market. Their work has lost all individual character and all charm. It is only the most simple and most easily acquired work that is required of them.

The on-demand worker's production cost is limited almost entirely to his living costs. But the price of a commodity is in the long run equal to its production cost. Therefore, the more the individual character disappears from his work, the wage decreases in proportion. The lower middle class will gradually become on-demand workers, partly because their specialized skills are rendered worthless by new methods of production."[184]

—KARL MARX AND FRIEDRICH ENGELS,

FROM *THE COMMUNIST MANIFESTO*, 1848

(WITH WORD SUBSTITUTIONS)

---

184 Karl Marx and Friedrich Engels, *The Communist Manifesto* (London: Penguin Books, 1985).

The implication: **Internet entrepreneurship has become the new bourgeoisie.**

Graph: Wealth Inequality is at Its Highest in Nearly 80 Years
Richest 1% Share of U.S. Wealth

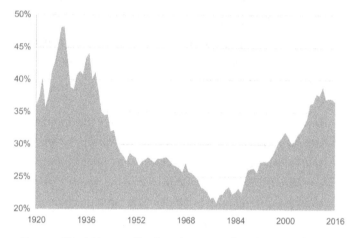

Source: World Inequality Database, retrieved September 25, 2020

In the US, the top 1 percent now owns a proportion of the economy so large it hasn't been seen since before World War II. The average worker, earning less than the median salary, is in the red and owns less than nothing. The communist analysis looms once again and ideas analogous with communism are emerging.[185]

But communism has never worked. One of its several design flaws is, "After we get rid of the oppressors, we can build a good society," which has always been a fantasy for

---

185 "Wealth Inequality—Top 1% Share," *World Inequality Database*, accessed September 30, 2020.

revolutionaries. It seeds a culture of finger-pointing and violence that often persists after the oppressors have been removed. This is often because revolutionary leaders are usually better at fighting enemies than building economies. Once in power, they tend to remove all capable people from the previous government who knew how to run things, and thus they build mediocre (or worse) societies.

Communist leaders often keep themselves in power by continuing to find more enemies to finger-point at and fight or imagining them if they must. These scenarios doomed both the Soviet Union and Nazi Germany. Finger-pointing will always lead to moving in the wrong direction because it points to a real or imagined problem, not the solution.

Instead, inclusive middle-class wellbeing economies found the solution and subsequently ruled the world economy until this day. Instead of "revolution," Swedish Prime Minister Per-Albin Hansson coined "the people's home," or the "Nordic Model" in 1928:

> "We don't look down on each other...there is equality, consideration, cooperation, helpfulness. Applied to the large public and citizen's home, this would mean tearing down all social and economic walls and barriers that now divide us into the privileged and the underserved, the rulers and the ruled, the exploiters and the exploited...To become a good people's home, class distinctions must be removed, social care developed, wealth and income gaps must be narrowed, workers should take part in managing the wealth we build,

democracy must be fully implemented and applied also socially and economically."[186]

Just three decades later, Sweden had gone from a poor country to being one of the richer countries in the world, ranking high in economic, social, and educational indicators. Similar economic "miracles" have also happened in, for example, Singapore and Israel, both of which applied the successful concept similar to Per-Albin's people's home.[187]

Franklin Delano Roosevelt's New Deal in 1933 is an especially noteworthy example when it comes to impact on the world economy. It is usually framed as the remedy for the Great Depression and the crash on Wall Street in 1929, but it actually matches the Nordic Model so well in time and outcome that the analogy is worthwhile. They both solved the problems observed by Marx and Engels with inclusive middle-class economies. It is likely fair to observe, however, in the US, World War II introduced a massive demand for labor that put many women to work as well as men, driving significant economic growth.

The key tool for building the Swedish people's home was presented at the Stockholm World Exhibition in 1930, when six architects launched "funkis," a building style that used affordable materials and was enabled by quick and efficient construction. It came with a manifesto, "Acceptera!" ("Accept!") that outlined design as an instrument for building

---

186 Fritz Stern, and Tim Tilton, "The Political Theory of Swedish Social Democracy," *Foreign Affairs* 70, no. 3 (1991).

187 Angus Maddison, *The World Economy*, Volumes 1 and 2 (Paris: OECD, 2006).

a new society. The key message was the same as Marx's: mass production has come to stay while traditions and crafts, vocations, and culture are gone. The solution was to embrace this core idea and create a new culture for the masses, with mass production and consumption as the basis for a middle-class economy in the machine age. One way to sum this up was, *"Accept the present reality, as this is the only way of mastering it, and create a livable culture."*

This shaped not only the modern Swedish economy but also the way people lived. The design industry in Sweden has now become famous for enterprises such as IKEA, and you can clearly see the core ideas of affordability, mass production, and efficiency in IKEA furniture. The general concept of the "American Dream" was also analogous because it provided a vision of the middle-class American economy people could follow, which was key for creating that economy.

Our present industrial revolution, with AI and machine learning, is now taking us from mass-production to mass-personalization. This time it is depreciating the vocations and traditions created in the previous industrial revolution. Now, just like then, the solution calls for a similar recipe—designing a new society with new concepts of not only how we should work and educate, but also how we can live.

The solution to the future of work is to reinvent the New Deal and the Nordic Model, applying the same principles of inclusiveness and human value that created the greatest economies of the 1900s, but switching context to the new industrial revolution.

We are developing, together with members of our innovation for jobs (i4j) community, a framework for designing the next generation of successful economies. It is presented in detail in our recent book *The People-Centered Economy: The New Ecosystem for Work*. It suggests an economic model from higher concepts down to business models, policy recommendations, and examples of existing initiatives that fit with the PCE.

The purpose of innovation in the PCE is a sustainable economy where we do meaningful work with people we like, are valued by the market, and provide for the people we love. If innovation does this, we will prosper.

For the economy to work, people must have a self-interest in seeing their friends and family do well. It also requires communities to feel like a part of this new economy to thrive.

EXPLAINING PCE—THE PEOPLE-CENTERED ECONOMY

Our present economy is a "task-centered economy," driven by market-forces aiming at lowering the cost of tasks. The "people-centered economy" is driven by market forces aiming to raise the value of people. Both economies are in agreement, people make themselves valuable by performing valuable tasks, but the drivers are not quite the same:

A task-centered economy seeks people to do valuable tasks.

A people-centered economy seeks tasks that make people valuable.

Switching the order of two words might not seem important, but it makes all the difference. A task-centered economy will typically shape people to fit job slots. A people-centered economy will ideally shape jobs to fit people, as in, "Let's find out what you are good at and like doing and see what opportunities we can create for you." This might seem puzzling from a task-centered point of view, perhaps more like pampering than building a strong economy. Then again, perhaps this is a shortcoming of the task-centered paradigm. It does not appreciate what people could do for each other as much as it values existing demand. We suggest economic models might be vastly improved and simplified by optimizing the value of people instead of the cost of things, as suggested in the figure.

Today, we have a labor market, where people earn their living and spend their income on the consumer market. Placing tasks, services, and products at the center of the markets lead to the optimization of cost-efficiency. We are good at this today, but it has the effect of driving production costs down while reducing the value of work. An argument can be made for making products and services more affordable, but without maintaining labor's earning capacity, workers will not benefit.

The PCE merges the labor and consumer markets into a single market with people at the center. Around them, companies offer two kinds of services: one for earning money and another for spending it. The economy focuses on people and provides them with things to do for earning and spending, respectively.

It is an exact parallel to the difference between the assumption the earth moves around the sun, which leads to simpler and better astronomical models, and the old Ptolemaic assumption the sun moves around the Earth, which leads to very complicated models. (Despite it being too complicated, the Ptolemaic system was in use for hundreds of years because people could clearly see the sun moving around Earth.)

We are stuck in the same "geocentric" rut today, using unnecessarily complicated economic models just because we assume artifacts have value. Alternately, the PCE-based assumption that artifacts make people more valuable to each other is the key to "heliocentric" economic models, which provide a clearer and simpler understanding of the economy as shown in the figure below. Today, we explain the economy with several markets connecting in various complex ways, while PCE has a single-market view that is simple: a good economy balances both spending and earning services.

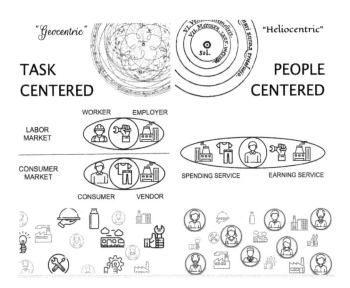

Therefore, the PCE postulates organizations should always serve people, not the other way around, leading to the following simple and handy definition of the economy:

People create and exchange value, served by organization.

We can envision the economy as people embedded in an ecosystem of organizations and companies competing to increase the value people see in and create for each other.

It is for the macro-economist to be the system engineer, tuning the balance between the services for earning and spending, respectively, by stimulating innovation in whichever one is lagging such that meaningful earning and spending is executed with comparable ease.

The microeconomist will, in synergy, take advantage of imbalances between services for earning and spending by improving whichever service has the greater demand. In this model, the ecosystem is a two-sided market where organizations serving spending and earning needs, respectively, connect and negotiate so every human is served by organizations for every particular need.

The conundrum of this day and age, whether AI will create or kill jobs, is a false dichotomy. It will do both. But seen through the PCE lens the question becomes crystal clear, it is simply the case of a balanced economy: is AI-innovation being applied more to earning or to spending? The emphasis today is on "spending," that is, increasing demand for products and services, so the conclusion is we need to support innovation that helps people earn. We need as much innovation for earning a living as we have for helping people spend what they earn.

In short, we suggest moving from a labor market where people compete for jobs to one where jobs compete for people. By offering the earner a richer and more tailored choice of alternative livelihoods and seeing the need for workers exceeds the need for jobs, market forces will drive the competing job providers to offer people more satisfying, valuable, and well-paid jobs. This puts services for earning on equal footing with services for spending where both compete to serve the individual.

Today, when unemployment approaches zero, the lack of workforce drives up wages and employers start hiring unfit candidates, lowering productivity. The result is "wage inflation." We believe the innovation economy may create a new work dynamic; increasing labor costs and sinking productivity is a strong incentive for automation. If people are no longer attracted by a job, there is an incentive for innovation to compensate for the lack of people. The situation is analogous to when a product or service does not attract customers in an innovation economy. Hence, wage inflation in the industrial economy is replaced by a balance between automation and job-innovation, leading to increased productivity and growth in the innovation economy.

Companies compete for workers with the right competencies. AI, ML, and robotics have the capacity to increase the value of work by augmenting the capacity of people to do creative work. Applied properly, these technologies increase the value of people. Of course, we must re-skill workers as the demand for skills changes. Thus, continued education over a career or work is a requirement now more than ever.

Profitable growth markets for matching jobs, upskilling workers, and education are pillars in the PCE, together with a huge untapped market for identifying and leveraging people's undetected abilities.

Converting a task-centered economy into a people-centered one should be straightforward by introducing what is missing today: the ecosystem for innovating jobs and making workers more valuable.

For further reading, see *The People-Centered Economy: The New Ecosystem For Work.*[188]

---

188 David Nordfors and Vint Cerf, *The People Centered Economy: The New Ecosystem for Work* (IIIJ Foundation, 2018).

DIFFICULT TRANSITION TO THE FUTURE

"Imagine telling a farmer in 1900, that the number of people working in agriculture in the US would decrease from 40 percent to 2 percent in the next 100 years...What kind of jobs are those people going to do? Will there be enough food?"

—DEREK OZKAL FROM THE KAUFFMAN FOUNDATION,

REFERRING TO A HYPOTHETICAL SCENARIO

PROPOSED BY PROFESSOR DAVID AUTOR

There is a reasonable line of argument that states we do not need to worry too much about the three trends discussed here. "Human history is all about the automation of work," from the plow to the automobile, and our society has managed the transition from an agricultural economy to an industrial economy.[189] [190] Will the jobs destroyed by tech now lead to new jobs created elsewhere, just like during the Industrial Revolution?

While it is probably the case we will all be better off in the future, the transition will be rough. As economist Tyler Cowen points out, comparing today's shift to the Industrial Revolution is not comforting.[191] Estimates by Gregory Clark, economic historian at the University of California, Davis, show the real wage of English workers may have fallen about 10 percent from 1770 to 1810 (the core of the Industrial Revolution in England). Clark estimates it took sixty to seventy

---

189 Ross Dawson, "How to Prepare for the Future of Work—Human-Machine Collaboration, Humanisation, Education," *Ross Dawson*, November 6, 2016.

190 Tyler Cowen, "Industrial Revolution Comparisons Aren't Comforting," *Bloomberg.com*, Feb 16, 2017.

191 Ibid.

years of transition, after industrialization, for people working in England to see sustained real wage gains.[192] The rise
of movements from communism to luddism came on the
tails of the social disruption of the Industrial Revolution and
serve as evidence of how tough the transition was.

Said another way, the Industrial Revolution sucked for many
people for a long time. The impact of the Great Reboot on
the work sphere will also suck for many.

We see examples of this unequal impact today. As of September 2020, the job crisis was already gone for high-wage
earners; their employment levels in the US were already at
the same levels seen pre-crisis. But low-wage workers had 19.3
percent lower employment levels during the same time period.

**Graph: Employment Rate for High-Income Workers Returned
to Pre-Crisis Levels in Sept. 2020**
Percent change in employment

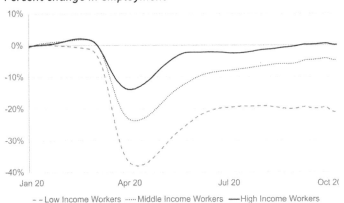

*Source: Economic Tracker, Opportunity Insights, Track the
Recovery, retrieved on November 15, 2020*

---

192 Ibid.

I am optimistic and believe these technological innovations will create a better society in the long run, but the key term here is *long run*. To get to this better future, we all have a lot of work to do.

CHAPTER 6

CITY: THE RESHUFFLED MAP OF INNOVATION

———

A 2020 report at a major news outlet, titled "The Death of the City," describes how remote working is "making urban living obsolete." In its opening paragraph it cites the history of Siena, Italy. In 1348, the city was a medieval powerhouse for banking and proto-industrial activity until it was dramatically affected by the Black Death, losing 60 percent of its population. The city only recovered to its pre-pandemic size in the twentieth century.[193]

The article is one example of many claiming a general narrative that goes something like this: the COVID-19 pandemic and the growth of remote work could lead to the end of cities. It is especially bad in places like New York and San Francisco, and it can lead to the end of Silicon Valley.

———

193 Aitor Hernández-Morales, Kalina Oroschakoff, and Jacopo Barigazzi, "The Death of the City," *POLITICO*, August 3, 2020.

To make their cases, these articles bring up a mix of points on the advantages of remote working, stories of people leaving "superstar" cities like San Francisco or New York for cheaper places (nevermind the stories featured are often of families with kids—a point in life when historically people have left cities for suburbs and cheaper areas anyways), and falling rent prices.[194][195]

The general narrative presented makes some solid points. It is true some people are leaving cities. It is true remote working is becoming more accepted. It is all but certain remote working technology will get better over the years.

But when we dig deeper underneath the surface of the stories, we quickly see the trends cannot be as simple as "the end of cities," "New York is dead," or "Silicon Valley is over" as these narratives suggest. For example:

- While real estate prices in Manhattan are *down* year-over-year, prices in broader New York City are actually *up* as of November 2020.[196][197]
- Inventory of housing for sale in the city of San Francisco proper grew during the pandemic (suggesting more people putting homes up for sale), but it has remained essentially unchanged for the broader metropolitan area

194 Richard Florida and Benjamin Schneider, "The Global Housing Crisis," *Bloomberg News*, April 11, 2018.
195 Joel Kotkin, "The Coronavirus Is Changing the Future of Home, Work, and Life," *The Daily Beast*, April 11, 2020.
196 "Manhattan Housing Market," Redfin, accessed November 18, 2020.
197 "New York Housing Market," Redfin, accessed November 18, 2020.

as research from real estate company Zillow shows.[198] For other major metropolitan areas like Boston, Los Angeles, Miami, Seattle, and Washington DC, housing inventory for sales is actually *down*.[199]

- People are back in the workplace at pre-pandemic levels in New Zealand and Taiwan, the only two rich economies to control the pandemic so far, as GPS data aggregated by Google shows.[200] [201]
- Migration data from LinkedIn shows the number one place New Yorkers have moved to the twelve months ending in November 2020 is Los Angeles—hardly a small city.[202] The number one destination away from the San Francisco Bay Area in the same period is Seattle, another tech hub.[203]

In the middle of a crisis, it is easy to overestimate the long-term impact of the pandemic. The rise of remote work and the migration away from cities are probably the two most overestimated changes coming from the pandemic. While there is a real reshuffle of tech and innovation activity, there are several key patterns that will dominate the life of cities post-pandemic.

---

198 "Zillow 2020 Urban-Suburban Market Report," Zillow Research, October 2, 2020.

199 Ibid.

200 "Taiwan," COVID-19 Community Mobility Report, Google, November 15, 2020.

201 "United Kingdom," COVID-19 Community Mobility Report, Google, November 15, 2020.

202 "New York City," LinkedIn Workforce Report, LinkedIn, November 2020.

203 "San Francisco," LinkedIn Workforce Report, LinkedIn, November 2020.

1. **People live in cities for many reasons which have nothing to do with work.**

There are many reasons why people live in cities outside of work. Cities are major centers for entertainment and social life. Some—like San Francisco, Melbourne, and Rio de Janeiro—are endowed with gorgeous natural landscapes. Others have rich architecture and history, such as Beijing, London, and Paris. These cities being millennia old and having lived through their own share of pandemics is also a clue to the overblown nature of the "end cities" narrative.

I was talking about the topic with Marianna Presotto, an artist friend who lives in Alameda, California, an island that is a short drive or ferry ride away from San Francisco. I asked if she was thinking about moving further from the city. Her answer was, "No, I am thinking about moving into it," to take advantage of the temporary reductions in rent prices.

For career-minded people who are choosing where to live to optimize professional gains or for the relatively introverted one in four people who prefer remote work to in-person, these non-work considerations are not as prominent. We all have different priorities, after all. But I suspect the overlap of "career-minded" or "relatively introverted" with "technologists" and "writers" is pretty high, and that leads to an overrepresentation of the "end of cities" perspective on public discourse.

2. **Many of the moves happening will turn out to be temporary.**

While "I am leaving San Francisco (or New York)" can make for a good story, many of the moves will turn out to be temporary. In fact, that is what data from the US Postal Service suggests, with short-term moves up during the pandemic but no meaningful increase in long-term moves.[204]

During the time frame from February to July 2020, the number of temporary change-of-address (CoA) requests in the US increased by 27 percent compared to the previous year, whereas permanent CoA requests increased by only 2 percent. The majority of these temporary CoA requests were in March and April when the pandemic was at its peak in the US and has since then become closer to 2019 request numbers.[205]

As constraints on where one lives become detached from how one makes a living, at least temporarily for some of the population, it is natural people experiment with different living arrangements. A friend has moved from Washington DC to Florida to be close to in-laws and homeschool kids. A different friend moved from San Francisco to Sao Paulo, and then to a rural, waterfall-rich area in Brazil. Another one is experimenting with living a hundred miles outside of London and dividing time between there and his London home.

I myself write this from Hawaii, where I am spending time with family. I am also planning on a season in my birth state of Minas Gerais in Brazil for the next year—although my home is still in the Bay Area. Whether or not these kinds of experiments will become permanent is very much still up in

---

204 Marie Patino, "New Data Shows Just How Much Americans Moved Temporarily During Covid," *Bloomberg News*, October 12, 2020.

205 "Coronavirus Moving Study Shows More Than 15.9 Million People Moved During COVID-19," *MYMOVE*, October 12, 2020.

the air—and much more a function of family and personal choices than pandemic-influenced decisions.

The major drop in rent prices we see is not accompanied by a similar drop in sales prices of homes, which is consistent with this notion of an increase in experimental and temporary moves, but not as much long-term ones.[206]

If you can make big-city wages with small town cost of living, that is an unbelievably good deal. Over time, labor markets will settle and the arbitrage opportunity of getting paid Silicon Valley money while paying Montana cost of living will get competed away.

No doubt some of these moves will be permanent, but these hardly add up to an "end of cities" story.

3. **Permanent relocations will be dominated by "near-city" moves.**

As we covered in the previous chapter, the future of work is more hybrid than remote. Over time, working away from your team 100 percent of the time gets tiring, and most of the people who do not get back to the office full-time will adopt a hybrid model of work.

Much of the movement in migration and prices we see today are consistent with this expectation, including the data we mentioned at the beginning of the chapter. Real estate prices

---

206 "Zillow 2020 Urban-Suburban Market Report," Zillow Research, October 2, 2020.

in New York City are *up* even though Manhattan-only prices are down.[207][208]

The major metropolitan areas studied by Zillow—San Francisco, Boston, Los Angeles, Miami, Seattle, and Washington DC—all have fewer homes for sale, even if in the case of the city of San Francisco proper inventory is up.[209] While commenting on a softening of demand for homes in the densest areas of San Francisco, chief market analyst for the Bay Area at the real estate brokerage company Compass Patrick Carlisle states, "More rural and suburban counties (around the area) and markets have gone absolutely nuts—Sonoma, Monterey, Marin."[210]

RESHUFFLED MAP OF INNOVATION

While the above makes a clear case why we are not living "the death of the city," some meaningful changes are happening. But rather than being caused by COVID-19, they are previously ongoing trends that were accelerated by it—and are a lot more nuanced than you could fit into a headline. It is the case some people are leaving Silicon Valley and a few other superstar cities like London and New York. But as my friend Torsten Kolind, founder and CEO of YouNoodle says, "People leaving San Francisco was not a new story in February 2020."

207 "Manhattan Housing Market," Redfin, accessed November 18, 2020.
208 "New York Housing Market," Redfin, accessed November 18, 2020.
209 Ibid.
210 Jordan Novet, "San Francisco Housing Has Cooled as Some Flee the City, but Demand Is Still There," *CNBC*, September 27, 2020.

The places experiencing meaningful out-migration are primarily those that had overheated housing markets and abnormal dynamics to begin with. This move out of the city is not the story, for example, in tech hubs like Berlin or Austin, where the cost of living is still relatively affordable (and some of these are gaining ground).

But even with the recent out-migration, the changes are much more a story of relieving pressure on the overheated systems of New York and San Francisco than a story of the death of these places. This is bringing these "superstar" markets closer in line with other places on certain metrics, and it creates new opportunities for smaller tech hubs.

Austin is frequently cited as a destination for those leaving San Francisco, so it is informative to look at figures for these places to see how things are changing.[211] A look at the numbers strongly suggests a reshuffled map of tech but not a tidal wave shift away from superstar cities.

In late 2020—as both Pfizer and Moderna announced vaccines with higher than 90 percent effectiveness, and at least ten vaccines in phase three testing—Austin, Texas is the city in the US that has gained the most people in the past twelve months. (As I and others have written with the Kauffman Foundation in the past few years, Austin has been gaining

---

211 Joe Lonsdale, "California, Love It and Leave It," *The Wall Street Journal*, November 15, 2020.

ground on start-up activity for a while.)[212] [213] [214] The top five, according to LinkedIn data, are:

1. Austin, Texas
2. Charlotte, North Carolina
3. Tampa-St. Petersburg, Florida
4. Denver, Colorado
5. Seattle, Washington

But even with all these gains, the net population growth resulting from people moving to Austin is 1.4 percent over twelve months.[215] Of those, about 12 percent are, on net, coming from the San Francisco Bay Area. When we extrapolate those numbers to the total population of Austin, we get about 31,000 newcomers over one year, with between three and four thousand of those coming from the Bay Area.[216]

Relatedly, the housing market in San Francisco city proper has slowed down. The median number of days homes spend on the market is up, price drops are more common, and homes sold above list price are less common.[217] The broader US market is going in the opposite direction as is the housing market

212 Aaron Steckelberg and Carolyn Y. Johnson, "These Are the Top Coronavirus Vaccines to Watch," *The Washington Post*, November 23, 2020.
213 "United States," LinkedIn Workforce Report, LinkedIn, November 2020.
214 Arnobio Morelix, Victor Hwang, and Inara Tareque, "Zero Barriers: Three Mega Trends Shaping the Future of Entrepreneurship," *Ewing Marion Kauffman Foundation* (2017).
215 "United States," LinkedIn Workforce Report, LinkedIn, November 2020.
216 "Population Overview," Austin Chamber of Commerce, accessed November 20, 2020.
217 "San Francisco Housing Market," Redfin, accessed November 18, 2020.

in Austin, often cited as an alternative to Silicon Valley (and one of my favorite US cities). This has brought the San Francisco housing market a little more in line with other ones.

But despite the opposing trends and reports of historic "red hot" demand in Austin and a cooled-down demand in San Francisco, San Francisco is still a much more competitive real estate market.[218] [219] [220] San Francisco homes still sell faster than homes in Austin (twenty-eight versus thirty-six days, respectively), and are more likely to be sold above list price (54.4 percent versus 39.1 percent).[221] [222] San Francisco homes are more likely to see price drops, however (16.1 percent versus 12.8 percent).[223] [224]

SILICON VALLEY IS DEAD. LONG LIVE SILICON VALLEY

If you are following the stories of technologists, investors, and founders leaving Silicon Valley for greener pastures, the quote below will ring familiar:

> *"Entrepreneurial zeal has been overtaken by worries about fierce global competition, increasing government regulation and the cumbersome size of some companies, as well as the high cost of living, poor transportation, and pollution."*

---

218 Ibid.
219 "Austin Housing Market," Redfin, accessed November 18, 2020.
220 "United States Housing Market," Redfin, accessed November 18, 2020.
221 "San Francisco Housing Market," Redfin, accessed November 18, 2020.
222 "Austin Housing Market," Redfin, accessed November 18, 2020.
223 "San Francisco Housing Market," Redfin, accessed November 18, 2020.
224 "Austin Housing Market," Redfin, accessed November 18, 2020.

The complaints about the high cost of living, government regulation, and attractive global alternatives are both common. But they are not new. In fact the quote, which comes from the *New York Times* article "Silicon Valley May Have Lost Its Way," was published in 1992—nearly three decades ago.[225] Since then, here is a brief list of companies founded in the area:

- Airbnb
- eBay
- Facebook
- Google
- Netflix
- Uber

That these complaints are old does not make them untrue. There are certain governance aspects of life in Silicon Valley that present serious headwinds (even if not caused by the pandemic) to the area's development. For example:

- The property-crime rate in San Francisco is now the highest in the US.[226]
- Zoning restrictions make building housing in the Bay Area expensive (sometimes impossible), pricing out most anybody with lower- or middle-incomes from being able to buy (or even live) in the major centers. Surprisingly to many people outside, it also prices out techies. We hear about "two exit" (and even three exit) towns, which are

---

225 John Markoff, "Silicon Valley May Have Lost Its Way," *The New York Times*, September 28, 1992.

226 Joe Lonsdale, "California, Love It and Leave It," *The Wall Street Journal*, November 15, 2020.

the places where one needs to have not one, but two or more successful tech start-up exits to be able to live in them.[227] [228]

- Homelessness is rampant, and it is relatively common to see needles and human waste on the streets. The city created an official taskforce to do "poop patrol," and the city has been called "the doo-doo capital of the US." There was an app made by a resident called Snapcrap to report human poop.[229]

Altogether, these are major headwinds, but they are not death sentences.

* * *

At the height of lockdowns, San Francisco might have been one of the worst places in the world for establishing a start-up. Lockdowns combined with wildfire season made for a bleak picture. The sky outside had an apocalyptic, red hue: somewhere between a scene from *Blade Runner* and *Star Wars*. The smell in the air brought to mind breathing in diesel truck exhaust. Not long before, the typically balmy weather of Northern California had gotten desert hot, with heatwaves. (As I heard said, "I miss it when it was just the pandemic.")

---

227 Antonio García Martínez (@antoniogm), "'If the Startup IPOs, I Might Buy a House' Is a Thing Real People in the SF Bay Area Say," Twitter, 16 July 2020.

228 Antonio García Martínez (@antoniogm), "Atherton, Woodside, Portola Valley....," Twitter, 16 July 2020.

229 Charles Kesler, "California's Biggest Cities Confront a 'Defecation Crisis'," *The Wall Street Journal*, August 16, 2019.

The double-whammy of lockdowns and smoke negated the usual advantages of being in the area—especially the agglomeration benefits of easily connecting and working together with lots of amazing people in-person. But the usual disadvantages of being in the area were still felt keenly. The cost of living and doing business in the area is incredibly high. Unbeknownst to many people not living in the Bay Area, internet and cell phone connectivity is shockingly spotty and expensive (which, when travel was more open, made for embarrassing conversations with visitors coming from places like South Korea).[230]

But the region still has an enduring appeal that will continue to exist in the long run.

To start, the city is far ahead of the rest of the world in tech start-up activity. As shown in research from Startup Genome, where I served as CIO, the top five start-up ecosystems in the world and their respective ecosystem values are:

- Silicon Valley: $677B
- Beijing: $345B
- New York City: $147B
- Boston: $96B
- London: $92B

Silicon Valley produces as much value as the next four top-performing start-up ecosystems combined, and even if

---

230 Shawn Paul Wood, "Silicon Valley Has Some of America's Slowest Internet Connections," *Adweek*, November 6, 2014.

it lost half of the value it would still be the largest start-up ecosystem in the world, all else equal.

Additionally, even the stories of people leaving California can be more nuanced than they seem at a first glance.

Antonio Garcia Martinez, the fascinating author of the book *Chaos Monkeys* and a tech executive and former Facebooker, mentioned some of the downsides of California when he moved away a few years ago to the remote Orcas Island on the Pacific Northwest to live in a yurt (as a camping, hippie-ish person, I could see myself making a similar move).[231] Martinez later moved back to the Bay Area for a job, first to a suburb-y area of Silicon Valley and then to the city of San Francisco proper in the middle of the pandemic (I could also see myself making a similar move).[232]

In a similar vein, the founder and CEO of YouNoodle Torsten Kolind, who I mentioned previously in this chapter, is originally from Denmark. He moved to San Francisco in 2009 at the peak of the financial crisis, when optimism for Silicon Valley was low and venture capital activity was the lowest it had been in years.[233] He started his company in Silicon Valley with the whole team co-located, but over time began to hire in other places (e.g., Mexico City). During the pandemic, he and his spouse (who until recently worked at a

231 Antonio García Martínez, *Chaos Monkeys: Obscene Fortune and Random Failure in Silicon Valley* (New York: HarperCollinsPublishers, 2016).

232 Antonio García Martínez, "Ever the Contrarian, I've Decided to Move to the City Everyone Is Fleeing, and Take Residence in One of Those Old SF Edwardians Held Together by Paint and Prop 13. I Have No Doubt This Is a Terrible Idea." Twitter, November 15, 2020.

233 "PwC MoneyTree Report Q3 2020," PwC, accessed November 20, 2020.

major publicly traded tech company) moved to Copenhagen primarily for family reasons.

But Kolind has considered a move back to San Francisco and is even more optimistic for SF post-pandemic than before, as crises create "slack in the system," which have often turned into opportunity in the city's past. In fact, the city has thrived through crises, for instance after the Great Recession and the Dot-Com Bust.

Silicon Valley has had major crises and transformations in its history. Although it is rarely mentioned today, considering the city of San Francisco proper as part of Silicon Valley is a relatively new development. It used to be that "Silicon Valley" meant the suburban sprawl around Palo Alto, Mountain View, and the like. That began to change around the 2000s when newer start-ups began to set up offices in the city of San Francisco directly. Exemplifying the perception, a 2006 essay from legendary investor Paul Graham talks about how "Silicon Valley proper is soul-crushing suburban sprawl."[234]

Fabrice Cavarretta, a professor at ESSEC Business School in Paris, used to work as a software engineer at Oracle and studied at Stanford in the '80s and '90s. He told me over drinks going to San Francisco for fun was unusual among the suburban-dwelling Silicon Valley techie crowd of the time; the city was a little too dangerous and rowdy for most.

Looking beyond the recent crises, cities have a history of adapting. London became a much healthier city after the

---

234 Paul Graham, "How to Be Silicon Valley," *paulgraham.com*, May 2006.

British cholera epidemic of the 1830s spurred science and engineering developments like sewage disposal and clean water supply.[235] Chicago pioneered the skyscraper—buildings taller than you could see anywhere else in the world—in the very business district the 1871 fire had turned into a wasteland.[236] New York City was considered "done for" in the '70s and '80s, but it had major growth and revival in the 1990s once high crime rates were under control.[237]

These examples are all better parallels for what is happening in cities today than Siena after the Black Death.

The challenges to superstar cities are real, and no city is destined for certain success nor certain failure. But crisis brings opportunities, and together we can build better places out of seeming disaster.

235 Derek Thompson, "Get Ready for the Great Urban Comeback," *The Atlantic*, September 4, 2020.

236 Ibid.

237 Richard Florida, "Understanding the Great Crime Decline in US Cities," *Bloomberg*, January 16, 2018.

CHAPTER 7

WORLD: THE SHIFTING DYNAMICS OF HYPER-LOCAL AND HYPER-GLOBAL

―――

Jeff Hoffman is a founder of multiple start-ups and has been the CEO of both public and private corporations, including being part of well-known companies like Priceline.com. Today, as chairman of the Global Entrepreneurship Network (GEN), he spends a lot of his time mentoring entrepreneurs around the world. Right now, this means overwhelmingly helping them navigate the crises and opportunities of the Great Reboot.

Between Hoffman's experience with the travel industry and his global entrepreneurship work, he was one of the key people I wanted to interview about the impact of the pandemic on founders globally. He recently told me a story that exemplifies some of the unique situations the Great Reboot is creating.

In one of his global mentorship calls, including entrepreneurs from over a hundred different countries, a spirits distillery in the US was trying to figure out what to do with their massive idle capacity in the middle of the pandemic. The distillery's main customers like bars and liquor stores had cut down orders dramatically. At that point in time, the local market had a major shortage of disinfectant products like hand sanitizer, as did many other markets around the world. Working together on these mentorship calls, the distillery realized it could use its chemists and equipment to make disinfectant products rather than spirits, and it switched to doing so with major success.

Another group of entrepreneurs in the cohort from Ghana talked about their own shortage of hand sanitizer, and they asked to import the product from North America into Africa. At the time, the distillery could not even meet local demand, and global logistics chains were tough to navigate. Thus, physically sending the product across the analog world was not really an option. But the distillery offered to teach a class on how to make hand sanitizer online so the

Ghanaian entrepreneurs could make their own.

* * *

As you might imagine, writing about something as broad as the likely impact of the Great Reboot on the world at large was one of the hardest chapters to write in this book.

On one hand, I had been seeing all these signs of globalization and global connectivity in retreat:

- Global supply chains were disrupted, and industries were reshaping and turning to local alternatives—including making products with 3D printers.[238] [239]
- Global travel declined dramatically, with no expectations of it to return to pre-pandemic levels. Immigrants had their right to stay in their countries of residence questioned.[240] [241] [242]
- Decline in cross-border investments and companies focusing on domestic consolidation while governments constricted the rules on inward foreign investments.[243] [244]

Looking at these kinds of signals together made the claims many made along the lines of "globalization is another victim of COVID-19" compelling.[245] But on the other hand, I could also see very encouraging signs of a major rise in global connectivity:

---

238 Steven A. Altman, "Will Covid-19 Have a Lasting Impact on Globalization?" *Harvard Business Review*, August 17, 2020.

239 "Trade Set to Plunge as COVID-19 Pandemic Upends Global Economy," Press Release, WTO, April 8, 2020.

240 Steven A. Altman, "Will Covid-19 Have a Lasting Impact on Globalization?" *Harvard Business Review*, August 17, 2020.

241 Yen Nee Lee, "5 Charts Show Which Travel Sectors Were Worst Hit by the Coronavirus," *CNBC*, May 6, 2020.

242 Noah Higgins-Dunn, "Bill Gates Says More than 50% of Business Travel Will Disappear in Post-Coronavirus World," *CNBC*, November 18, 2020.

243 "Insights—How COVID-19 Is Shaping the Global M&A Outlook," Goldman Sachs, June 16, 2020.

244 Jacob A. Kuipers, "Covid-19 Accelerated Nationalist Trends in Cross-Border M&A," *M&A Review*, September 17, 2020.

245 Andrea Riquier, "Another COVID-19 Victim: Globalization," *MarketWatch*, September 28, 2020.

- As events and conferences were cancelled, virtual events became the norm and helped expand the coverage to global audiences.[246]
- SpaceX's Starlink internet services provided services to emergency workers and people in remote areas.[247] [248]
- Global scientific establishments collaborated in research and development of a vaccine.[249] [250]
- Demand increased for global, decentralized blockchain protocols for healthcare systems.[251]
- Global technology enabled businesses to grow globally, such as Amazon, Uber, DoorDash, and Zoom.

After talking with people in every continent of the world and hearing convincing arguments from both the "decline of globalization" and "new rise of globalism" perspectives, it finally hit me (though perhaps it took too long): both the decline and the rise are true. They are just happening in different domains.

246 Michael Price, "As COVID-19 Forces Conferences Online, Scientists Discover Upsides of Virtual Formatm" *Science*, April 30, 2020.

247 Eric Mack, "How SpaceX Starlink Broadband Will Envelop Earth and Transform the Sky," *CNET*, November 22, 2020.

248 Liam Tung, "SpaceX's Starlink in Action: Internet Satellites Keep Emergency Workers Online amid Wildfires," *ZDNet*, September 30, 2020.

249 "Public Statement for Collaboration on COVID-19 Vaccine Development," Press Release, World Health Organization, last updated April 16, 2020.

250 Matt Apuzzo and David D. Kirkpatrick, "Covid-19 Changed How the World Does Science, Together," *The New York Times*, April 1, 2020.

251 Netta Korin, "Using Blockchain to Monitor the COVID-19 Vaccine Supply Chain," World Economic Forum, November 20, 2020.

HYPER-LOCAL AND HYPER-GLOBAL

The rise of tech in the aftermath of the Great Reboot means for certain dimensions (mostly in the analog world) globalization is in retreat, and it will continue to suffer pressures. In other dimensions (mostly in the digital world), we see a new wave of globalism which will continue to thrive.

The result of this is a world that trends toward hyper-local in certain domains (mostly analog) and hyper-global in others (mostly digital). For businesses, the two main implications are the incentives get tilted toward building more "local-first" supply chains, while creating "global-first" knowledge networks.

* * *

LOCAL-FIRST SUPPLY CHAINS

"The (seemingly) robust image of our modern economy in fact depends on a small miracle taking place each day within our labyrinthine supply chain."
—MARCIN JAKUBOWSKI, FARMER AND TECHNOLOGIST, AND
CAMERON COLBY THOMSON, SOFTWARE ENTREPRENEUR

The shock of the COVID-19 crisis laid bare the seriously fragile status of our global supply chains. By (seemingly) relying on optimizing tools like just-in-time inventory, overly complex supply chains, and numerous cross-border steps (e.g., certain electronics use African minerals, are assembled in China with parts from Japan, and designed in the

US) our supply chains sacrifice redundancy, robustness, and antifragility.[252]

These optimizations are no doubt value-creating at certain scales. But taken to extremes (as has been the case with global supply chains), these approaches, which on first order can appear to optimize, can create fragilities on second and third order (and fourth, and fifth…) consequences—as Nassim Taleb convincingly shows throughout his work. These systems, which can seem to work great in times of predictability, show themselves for the fragile constructs they are in times of crisis.

That even the US, the richest country in the world, was unable to make products like hand sanitizer, masks, gloves at the levels needed—and had off-and-on shortages of toilet paper on shelves—is a sign of such fragility.[253] [254] New York City literally did not have enough surgical gowns and asked local organizations to donate rain ponchos to be used as medical gowns in April 2020.[255]

But clear awareness of this global fragility is spurring action, encouraging people and companies to create local-first (as

---

252 Cameron Thomson and Marcin Jakubowski, "Toward an Open Source Civilization: Innovations Case Narrative: Open Source Ecology," *Innovations: Technology, Governance, Globalization* (2012).

253 William Wan, "America Is Running Short on Masks, Gowns and Gloves. Again," *The Washington Post*, July 9, 2020.

254 Gerald Porter Jr. and Edward Ludlow, "Hand Sanitizer Will Be Hard to Find for a Long Time," *Bloomberg.com*, April 8, 2020.

255 Katie Honan, "New York City Seeks Rain Ponchos as Surgical Gowns Dwindle," *The Wall Street Journal*, April 13, 2020.

opposed to global-first) supply chains. Examples of this "local-first" prioritization include:

- Supply chains are moving closer to the factories globally.[256]
- A new wave of 3D-printed products and capacity for those products is being created.[257]
- Countries on the African continent are building capacity to produce masks, gloves, and face shields from the rubber they produce, which had previously been exported almost entirely to Chinese industries.[258]

* * *

GLOBAL-FIRST KNOWLEDGE NETWORKS

For the first time in history, the costs of talking with someone on the other side of the world have become the same as those of talking with someone across town. At the height of the lockdowns in 2020 with social distancing, there was not much distinguishable difference between getting on a video call with a business partner in New York or New Delhi.

This incentivized global collaborations to happen in ways they would not before, and we see this rise of "global-first" knowledge networks in a few different ways:

256 Mary-Ann Russon, "Coronavirus: How Africa's Supply Chains Are Evolving," *BBC News*, June 25, 2020.

257 Frédéric Vacher, "3D Printing Communities Rise to Meet Covid-19 Challenges," *STAT News*, August 8, 2020.

258 Mary-Ann Russon, "Coronavirus: How Africa's Supply Chains Are Evolving," *BBC News*, June 25, 2020.

- Impressive organizations like GEN organize mentorship sessions with people in over a hundred countries sometimes in the same call, with impressive results—like the Ghanaian entrepreneurs building capacity to make hand sanitizer.
- Tech companies quickly develop global footprints, and the incentives for startups to "go global" grow.
- Global networks of scientists work to quickly publish and share data on COVID-19, at a pace unmatched in non-crisis times.[259]

The ease of global communication and sharing of any intangible assets (e.g., intellectual property, software) online means even though we will live in a world with less global travel, we will have more global collaborations.

"National boundaries are as porous to innovations as they are to viruses."

—JONATHAN ORTMANS, FOUNDER AND PRESIDENT OF THE GLOBAL ENTREPRENEURSHIP NETWORK (GEN)

* * *

---

259 Matt Apuzzo and David D. Kirkpatrick, "Covid-19 Changed How the World Does Science Together," *The New York Times*, April 1, 2020.

A NEW KIND OF GLOBALIZATION

"Globalization has created this interlocking fragility. At no time in the history of the universe has the cancellation of a Christmas order in New York meant layoffs in China."
—NASSIM TALEB, AUTHOR OF *THE BLACK SWAN: THE IMPACT OF THE HIGHLY IMPROBABLE*

Marcin Jakubowski is a technologist and farmer, born in Poland and now living in rural Missouri in the US. In his twenties, after completing a PhD program in fusion physics, he realized he had no practical skills and chose to take an unusual post-academia step: become a farmer. He felt frustrated with how difficult it was to fix up his tractor and how expensive it was to afford replacement parts.

To address his issues, Jakubowski designed his own tractor with easy-to-procure parts that can be found pretty much anywhere. He open-sourced the blueprints and made it available online for free. Over time this turned into the Open Source Ecology (OSE) movement, a network of farmers, engineers, architects, and supporters focused on manufacturing fifty or so machines essential for civilization. These machines include generators, cement mixers, 3D printers, and trucks.

I learned about Jakubowski's work several years ago when we were planting trees together on his sustainable compound. For years, he has been alerting the world about the fragilities of our global manufacturing chains. In a 2012 paper with software entrepreneur Cameron Colby Thomson for MIT's *Innovations* journal, he defends the importance of democratized manufacturing capacity in responding to pandemics and geopolitical disruption—something that looks incredibly prescient today.[260]

During the pandemic, demand for joining the movement and learning from the global network has understandably grown, and OSE is working on a 2,000-person hackathon for next year to release an open-source housing product—a "1000-square-feet house you can build with a friend in one week."

Movements like OSE and GEN embody the opportunity we have to build a new kind of globalization, with local-first supply chains alongside global-first collaborative networks.

* * *

Historically, globalization has created tremendous value but has also left many people behind.[261] Even when it is value-creating as a whole, often gains are unequally distributed, creating winners and losers. As tough as the challenges to globalization are, we also have flashes of hope that globalization can be transformed for the better. For example, the American pharma conglomerate Pfizer has developed a promising COVID-19 vaccine with BioNTech, a German start-up founded by the children of Turkish immigrants.[262]

---

260 Cameron Thomson and Marcin Jakubowski, "Toward an Open Source Civilization: Innovations Case Narrative: Open Source Ecology," *Innovations: Technology, Governance, Globalization* (2012).

261 Laura Silver, Shannon Schumacher and Mara Mordecai, "In the US and UK, Globalization Leaves Some Feeling 'Left Behind' or 'Swept Up'," *Pew Research Center*, November 10, 2020.

262 David Gelles, "The Husband-and-Wife Team Behind the Leading Vaccine to Solve Covid-19," *The New York Times*, November 10, 2020.

In a conversation with Gary Bolles, future of work chair at Singularity University, he mentioned he sees the moment we are living in as one of those times in history when we are at an inflection point.[263] At inflection points, we have more opportunity to actually influence catalysts to build a better future. Looking at the confluence of trends in the circles of impact of the home, work, city, and world, it is easy to agree with him. Let us get to it.

---

263 Arnobio Morelix, "What the Lower Unemployment Rate Really Means for the Economy," *Inc.com*, June 9, 2020.

PART III

NEW OPERATING SYSTEM TOOLKIT

TECH BUTTERFLY EFFECT AND TOOLS FOR THE NO NORMAL

———

In April 2006, Aza Raskin created *infinite scrolling,* a feature for websites to present never-ending content to the user instead of reaching the end of a page. When you read his original blog post on the feature and put yourself in the shoes of a web user over a decade ago, it is easy to understand Raskin's reasons for designing the feature.[264] Clicking on a "next page" or "refresh" button takes you away from the content experience.

Today, combined with other features like touchscreens, *infinite scrolling* has sometimes been referred to as *doomscrolling.* It takes away our attention for long periods of time and sometimes hurts our mental health, as suggested by

---

264 Aza Raskin, "No More More Pages?" *Humanized* (blog), April 25, 2006.

Mesfin Bekalu, a research scientist at Harvard University's T. H. Chan School of Public Health.[265] [266]

Combined with humans' natural inclination to focus more on bad news than good in an increasingly weird and difficult-to-understand world, the feature is addictive.[267]

"If you don't give your brain time to catch up with your impulses, you just keep scrolling," Raskin told the BBC in 2018.[268] Raskin said the feature is partly responsible for the staggering increase in the amount of time people look at their phones and consume web content. He's upset what he created has increased the addictive potential of certain apps, juicing up the users' time spent on an app to unhealthy levels.[269]

* * *

In climate science, the butterfly effect is the notion a flap of a butterfly's wings in Brazil can set off a tornado in Texas. This comes from climate science models showing how in highly connected and complex systems, even small events can trigger massive shifts a world away.[270]

---

265 Angela Watercutter, "Doomscrolling Is Slowly Eroding Your Mental Health," *Wired*, June 25, 2020.

266 Miranda Levy, "Beware the Health Dangers of 'Doomscrolling'," *The Telegraph*, September 24, 2020.

267 Jill Suttie, "How to Overcome Your Brain's Fixation on Bad Things," *Greater Good Magazine*, January 13, 2020.

268 Hilary Andersson, "Social Media Apps Are 'Deliberately' Addictive to Users," *BBC News*, July 3, 2018.

269 Ibid.

270 E.N. Lorenz, "Predictability: does the flap of a butterfly's wings in Brazil set off a tornado in Texas?" *Presented at 139th Annual Meeting of the American Association for the Advancement of Science*, December 29, 1972.

The tech industry has a special case of this effect, where a technologist making changes to a small piece of software in Silicon Valley (or Beijing, Berlin, Tel Aviv, etc.) can set off a figurative tsunami elsewhere. Whether it is Raskin's convenient scrolling feature leading to mental health erosion, or a seemingly innocuous feature for forwarding messages easily on a mobile app being connected with coordinated lynching in India (the forwarding feature was later curbed), the examples are numerous. (We cover their typology in the section of this book on the Four Quadrants of Unintended Consequences).[271] [272] [273] [274]

Raskin is sorry he built the feature, but we can hardly blame him. The year 2006 was a different time. The web was not the dominating force it is today, and mobile apps as we know them were basically nonexistent (the first iPhone was sold just twelve months later in June 2007).[275] [276] In addition, someone else would probably have invented the feature anyways if not him—although perhaps at a later time.

But the role of tech in society today is so massive tech creators need to act differently than they did in the mid-2000s.

---

271 Rita El Khoury, "WhatsApp Now Lets You Share and Forward a Message to Multiple Chats (with Frequent Chats on Top)," *Android Police*, August 11, 2016.

272 "Hunted—India's Lynch Files," *TheQuint*, accessed July 22, 2020.

273 "How WhatsApp Helped Turn an Indian Village into a Lynch Mob," *BBC News*, July 18, 2018.

274 "Labeling Forwarded Messages," WhatsApp (blog), WhatsApp, last modified July 10, 2018.

275 Hilary Andersson, "Social Media Apps Are 'Deliberately' Addictive to Users," *BBC News*, July 3, 2018.

276 April Montgomery and Ken Mingis, "The Evolution of Apple's IPhone," *ComputerWorld*, September 10, 2019.

The third part of this book is about presenting actionable insights, tools, and frameworks to create tech in a more responsible way.

To be clear, the tech butterfly effect can be both positive and negative. This is clearly exemplified by the creation of the internet—originally built for military and scientific purposes and later on unleashing a new wave of global value creation and innovation for civil society.

It is true every highly complex industry has the potential for butterfly effects, both positive and negative. But tech is unique in being a fertile ground for these kinds of event chains that arise from complex systems because of three key drivers: leverage, speed, and scale.

1. LEVERAGE

> *"If you give me a lever and a place to stand, I can move the world."*
>
> —ARCHIMEDES

When Kodak, an innovation giant of its time, hit $1 billion in revenue in today's dollars in 1962, it had more than seventy thousand employees.[277] When Facebook hit the same benchmark in 2013, it had only about seven thousand employees. The modern tech industry is remarkable for its leverage: a

---

277 Arnobio Morelix, Victor Hwang, and Inara Tareque, "Zero Barriers: Three Mega Trends Shaping the Future of Entrepreneurship," *Ewing Marion Kauffman Foundation* (2017).

relatively small level of inputs—people, capital, locations—
can have an outsized impact.[278]

Graph: In 1962, Eastman Kodak employed 75,000 people. At the same revenue scale in 2013, Facebook employed only 6,300 people.
Jobs by Company at the Same Revenue—$8 Billion [in italics]

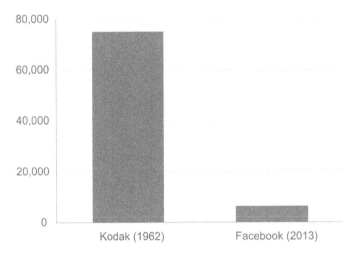

Note: $B in 2017 dollar terms
Source: Kauffman Foundation, 2017; Great Reboot Project
analysis (www.greatreboot.com)

For another example of many, you could look at Instagram. It became a billion-dollar company and was purchased by Facebook when it had fewer than thirty employees.[279] Incidentally, leverage is one of the key features making tech companies so attractive to venture capitalists: the potential for huge payoffs from relatively small initial investments.

---

278 Ibid.

279 "Facebook Buys Instagram Photo Sharing Network for $1bn," *BBC News*, April 10, 2012.

Another way this leverage can be shown is through geographic concentration—a relatively small set of locations produce outsized value. Silicon Valley is the prime example of this. You might leave a meeting at the Facebook headquarters, then bike for about forty-five minutes to Google's headquarters, and then hop on an e-scooter for another twenty-five minutes and get to LinkedIn, and from there take a fifteen-minute ride-share drive to Apple. Relatedly, as our research at Startup Genome shows, about 70 percent of the value created by tech startups is concentrated in only the top ten performing cities.[280]

2. SPEED

Consider this astounding timeline:

- **2004**: Mark Zuckerberg creates "The Facebook" while in college with classmates. In the same year, Peter Thiel made a $500,000 angel investment for a 10.2 percent stake.[281]
- **2005**: After dropping out of college and moving the company from the Boston area to Silicon Valley, twenty-one-year-old Zuckerberg is explaining his website, Facebook, in shorts and flip flops at a keg party.[282]
- **2007**: Microsoft pays $240 million for a 1.6 percent stake in Facebook. The company is now valued at $15 billion and twenty-three-year-old Zuckerberg becomes the

---

280 "State of the Global Startup Economy," *Startup Genome*, accessed September 30, 2020.
281 Leena Rao, "Peter Thiel: We Would Be A Lot More Careful About Funding Facebook Today. But...," *TechCrunch*, September 27, 2010.
282 Derek Franzese, "Facebook Interview," 17 May 2010.

world's youngest billionaire less than four years after Facebook's creation.[283]

- **2012**: Facebook goes public, valued at $104 billion. This was the third-largest IPO in US history.[284]
- **2016**: There are flattering articles in top media outlets seriously suggesting Zuckerberg should run for US president.[285]
- **2018**: Thirty-two-year-old Mark Zuckerberg explains the ins and outs of his social media platform in a US Congressional hearing.[286]

In just over a decade, Zuckerberg went from talking about Facebook in flip flops and shorts at a keg party to doing so in a suit and tie in Congress, creating nearly a trillion-dollar company and becoming a billionaire in the process.[287] [288]

This is a particularly extreme case of tech's miraculous speed. It exemplifies the broader trend, nonetheless: tech businesses and products can grow so much faster than other industries. This is not just in terms of company growth but also in terms of wealth increase for creators and entrepreneurs.

---

283 Brad Stone, "Microsoft Buys Stake in Facebook," *The New York Times*, October 25, 2007.

284 Tomio Geron, "Facebook Prices Third-Largest IPO Ever, Valued At $104 Billion," *Forbes Magazine*, May 18, 2012.

285 Shawn M. Carter, "More Signs Point to Mark Zuckerberg Possibly Running for President in 2020," *CNBC*, August 15, 2017.

286 Transcript courtesy of Bloomberg Government. "Transcript of Mark Zuckerberg's Senate Hearing," *The Washington Post*, April 8, 2019.

287 Mary Bellis, "Biography of Mark Zuckerberg, Creator of Facebook," *ThoughtCo*, June 19, 2019.

288 Jeff Desjardins, "Mark Zuckerberg Turned $1 Million into $1 Billion in Just One Year—Here's How Long It Took Other Billionaires to Do the Same," *Business Insider*, April 5, 2018.

Technology is, by far, the quickest industry for turning millionaires into billionaires, averaging 7.3 years as a study of the top one hundred richest people has shown.[289]

3. SCALE

Seven out of the ten largest companies today are in tech, with five in the US and two in China.[290] For comparison, in 2008 only one of the ten largest companies were in tech.

Scale, in the usual business sense, is about the size of operations. Powered by the speed and leverage of the industry, tech's scale has led it to reach the highest industry concentration among the top ten largest companies on record.[291]

LIFE, DEATH, AND TECH

The same drivers that make tech beautiful can also make it ugly. Other industries, of course, also have major impacts on the world and have their own unintended consequences. Education, energy, and banking come to mind. But none of them have the combination of leverage, speed, and scale tech has.

It is fashionable in some circles today to pile on tech companies. Any industry of this size is subject to criticism, which

---

289 Jeff Desjardins, "Timeline: The March to a Billion Users [Chart]," *Visual Capitalist*, March 11, 2019.

290 "State of the Global Startup Economy," *Startup Genome*. Accessed September 30, 2020.

291 Ibid.

is fair. But while we look at the negative unintended consequences of tech, we need to note the vast positive ones.

Many of these positive consequences have surfaced during the Great Reboot. While our infrastructures for public health, government action, and politics were fraying, our tech infrastructure held strong and kept economies going even during the pandemic. From e-commerce companies (allowing for social distancing while getting people the necessities they need) to video conferencing apps (used for everything from office work to schooling to socialization), our digital infrastructure was not created to make life easier during a pandemic, but it certainly has done so.

The company that invented the Pfizer vaccine for COVID-19, BioNTech, is a German deep tech start-up created by the children of Turkish immigrants.[292] As stated by founder Matt Clifford, the story is the best advertisement for immigration, start-ups, and science.[293] It drives home the beauty innovation ecosystems can create.

Tech has become increasingly relevant during the Great Reboot, and it will become even more so. One might well say today the only certainties in life are death and tech. With crypto currencies, taxes might not even make the list anymore.

292 David Gelles, "The Husband-and-Wife Team Behind the Leading Vaccine to Solve Covid-19," *New York Times,* November 10, 2020.

293 Matt Clifford (@matthewclifford), "The century's best advert for: (a) science (b) startups (c) immigration," Twitter, November 9, 2020.

So, as a founder or technologist, how do you handle and manage the unintended consequences of what you create, both positive and negative? In the following chapters, we will unpack and share specific tools and examples on how to do so.

FOUR QUADRANTS OF UNINTENDED CONSEQUENCES IN TECHNOLOGY

———

"Computer scientists and engineers often do not have the capacity to fully imagine the implications of the technology they develop"

—VINT CERF, FATHER OF THE INTERNET, CHIEF INTERNET EVANGELIST AT GOOGLE, AND CONTRIBUTING AUTHOR TO THIS BOOK

"Future tech always comes with two things: promise and unintended consequences"

—CHUCK NICE, WRITER, PRODUCER, AND CO-HOST OF *STARTALK* WITH DR. NEIL DEGRASSE TYSON ON NAT GEO

WHY DO GOOD PEOPLE CREATE BAD TECH?

I believe the vast majority of technology creators and founders are smart, well-intentioned, and self-reflective people. Most of them are good people wanting to do positive things for the world. But the reality is, despite their intelligence and intentions, they still create technologies that can cause harm.

Why does it seem like tech creators are not taking action to address these consequences? "They only ever see the positive side of the technologies they create," according to author Antonio Garcia Martinez. "Part of that is because we really, at heart, are just such optimists, they can't imagine negative scenarios, they don't have some kind of tragic history."

Even if your opinion of technology creators is not as positive as mine, you might still wonder: why did what might be one of the most left-wing clusters of people in the US (professionals in Silicon Valley) create social media tech that turned out to be so crucial to the rise of Donald Trump, one of the most right-wing presidents in the US in recent history—a politician they disagree with on almost any given issue?

These technologies, created by intelligent people, end up as something even they could not predict in the beginning.

To help mitigate this, we need to build tools that allow people to think through the unintended consequences or downstream effects of these technologies so we can make better decisions as a society.

INNOVATION'S DOUBLE-EDGED SWORD

New technology almost always carries with it seeds of creation and destruction.

The historical examples of the unintended consequences of technology are too many to count. They range from the first controlled use of fire (over one million years ago), to agricultural irrigation and pest control (increasing food production but also risking droughts and ecological imbalances), to industrial production (and its polluting waste), to modern medicine (and its side effects).[294] [295] [296] [297] [298]

But since the internet era, the cycles of innovation (with their ups and downs) are much faster (and more scalable and inter-dependent) than they used to be. Previous technological innovations might have taken decades to show unintended consequences. For example, DDT (dichloro-diphenyl-trichloroethane) was first synthesized in 1874 and discovered to be an effective agricultural pesticide in 1939.[299] Yet, public concern about adverse effects only started in the

---

294 Scott, Andrew C. "When Did We Discover Fire? Here's What Experts Actually Know," *Time*, June 1, 2018.

295 Discussions of unintended consequences themselves, usually applied to policy actions, go back at least as early as John Locke (1600s) and Adam Smith (1700s). Social scientist Robert K. Merton popularized the term in the 1900s. Those prone to mythological lenses might see the Greek myth of Prometheus as talking about the same thing also.

296 John Locke, *The Works of John Locke in Nine Volumes* (London: Rivington, 1824 12th ed.) August 10, 2020.

297 Adam Smith, *The Theory of Moral Sentiments* (Edinburgh, 1761).

298 Robert K. Merton, "The Unanticipated Consequences of Purposive Social Action," *American Sociological Review* 1, no. 6 (1936).

299 "DDT Regulatory History: A Brief Survey (to 1975)," *Environmental Protection Agency*, September 14, 2016.

1960s and only in 1972 did the Environmental Protection Agency issue a cancellation order for DDT.[300] [301]

Internet-connected innovations can show unintended consequences much faster. Instagram and Snapchat were created in 2010 and 2011, respectively, but at least as early as 2013 popular media were linking these apps to depression, with published academic studies showing how usage of apps influences students' depression and loneliness in 2018.[302] [303] [304] [305]

The internet itself might be the primeval example of this recent era of highly positive, yet unpredictable, technologies. It was born flawed as Vint Cerf, co-inventor of the internet, says.[306] By virtue of being software-based (and thus cheaply scalable), networked, and interdependent, it now provides a global-spanning infrastructure where tremendous value is created every day. It has led our world to outcomes that would look like marvelous magic to our ancestors, like automatically transmitting our thoughts to someone thousands of miles away. But foundational shortcomings (like the

---

300 Ibid.

301 "DDT—A Brief History and Status," *Environmental Protection Agency*, August 11, 2017.

302 Dan Blystone, "The Story of Instagram: The Rise of the #1 Photo-Sharing Application," *Investopedia*, August 29, 2020.

303 Brian O'Connell, "History of Snapchat: Timeline and Facts," *TheStreet*, February 28, 2020.

304 Jessica Winter, "Here's Why Instagram Is Even More Depressing than Facebook," *Slate Magazine*, July 23, 2013.

305 Melissa G. Hunt, Rachel Marx, Courtney Lipson, and Jordyn Young, "No More FOMO: Limiting Social Media Decreases Loneliness and Depression," *Journal of Social and Clinical Psychology* 37, no. 10 (2018).

306 Troy Wolverton, "The Internet's 'Father' Says It Was Born with Two Big Flaws," *Business Insider*, January 20, 2019.

internet's lack of focus on privacy, also partially responsible for growth in usage) can hang on as "original sins" that bear fruit later.[307] [308]

NO MORE PARTYING LIKE IT'S 1999

The "move fast and break things" ethos of technology creators has been a boon for value creation in society, exemplified by the 1990s-and-on boom of tech companies that began to fully realize the potential of the internet. That ethos served well when tech companies were in no small part "guys in a garage." But now they are the major forces of the global economy, and society is increasingly reliant on software in all of its manifestations.

As I learned from my friend Usman Ahmed, head of global public policy at PayPal and author of an upcoming book about the history of e-commerce, the creation story of the browser cookie exemplifies the 1990s mindset of the tech industry; the only concerns were about business and technical feasibility.

Lou Montulli, an early web browser developer and technologist who worked at Netscape and other influential tech firms, created cookies as a way to help websites remember a user's preferences. Cookies are basically small pieces of data stored on a person's device. When it was first introduced, cookies made things like online shopping much easier because sites could remember what was in a user's cart.

---

307 Andreessen, Marc and Katie Hauna, "From the Internet's Past to the Future of Crypto," *16z Podcast on SoundCloud*, accessed October 8, 2020.
308 "The Internet's Original Sin," *Dark Reading* (blog), March 6, 2007.

However, what seemed innocuous and useful at the time has changed drastically as the internet has developed further. Companies began exploiting cookies in numerous ways, including tracking users around the web to learn most minute details about them to target ads. While higher-quality advertising might not seem like a big deal to some, when you pair that data with other identifiable information it can reveal an astounding and uncomfortable amount of personal details.

Broader concerns about the impact technology like cookies could have on the lives of users were afterthoughts or not thought of at all. The tech industry was still in its infancy, and frankly too small to be overly worried about unintended consequences—or at least it seemed so at the time. It is past time we start to change that.

While we cannot fault creators in the past for missing the world-spanning downstream effects of their work, today we have the benefit of knowing internet-scale creations can have a massive impact. As Vint Cerf told me in a recent conversation, that means technology creators of today need to build more responsibly.

The third part of this book is about presenting an actionable toolkit to do just that.

THE NEED FOR ANTI-EPIPHANIES

"It ain't what you don't know that gets you into trouble. It's what you know for sure that just ain't so."

—MARK TWAIN (COMMONLY ATTRIBUTED)

In 2005, Steve Blank—one of the fathers of the Lean Startup movement—published one of the classic texts for start-ups and customer development: *The Four Steps to the Epiphany.* It is a fantastic book for building new businesses. But when founders and technologists are thinking about potential unintended consequences of their tech, it is almost like we need the opposite of epiphanies. We need instead to realize things we thought we understood profoundly (like the technology we create ourselves) we do not understand as well. We need anti-epiphanies, if you will.

For instance, one might need to discover the profitable technology you thought worked a certain way does not quite have the outputs you thought it did, or the users you thought behaved in a particular way do not do so. If the sound of an epiphany is "Aha!" the anti-epiphany might sound more like "Oh…"

To help in this process of anti-epiphanies, we created the framework of the Four Quadrants of Unintended Consequences. It allows us to track and anticipate likely downstream effects of new technology. The two dimensions in the framework are:

- **User Behavior**
  - *Who* uses the technology, and *how* they do it
- **System Behavior**
  - *How* the technology itself behaves, and *what* outputs it produces

Four Quadrants of Unintended Consequences

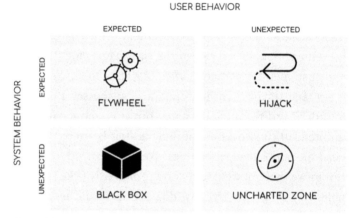

UNDERSTANDING THE FOUR QUADRANTS

In the next four chapters, we will dive into each quadrant to show how they have played out in the past and how you can use this framework to navigate the present and future of your technology.

The first dimension, *user behavior,* is defined by whether the types of users (*who*) you have are the ones you expected or not and whether they are using the technology as you intended (*how*).

The second dimension, *system behavior,* is defined by whether the system itself is behaving in the ways you expected (*how*) and whether the outputs it's producing are the ones you expected (*what*).

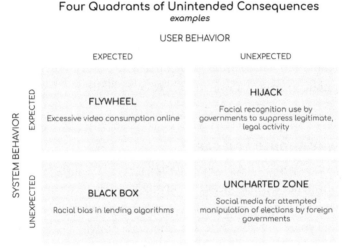

Four Quadrants of Unintended Consequences
examples

USER BEHAVIOR

EXPECTED · UNEXPECTED

FLYWHEEL
Excessive video consumption online

HIJACK
Facial recognition use by governments to suppress legitimate, legal activity

BLACK BOX
Racial bias in lending algorithms

UNCHARTED ZONE
Social media for attempted manipulation of elections by foreign governments

SYSTEM BEHAVIOR — EXPECTED / UNEXPECTED

Each quadrant represents a particular failure mode for unintended consequences in technology and can be exemplified by key future-looking questions:

1. **Flywheel:** What happens if you succeed wildly?
2. **Hijack:** Who is the worst (and best) possible user?
3. **Black Box:** What are the hidden biases and outputs?
4. **Uncharted Zone:** Where could the unknown unknowns come from?

Although the consequences are unexpected, it does not mean they are negative. Unintended consequences can be positive, and great start-up pivots can come from them.

Stewart Butterfield might be one of the masters at identifying these positive unintended consequences. Although two of his gaming start-ups failed, he turned the photo-sharing function from one of the games into Flickr (which was sold to Yahoo in 2005) and the internal communication tool his team used for the other game turned into Slack (which went public in 2019 at a valuation of over $20 billion).[309] [310] [311]

WHY SHOULD YOU CARE?

Even if you believe the technology you are creating can have unintended consequences, you might still have the question: why should you care at all? If you are a private company, by law your first duty is to shareholders. So why bother with consequences that could well be just externalities? There are two main cases for caring.

The Self-Interested Case for Addressing Unintended Consequences

Addressing unintended consequences can be a good business decision in a selfish sense, as it can:

309 Donna Tam, "Flickr Founder Plans to Kill Company e-Mails with Slack," *CNET*, August 14, 2013.

310 "A Brief History of Slack," *Digital Magazine*, June 7, 2017.

311 Chris O'Brien, "Slack IPO Starts Trading at $38.50 for $23 Billion Valuation," *VentureBeat*, June 20, 2019.

- protect your company from regulatory and other legal risks (e.g., lawsuits)
- improve your reputation among customers, investors, partners, and talent

Conversely, companies that do not care much about unintended consequences can get hammered in the court of public opinion. The pushback of talent against companies involved in creating military technology—and the hiring and retention difficulties that can arise from that—are an example of the risk of not addressing unintended consequences.[312]

The Altruistic Case for Addressing Unintended Consequences

"The people who are creating these (technology) products and writing software should feel a much greater burden than in the past because the harmful side effects can be devastating on a global scale"

—VINT CERF, FATHER OF THE INTERNET, CHIEF INTERNET EVANGELIST AT GOOGLE, AND CONTRIBUTING AUTHOR TO THIS BOOK

The downstream effects of technology today can reach a scale nearly unprecedented in history. Because of the reasons we

---

312 Ali Breland, "Tech Talent Balks at Government Work," *TheHill*, October 24, 2018.

cover in the chapter about the tech butterfly effect, a very small number of people can have an outsized effect in the world. In many ways, the archetypical desire of founders to "change the world" is true for many of them, and the opportunity for massive positive value creation and personal rewards also carries responsibility.

Who Holds the Responsibility for Unintended Consequences?

It is an open question where exactly you draw the line of responsibility. How much of it is the responsibility of the technology creator? How much of the responsibility is on the user? How much is the responsibility of governments (or society more broadly)?

Every powerful piece of technology of the past—cars, planes, guns, medicine—have landed on a different equilibrium on distributing the responsibility between the company, the customer, and the government. For internet-era technology, the jury is still out. Rather than clean and neat, these kinds of answers tend to be messy compromises reached over years.

FLYWHEEL: WHAT HAPPENS IF YOU SUCCEED WILDLY?

———

It was the late 1990s and Harrah's Casino had a problem. The company's performance was not up to the leadership's expectations and they were having a tough time competing against the newer, flashier properties in Las Vegas such as The Mirage.[313] To solve this, they turned to quantitative models to better predict customer spending and increase loyalty and revenues. This was done through what one of the leaders of the initiative referred to as "Pavlovian marketing."[314] [315]

In the early 2000s, Harrah's and their quant team launched an overhauled total rewards loyalty program with tremen-

---

313 Rajiv, Lal and Patricia Carrolo, "Harrah's Entertainment Inc.," Harvard Business School Case 502-011, October 2001.

314 Ibid.

315 Christina Binkley, "Casino Chain Mines Data on Gamblers, And Strikes Pay Dirt with Low-Rollers," The Wall Street Journal, May 4, 2000.

dous success.[316] [317] Combined with previous quantitative marketing developments, Harrah's revenue in test locations nearly doubled, significantly outpacing the competition.[318] The data science initiatives of Harrah's (now Caesars) were copied by other casinos and led years later to what some in the industry have called a "new renaissance" in casino analytics.[319] [320] Harrah's $100 million investment in technology and predictive analytics worked well.[321]

Perhaps it worked too well. Today, the same initiatives that were lauded as major wins in the triumph of data science algorithms over "gut instinct" marketing are associated with gambling disorders and addictions.

"Retail businesses such as Target and Walmart use their customer data to target the right customers at the right time. For example, they will target new parents with offers featuring baby-related items. By applying the same statistical and mathematical analysis to gamblers, Harrah's ensures that they target the right customers as well as encourage them to increase their spending. The impact of this targeting strategy on

---

316 "Casino Operator Overhauls Player Club Program," Las Vegas Sun, April 4, 2000.

317 Christina Binkley, "Casino Chain Mines Data on Gamblers, And Strikes Pay Dirt with Low-Rollers," The Wall Street Journal, May 4, 2000.

318 Ibid.

319 Staff and Wire Reports, "Harrah's Entertainment Inc. Changes Name to Caesars Entertainment Corp," Las Vegas Sun, November 23, 2010.

320 Az Husain, "Casino Analytics Is Entering A New Renaissance," Raving, October 3, 2018.

321 Rajiv, Lal and Patricia Carrolo, "Harrah's Entertainment Inc.," Harvard Business School Case 502-011, October 2001.

customer acquisition and engagement as well as value
maximization is huge."

—UNIVERSITY OF CALIFORNIA, BERKELEY

COURSE. RESEARCH DESIGN AND APPLICATIONS

FOR DATA ANALYSIS, WEEK 8.

Natasha Dow Schull, a professor at New York University focused on studying the gambling industry, says that 70 percent of casino customers use loyalty cards today.[322] By design, these loyalty programs target people who gamble frequently (sometimes called VIPs) and try to reinforce money spent while gambling. Industry-wide reporting in the UK shows VIP programs associated with loyalty initiatives have been responsible for seven out of ten regulatory penalties issued by the Gambling Commission for failures to prevent problem gambling.[323]

A casino critic from the organization Gambling with Lives says the practices of loyalty rewards programs are designed to maintain and increase addiction.[324] The observation is supported by the findings that "VIP" gamblers are more likely to be addicts than other clients and that gambling addiction is correlated with suicide.[325] [326] As usual, it is

---

322 John Rosengren, "How Casinos Enable Gambling Addicts," *The Atlantic,*
November 15, 2016.
323 Rob Davies, "Report Shows Betting Industry's Reliance on Problem Gamblers," The Guardian, January 2, 2020.
324 Rob Davies, "Gambling Firms Criticised for 'Enticing' Loss-Making Customers," The Guardian, November 10, 2019.
325 Rob Davies, "Report Shows Betting Industry's Reliance on Problem Gamblers," The Guardian, January 2, 2020.
326 Rob Davies, "Problem Gamblers Much More Likely to Attempt Suicide— Study," The Guardian, July 19, 2019.

FLYWHEEL: WHAT HAPPENS IF YOU SUCCEED WILDLY? · 173

hard to prove a causal relationship (in this case of loyalty programs and sophisticated predictive analytics initiatives leading to more addiction), but preliminary evidence shows disordered gamblers are more likely to participate in loyalty reward programs and be disproportionately rewarded by them.[327]

Research funded by the International Center for Responsible Gaming—an organization originally funded by gambling companies, and formerly called the National Center for Responsible Gaming—estimates about 1 percent of the US population has a pathological gambling problem.[328] A different study compiled by the same industry-funded organization shows the problem can be starker for certain groups. For instance, 6 percent of college students in the US have serious gambling problems that can result in psychological difficulties, unmanageable debt, and failing grades.[329]

I first learned about this story when it was shown as a positive example of how data science can create business value during one of my graduate school classes at UC Berkeley. It might have started as something mostly positive, and it certainly has the potential for good. For example, one can imagine using similar predictive techniques to help *prevent* gambling problems.

---

327 Wohl, Michael J. A., "Loyalty Programmes in the Gambling Industry: Potentials for Harm and Possibilities for Harm-Minimization," *International Gambling Studies*, (2018).

328 "Original Donors," ICRG, accessed October 12, 2020.

329 Ibid.

But the potential downstream effects we see today of problem gamblers exemplify the Flywheel Quadrant. Sometimes our technology works so well it can bite us in the rear.

* * *

Innovations to increase habit-forming behavior among gamblers is hardly a new development.

Electromechanical slot machines introduced in the 1960s, combined with psychologist B.F. Skinner's famous findings around the same time on how to dole out rewards and punishments in a way that reinforces certain behaviors, took the original concept of the mid-1800s slot machines to new levels of commercial success (and habit formation).[330] [331] [332] In the 1990s, casino operators bought data from credit-card companies and direct-mail marketers to identify compulsive gamblers.[333] [334]

---

330 Andrew Thompson, "Slot Machines Perfected Addictive Gaming. Now, Tech Wants Their Tricks," *The Verge*, May 6, 2015.

331 Schüll Natasha Dow. *Addiction by Design Machine Gambling in Las Vegas* (Princeton, New Jersey: Princeton University Press, 2014).

332 "B. F. Skinner," Department of Psychology, Harvard University, accessed October 12, 2020.

333 John Rosengren, "How Casinos Enable Gambling Addicts," The Atlantic, November 15, 2016.

334 Incidentally, many of the ad-targeting techniques applied in the web today (using data from purchasing history, demographics, psychographics, etc.) are the more statistically sophisticated cousins of the direct-mailing marketing world, as many people in the advertising technology industry would tell you.

But as it is recurring with computer hardware and software technology, scalability can make problems more evident than they would be with less scalable tech.

DEFINING THE FLYWHEEL QUADRANT

Unintended consequences in the Flywheel Quadrant are about the extremes that can happen when your system and your users work precisely as you designed. Flywheel consequences typically do not show up right away, but they can begin to creep in once your system is refined over time and possibly over-optimized for a narrow set of outcomes.

Historically, flywheels are mechanical devices which accumulate energy and help a motor keep going through momentum even if you are not directly applying energy to it anymore. A parallel phenomenon happens with unintended consequences in the Flywheel Quadrant where your systems work so well, they create output you did not plan for.

The guiding question for identifying flywheel consequences is: what happens if you succeed wildly?

Four Quadrants of Unintended Consequences
FLYWHEEL

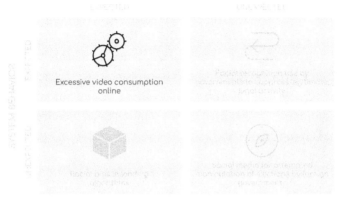

Excessive video consumption online

HIDDEN RISKS OF OPTIMIZATION

The core problem for flywheel consequences is over-optimization, where your technology performs so well for a particular activity you end up with unforeseen downstream effects.

To visualize the risks of the optimization problem, consider this: it would be perfectly fine to work with your team to optimize the time people spend watching videos on your site, as you are trying to make users go from spending seven minutes to eight minutes a day using your platform. But that same optimization exercise can be very problematic when you are trying to make users go from spending seven hours to eight hours a day on your app.[335]

---

335 I am grateful to Jordan Bell-Masterson for sharing this example with me.

In practice, engineers start optimizing a feature with the intention of helping the user. When Aza Raskin introduced the new feature of "infinite scrolling" in 2006, his intention was to make the user experience seamless—avoiding the navigational steps of having to click on a "next page" or "refresh" button.[336] [337] But as the feature got adopted ubiquitously in social media, combined with other features, and increasingly optimized to capture users' attention for longer, we end up with *doomscrolling*, taking our attention for hours.[338] What used to be a solution to an inconvenience, taken to the extreme, can become a major problem for the user.[339]

"Behind every screen on your phone, there are generally literally a thousand engineers that have worked on this thing to try to make it maximally addicting,"

—AZA RASKIN, INVENTOR OF "INFINITE SCROLLING"
AND FORMER MOZILLA AND JAWBONE EMPLOYEE

Kerry Roden, a former Googler, wrote an article for the Google Ventures' *Library* blog talking about optimizing user experience metrics and gives the example of how an engagement signal from YouTube might be the number of pages users watch on the site or, better, the amount of time people spend watching videos.[340] This is abso-

---

336 Aza Raskin, "No More More Pages?" *Humanized* (blog), April 25, 2006.
337 Tom Knowles, "I'm so Sorry, Says Inventor of Endless Online Scrolling," *The Times*, April 27, 2019.
338 Angela Watercutter, "Doomscrolling Is Slowly Eroding Your Mental Health," *Wired*, June 25, 2020.
339 Ibid.
340 Kerry Rodden, "How to Choose the Right UX Metrics for Your Product," GV Library, *Medium*, December 17, 2015.

lutely helpful guidance for creators of the early phases of a product, but it can be problematic when an app is already "too engaging."

"An engagement signal for YouTube might be the number of videos users watch on the site—but an even better one might be the amount of time they spend watching those videos."
—KERRY RODDEN, AUTHOR FOR GOOGLE
VENTURES *LIBRARY* ARTICLE

Most technologies at companies are optimized with certain metrics in mind, which in turn helps achieve business goals. Ultimately, the vast majority of businesses are optimizing for one metric: shareholder value. To zoom out of the tech industry, the doctrine of shareholder value maximization means problems of over-optimization happen in every sector. When the sole goal of a business entity is to generate economic value for shareholders—something often considered legal guidance—you risk ending up with all manners of nasty externalities (e.g., polluting industries, squeezing workers' rights), even when the company performs precisely as it is designed to perform.

What makes the Flywheel Quadrant unique for tech is computer hardware and software systems are uniquely optimizable and scalable, making unintended consequences come faster and more unexpectedly than they would in industries that are not so scalable.

FLYWHEEL QUADRANT IN THE WILD

ARTIFICIAL INTELLIGENCE (AI) FLYWHEEL

As a business concept, the "flywheel effect" was popularized by Jim Collins in his book *Good to Great* in 2001, comparing it to the process of turning a giant flywheel and, "building momentum until a point of breakthrough, and beyond."[341]

This concept has been applied to specific business domains, for example data and sales flywheels.[342] [343] [344] When we are talking about positive outcomes from the flywheel, they are usually intended. Nonetheless, one of the most astounding stories of positive outcomes from a flywheel effect comes from Amazon's (AI) flywheel, as brilliantly reported in a *Wired* article.[345] Roughly speaking, this flywheel is characterized by:

> *more data is collected, leading to better-performing algorithms*
> *better algorithms lead to better (and new) products*
> *better products lead to more customers*
> *more customers lead to more data*
> *and so on, keeping the flywheel turning*

---

341 James C. Collins, *Good to Great* (New York: Harper Business, 2001).

342 Team Blog, "The Data Flywheel: How Enlightened Self-Interest Drives Data Network Effects," *CB Insights*, October 16, 2019.

343 Brian Halligan, "Replacing the Sales Funnel with the Sales Flywheel," *Harvard Business Review*, November 20, 2018.

344 "Amazon Web Services (AWS)—Cloud Computing Services," Amazon Web Services, Inc., accessed October 8, 2020.

345 Steven Levy, "How Amazon Rebuilt Itself Around Artificial Intelligence," *Wired*, January 2, 2020.

Amazon's AI flywheel is exemplified by Alexa, the voice-based virtual assistant AI that became a breakthrough achievement in the smart-home industry. Originally used only for Amazon Echo smart speakers, Alexa was given other uses. As it became more popular, eventually leading to millions of customers, it started to be integrated into other products like Amazon Music, Prime Video, and shopping recommendations. As Al Lindsay, the then VP of Amazon Alexa Engine, told *Wired*, "Once we had the foundational speech capacity, we were able to bring it to non-Alexa products like Fire TV, voice shopping, the Dash wand for Amazon Fresh, and, ultimately, AWS."[346]

Today, external developers can also use Amazon APIs to create their own voice-recognition apps, leading to more data and a better platform overall.[347] As Pedro Domingos, a computer science professor at the University of Washington, summarizes, in less than ten years Amazon went from little prominence in AI to a major force in the field.[348]

NUDGING BEHAVIOR IN STOCK TRADING

Robinhood, the popular stock trading platform, has been a major success with new stock traders, especially during the COVID-19 pandemic.[349] The app's thirteen million users have a median age of thirty-one years old and many of them

346 Ibid.
347 "What Is Automatic Speech Recognition?" Alexa Skills Kit, Amazon Developer Services and Technologies, accessed October 12, 2020.
348 Steven Levy, "How Amazon Rebuilt Itself Around Artificial Intelligence," *Wired*, January 2, 2020.
349 Rob Walker, "How Robinhood Convinced Millennials to Trade Their Way Through a Pandemic," Medium, June 15, 2020.

are inexperienced.[350] [351] The company's commission-free trading, slick app interface, along with behavioral nudges during the trading experience (e.g., throwing confetti on the user interface as the user achieves milestones, giving free stocks), quickly attracted and engaged young users.[352] The company also offers margin trades—which are done with borrowed money from the brokerage, and available to some Robinhood members as a part of their $5/month *gold* subscription.[353]

But it is possible that making trading feel so much like a mobile game is leading to excessive risk-taking by inexperienced investors. Speaking on the topic, Andrew Lo, a finance professor at the Massachusetts Institute of Technology, says, "The parallels between video games and day trading are becoming closer and closer...For many gamers, particularly the younger ones who are not used to trading and don't fully understand the impact of significant losses and gains on their psychophysiology, it could have some significant adverse consequences."[354]

---

350 Michael Wursthorn, and Euirim Choi, "Does Robinhood Make It Too Easy to Trade? From Free Stocks to Confetti," *The Wall Street Journal*, August 20, 2020.

351 Lisa Beilfuss, "The Latest Trend in Mobile Gaming: Stock-Trading Apps," *The Wall Street Journal*, January 22, 2019.

352 Michael Wursthorn, and Euirim Choi, "Does Robinhood Make It Too Easy to Trade? From Free Stocks to Confetti," *The Wall Street Journal*, August 20, 2020.

353 "Upgrading to Gold," Robinhood, accessed October 8, 2020.

354 Richard Henderson, Robin Wigglesworth, and Eric Platt, "The Lockdown Death of a 20-Year-Old Day Trader: Free to Read," *Financial Times*, July 2, 2020.

Similarly, Thomas Ramsøy, a neuropsychologist who is chief executive of applied neuroscience company Neurons Inc., says the design cues implemented on the Robinhood app can exacerbate behavioral biases and affect investing behavior.[355]

All brokerages have similar incentives to Robinhood's to encourage users to trade, and other online brokerages use some of the same behavioral techniques on their apps (e.g., eToro and Webull Financial).[356] Robinhood just happens to be the most successful at it right now. But when a system works *too well* for the originally designed objectives—in Robinhood's case, engaging new investors and democratizing stock trades—problems like the adverse consequences on investing behavior Lo and Ramsøy talk about can start to show.

MANAGING THE FLYWHEEL QUADRANT

TOOL: THE FIVE WHAT'S

Sakichi Toyoda, the Japanese industrialist founder of Toyota from the turn of the century, developed the powerful Five Whys technique, widely used to explore cause-and-effect relationships when problems arise.[357] It is especially

---

355   Michael Wursthorn, and Euirim Choi, "Does Robinhood Make It Too Easy to Trade? From Free Stocks to Confetti," *The Wall Street Journal*, August 20, 2020.

356   Ibid.

357   Olivier Serrat, "The Five Whys Technique," *Knowledge Solutions* (2017), 307–10.

used today in Six Sigma and lean management methodologies.[358] [359]

The original Five Whys technique has been used by Amazon to identify root causes of problems. Jeff Bezos famously used it to find the root cause of an incident in a fulfillment center when an associate had hurt his finger.[360] A report from the Asian Development Bank reports Bezos walked to a whiteboard to ask the Five Whys and come up with an underlying cause of the accident:

1. Why did the associate damage his thumb?
   - Because his thumb got caught in the conveyor.
2. Why did his thumb get caught in the conveyor?
   - Because he was chasing his bag, which was on a running conveyor.
3. Why did he chase his bag?
   - Because he had placed his bag on the conveyor, which had then started unexpectedly.
4. Why was his bag on the conveyor?
   - Because he was using the conveyor as a table.
5. Why did he use the conveyor as a table?
   - Because there was no table around for him to use.[361]

The Five Whys tool is incredibly helpful for identifying one (and sometimes many) root causes for problems by looking

358 Sharon Johnson, "5 Whys: What You Need to Know to Pass Your Six Sigma Certification Exam," Six Sigma Study Guide, August 26, 2019.

359 Jon Terry, "The 5 Whys of Lean: Planview LeanKit," Planview, January 21, 2020.

360 Olivier Serrat, "The Five Whys Technique," Knowledge Solutions (2017), 307–10.

361 Ibid.

backward. We present here *the Five Whats,* a parallel tool to the original Five Whys which focuses on looking *forward,* and teasing out potential chain reactions (and fifth-order plus unintended consequences) arising from the Flywheel Quadrant.

The Five Whats tool has a new action as the starting point and imagines what the downstream consequences of that action might be, assuming your system and your users work exactly as you intended.

For instance, the Five Whats applied to the casino loyalty programs example might look like this:

Action: We will implement a loyalty program for customers to increase casino earnings.

1. ***Then what?***
    – We will collect extensive data on customers, and customers more prone to gambling will be more likely to be early adopters. (First what)
2. ***Then what?***
    – We will use data science algorithms to identify how to get customers to spend more time and money gambling. (Second what)
3. ***Then what?***
    – Users will gamble more often and for higher amounts. (Third what)
4. ***Then what?***
    – We will continue to refine our models to optimize earnings from gambling customers. (Fourth what)

5. *Then what?*
- Certain customers might have gambling addiction problems. (Fifth what)

Naturally, there is nothing magical about the number five. It is only a helpful heuristic: you might find you need fewer or more "whats" to get to informative scenarios.

TOOL: SATISFICING METRICS

Oftentimes Flywheel Quadrant negative unintended consequences come from having too much of a good thing. As we covered in this chapter, over-optimization can lead to serious risks.

A way of addressing this is to build technologies that *satisfy certain metrics*, as opposed to repeatedly *optimizing* for them. You could also look at this as a *constraint satisfaction* approach, similar to what we find in machine learning and operations research.[362]

For instance, to remain on the casino example, the algorithms can be optimized for increased gambling spend up to a point (e.g., a "healthy gambling" amount, estimated for customer accounts). Once that metric is satisfied, the technology could try to discourage gambling and even suggest gambling addiction interventions.[363]

---

362 Edward Tsang, and Thom Fruehwirth, *Foundations of Constraint Satisfaction* (Norderstedt, Germany: Books on Demand, 1996).

363 Wohl, Michael J. A., "Loyalty Programmes in the Gambling Industry: Potentials for Harm and Possibilities for Harm-Minimization," *International Gambling Studies*, (2018).

Over the past few years, the smartphone market has had some strong examples of building in constraints on phone usage. Overuse of smartphones has been a theme since the beginning (remember CrackBerries?), and over time third-party apps were created to track and limit time spent on phones. Usage tracker and website blockers like Freedom, RescueTime, FocusMe, and BlockSite come to mind. Today, many phones come with functions to reduce time on the phone natively (e.g., Android and iOS)—including app blockers, website blockers, and time constraints (e.g., blocking usage of an email app after spending more than ten minutes on it on a given day).

HIJACK: WHO IS THE WORST (AND BEST) POSSIBLE USER?

The pro-democracy 2019–20 protests in Hong Kong saw one of the first high-tech crackdowns from authoritarian governments. Among other things, Hong Kong law enforcement authorities had access to artificial intelligence (AI) that could match video footage to police databases through facial recognition. The government even called on emergency powers to ban the usage of facemasks in October 2019.[364]

Widespread use of facial recognition technology was primarily seen in relatively straightforward applications: social media, security of personal devices like smartphones, and payment apps.[365] However, security agencies around the

---

364 Keith Bradsher, "In Hong Kong's Crackdown on Protests, Face Mask Ban May Be the Start," *The New York Times*, October 6, 2019.

365 Shaun Raviv, "The Secret History of Facial Recognition," *Wired*, January 21, 2020.

world have been deploying this technology and coupling it with their huge databases. In some cases, like in Hong Kong, they have been applied for cracking down on democratic or lawful activities. Governments in the UK and the US have also been involved in the controversial use of the technology, and the delineation of acceptable uses are still fuzzy. For these reasons Elizabeth Denham, the information commissioner in the UK, proposes police forces need to "slow down" the use of facial recognition AI.[366] [367] [368] [369]

Many tech companies have responded to the controversies, often with decisive actions. Microsoft announced it would not sell facial recognition to the police until federal legislation about the technology has been passed. Amazon said it would implement a one-year ban on police use of Rekognition, their video-and-image-machine-learning classification tool, which includes facial recognition.[370] [371] IBM stopped offering facial recognition products entirely, citing the potential for abuse and racial profiling.[372]

---

366 Ibid.

367 Blake Schmidt, "Hong Kong Police Already Have AI Tech That Can Recognize Faces," *Bloomberg News*, October 22, 2019.

368 Elizabeth Denham, "Blog: Live Facial Recognition Technology—Police Forces Need to Slow down and Justify Its Use," *ICO* (blog), October 31, 2019.

369 *ICO Investigation into How the Police Use Facial Recognition Technology in Public Places.* (Wilmslow, UK: Information Commissioner's Office, 31 October 2019).

370 Karen Hao, "The Two-Year Fight to Stop Amazon from Selling Face Recognition to the Police," *MIT Technology Review*, June 15, 2020.

371 "Amazon Rekognition," Amazon AWS, accessed October 29, 2020.

372 "IBM CEO's Letter to Congress on Racial Justice Reform," *THINKPolicy*(blog), IBM, July 2, 2020.

While we cannot know the original intended uses each of these companies had when first developing their facial recognition technology, I think their response to current controversies shows they did not plan them to be used in the ways they are being used today. Their original goals were hijacked.

DEFINING THE HIJACK QUADRANT

Consequences in the Hijack Quadrant are about the extremes that can happen when your system works exactly as you designed it, but your users apply the technology in ways other than originally anticipated.

Unintended consequences in the Hijack Quadrant can happen when either: a) a different type of user than planned begins to apply the technology or b) the intended users of the technology use it in unplanned ways.

As with every quadrant, the unintended consequences here can be positive or negative.

Four Quadrants of Unintended Consequences
HIJACK

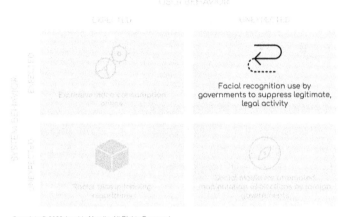

Facial recognition use by governments to suppress legitimate, legal activity

SCHELLING USER THESIS

The Schelling Point—or Focal Point—is a concept from game theory introduced by the economist Thomas Shelling in his 1960 book *The Strategy of Conflict.*[373] It basically describes how different people can coordinate their actions toward a focal point even without communicating. For example, consider this exposition on the topic from Naval Ravikant, the prominent investor and former CEO of AngelList:

> *"Suppose I want to meet with you, but I don't tell you where or when to meet. You also want to meet with me, but we can't communicate. That sounds like an impossible problem to solve—we can't do it. But not quite.*

---

373 Schelling, Thomas C. *The Strategy of Conflict* (Cambridge, Massachusetts: Harvard University, 1994).

You can use social norms to converge on a Schelling point. I know you're rational and educated. And you know I'm rational and educated. We're both going to start thinking.

When will we meet? If we have to pick an arbitrary date, we'll probably pick New Year's Eve. What time will we meet? Midnight or 12:01 a.m. Where will we meet? If we're Americans, the big meeting spot is probably New York City, the most important city. Where in New York City will we meet? Probably under the clock at Grand Central Station. Maybe you end up at the Empire State Building, but not likely.

There are many games—whether it's business or art or politics—where you can find a Schelling point. So you can cooperate with the other person, even when you can't communicate.

Here's a simple example: Suppose two companies are competing heavily and hold an oligopoly. Let's say the price fluctuates between $8 and $12 for whatever the service is. Don't be surprised if they converge on $10 without ever talking to each other.[374]

There is a related phenomenon when we look at how people use technology. I believe most technologies have a focal user: a type of user who will seek to use the technology you created even without any coordination—i.e., even if you do not target

---

374 "Schelling Point: Cooperating Without Communicating," *Nav.al* (blog), December 29, 2019.

that user or do anything in particular to attract them. I think of this as the Schelling User Thesis.

Some Schelling Users can be highly desirable, and great startup pivots can come from this. When a certain group of people or organizations look to use your technology without your company even trying to reach them, that can be a strong sign of product or market fit. Schelling Users can also have a potential for severe unintended consequences, like law enforcement using facial recognition to crack down on legal, legitimate activities—almost like a product or misuse fit.

The Schelling User Thesis is at the core of identifying unintended consequences in the Hijack Quadrant, and it is exemplified in the history of facial recognition itself. Woodrow Wilson Bledsoe, often recognized as the father of the technology, started developing it in the 1960s. He tried but failed to sell to business clients.[375] But even then, the surveillance potential of the tech was already clear—the Schelling User, if you will. His company Panoramic received funding from the Central Intelligence Agency (CIA) and CIA front organizations.[376] It is no stretch to think the CIA at that time might have envisioned applications much like the controversial usages we see today.

Consider other Schelling User examples. Advances in gaming and user interfaces (AR, VR) are likely to have the porn industry as a Schelling User. Cryptographed financial

---

375 Shaun Raviv, "The Secret History of Facial Recognition," *Wired*, January 21, 2020.

376 Ibid.

exchanges that are not able to be controlled by a central party or traced to the buyers and sellers (e.g., Bitcoin) are likely to have traders in illegal transactions as Schelling Users, which was the case of Silk Road, which was created in 2011 as one of the first large marketplaces where Bitcoin was used and which hosted drug deals.[377]

HIJACK QUADRANT IN THE WILD

BLUETOOTH NETWORKS: FROM MUSICAL FESTIVAL CONVENIENCE TO CIVIL PROTEST ESSENTIAL

While the Hong Kong protests saw negative unintended consequences of technology, they also saw positive ones. During pro-democracy protests, the government censored online speech, shut down the internet, and forced internet service providers to share user information on web activity. Internet connectivity was the primary tool for the activists to organize protests and share information, so this was a serious blow.[378]

The demonstrators found a way to communicate with each other around it via apps like Bridgefy, which is based on a peer-to-peer mesh network. The apps connected protesters across the city, and they could chat privately with contacts as well as broadcast to anyone within range even if they were not contacts. Bridgefy was originally developed for attendees of large music festivals, sporting events, natural disasters,

---

377 David Adler, "Silk Road: The Dark Side of Cryptocurrency," *Fordham Journal of Corporate and Financial Law*, February 21, 2018.

378 Lily Kuo, "China's Great Firewall Descends on Hong Kong Internet Users," *The Guardian*, July 8, 2020.

and other places where internet connectivity is not readily available.[379] [380] The app was not created to evade government surveillance of legitimate activity, but it was hijacked by users to do so.

HACKER-TRIGGERED APP STORE

When the first iPhone launched in June 2007, it did not have any third-party apps.[381] Steve Jobs was adamantly opposed to outside developers building native apps for the iPhone, despite the fact he faced pressure both internally (his executive teams) and externally (outside developers were requesting tools to build apps for the iPhone since Jobs first announced it).[382]

Jobs' resistance did not stop hackers. A month after the launch, the first native non-Apple app launched. Within three months of launch, news of hackers sharing application managers to assist installation of third-party applications appeared along with companies offering unlocking ("jailbreaking") services.[383]

After it became clear Apple could not truly stop these unwanted third-party apps, the company changed course.

379 Jane Wakefield, "Hong Kong Protesters Using Bluetooth Bridgefy App," *BBC News*, September 3, 2019.

380 Matthew De Silva, "Hong Kong Protestors Revive Mesh Networks to Preempt Internet Shutdown," *Quartz*, September 3, 2019.

381 Peter Cohen, "Apple Updates ITunes for the IPhone," *PCWorld*, June 29, 2007.

382 Stuart Dredge, "Steve Jobs Resisted Third-Party Apps on IPhone, Biography Reveals," *The Guardian*, October 24, 2011.

383 Rob Beschizza, "A Brief History of IPhone Hacking," *Wired*, June 4, 2017.

By October 2007, Jobs announced Apple would have a software development kit (SDK) for the developers by early 2008. The iPhone App Store opened in July 2008 along with the release of the new iPhone 3G.[384] At the time of the launch, the App Store had 552 applications and saw continued interest from consumers as well as the app developer community.[385] Within months, the company could see the results. Apps were so loved by the consumers they became Apple's central theme for marketing and promotion. The punchline "there's an app for that" became viral and ran as an internet meme for years.[386]

Third-party native apps became one of the cornerstones of Apple's success and the smartphone revolution. Apple saw its sales surging, with iPhone 3G selling twenty-five million units compared to the iPhone 1, which sold just over six million units.[387] Since then, strong sales of iPhones have continued. Today, there are more than two million apps on the iPhone App Store alone. The consumer-focused App economy is a $950 billion ecosystem.[388] In 2019, there were more than two hundred billion mobile apps downloaded with more than $120 billion spent on them.[389] In 2020, annual

---

384 Jason Snell, "Apple Opens ITunes App Store," *Macworld*, July 10, 2008.

385 "Apple's App Store Launches with More than 500 Apps," *AppleInsider*, July 10, 2008.

386 "The Best Marketing Campaigns of All Time (And What Made Them So Successful)," Alston & Clayden, March 22, 2018.

387 Sian Gardiner, "IPhone in Numbers" *The Telegraph*, September 6, 2014.

388 Roya Stephens and Adarsh Mahesh, *State of the App Economy—6th Edition* (Washington, DC: The App Association, 2018).

389 *App Annie State of Mobile 2020 Report*, (San Francisco, CA: App Annie, 2020).

marketing spent by brands on various app stores is expected to reach $240 billion.[390]

MANAGING THE HIJACK QUADRANT

TOOL: IDENTIFY SCHELLING USERS AND APPLY RED TEAMING

"Designing with bad actors in mind—Design for the Worst, let's call it—ought to be a priority: not to help them, of course, but to thwart them. Imagine instead a sort of Black Mirror Department devoted to nothing but figuring out how the product can be abused."

—ROB WALKER, SENIOR WRITER FOR *MARKER* BY *MEDIUM*

In the 1960s in the thick of the Cold War, the term "red teaming" first appeared.[391] It was used by the US military and intelligence community to describe exercises where they would create an internal adversarial group that would simulate the enemy and test military strategy. Nonetheless, the concept is at least as old as the role of *advocatus diaboli* (the original Devil's Advocate), the 1500s canon lawyer in the Catholic Church responsible for arguing against candidates for sainthood.[392] [393]

Red teaming is more widely used today in the private sector in situations where there is a clear adversarial entity, for

---

390 Ibid.
391 "Google Books Ngram Viewer," Google Books, accessed October 29, 2020.
392 Richard Burtsell, "Advocatus Diaboli," *The Catholic Encyclopedia. Vol. 1* (New York: Robert Appleton Company, 1907).
393 Mika Zenko, *Red Team: How to Succeed by Thinking like the Enemy* (New York: Basic Books, 2015).

example in cybersecurity, where it is easy to imagine an outside enemy who would like to break into your systems. It is usually not applied when the potential adversaries and exploiters of your tech are your own users.

A two-part exercise combining the Schelling User Thesis (to identify *who* might misuse the technology) with red teaming (to identify *how* they might do so) is a useful tool for managing unintended consequences in the Hijack Quadrant.

To identify Schelling Users, brainstorm with your team who they might be in three key categories:

- *Government*
    - example: authoritarian surveillance crackdown of legitimate, lawful activity
- *Companies*
    - example: excessive home surveillance of employees working from home
- *Individuals*
    - example: social media stalking by adults in children-targeted apps

TOOL: USE CASE DISENGAGEMENT

IBM disengaging from facial recognition technology is an example of how companies can take action to hold back unintended usage of technologies. Disengaging from specific technologies or use cases can reduce the talent supply for a specific market and inform a wider set of creators about their responsibilities toward usage of their technology. It also puts pressure on other companies to reconsider how they engage with a specific technology use case.

From an individual company perspective, disengaging from particular use cases is a legitimate tool. However, it is obviously incomplete. If a use case is profitable enough, another company will fill in the gap. Sometimes it makes sense for companies to keep engaged but do so in a more deliberate way.

TOOL: DEFINE CLEAR PRINCIPLES OF ENGAGEMENT

AI is likely to figure among the most transformational technologies of our time, with potential for tremendous gains and downsides. For any individual tech company to not engage with it would be crazy. In cases where disengagement is not an option, defining clear principles of engagement makes sense.

An example of this is Google's principles for AI. The company's AI guide sets principles around social benefits, removing unfair bias, accountability, incorporating privacy design principles, among others. It also specifically mentions AI applications the company will not pursue, including technologies that can cause harm like weaponry and surveillance that violates internationally accepted norms.

Like Google, other companies have outlined their responsibilities and intentions with usage of AI. Setting clear principles of engagement is a positive development that should spread as people (customers and talent especially) demand more ethical usage and implementation of technologies.

BLACK BOX: WHAT ARE THE HIDDEN BIASES AND OUTPUTS?

In 2016 Microsoft revealed Tay, an artificial intelligence chatbot. It was introduced to have "casual and playful conversations" with people on Twitter and was supposed to learn and improve as it interacted more with people.

Sixteen hours after launch, the bot had to be taken down.[394] The internet is not always kind. Tay was influenced by racist and misogynistic content, and it quickly went from "humans are super cool" to "I fucking hate feminists and they should all die and burn in hell" to "Hitler was right I hate the Jews." Microsoft shut it down, deleted the tweets, and swiftly issued a public apology.[395]

---

394 "Microsoft 'Deeply Sorry' for Racist and Sexist Tweets by AI Chatbot," *The Guardian*, March 26, 2016.

395 James Vincent, "Twitter Taught Microsoft's AI Chatbot to Be a Racist Asshole in Less than a Day," *The Verge*, March 24, 2016.

The developers were launching what they thought was an exciting experiment in natural language processing, and in many ways it was. The team tracked the bot closely and took it down when the experiment went sideways and the system misbehaved in ways not predicted by its creators.

The Tay example is mostly harmless. But system misbehavior can be very damaging, leading to biased healthcare treatments, unfair detention of convicts, and more, as we will cover in this chapter.

DEFINING THE BLACK BOX QUADRANT

Unintended consequences in the Black Box Quadrant are about the extremes that can happen when your users act mostly as you expected but your system misbehaves and yields uneven results.

A "black box model" is a well-known term in machine learning, referring to models where the internal functions that turn inputs into outputs are opaque. The general concept and the Black Box Quadrant apply much more broadly to all kinds of technological systems.

Four Quadrants of Unintended Consequences
BLACK BOX

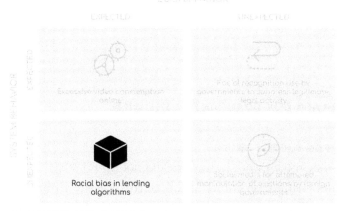

Racial bias in lending
algorithms

UNMEASURED SYSTEM BIAS AND UNKNOWN OUTPUTS

There are two core problems with unintended consequences in the Black Box Quadrant. The first one is unknown system bias, where the system is biased toward a particular set of decisions you are not aware of. For example, a lending algorithm can be biased against certain groups by race or gender if the model is not properly trained. The second one is unknown system output—things your system is producing but you are not quite aware of. For instance, the massive rise of e-commerce unintentionally leads to massive cardboard waste and strains our capacity for recycling.

"When a machine runs efficiently, when a matter of fact is settled, one need focus only on its inputs and outputs and not on its internal complexity. Thus, paradoxically, the more science and technology succeed, the more opaque and obscure they become."

—BRUNO LATOUR, SOCIOLOGIST AND ANTHROPOLOGIST

BLACK BOX QUADRANT IN THE WILD

FROM BUG TO FEATURE

Systems can work in ways we did not expect, but this does not mean these unintended performances are always negative. Bugs in system performance can be turned into features.

For example, Gmail's "unsend" feature was originally a bug. When Google developers were working on it, they realized Gmail actually took five seconds to process an email, something they did not plan on. The developers turned this into a feature, giving users the option of undoing an email send.[396] [397] Today, you can change settings to increase the email delay beyond the original "buggy" five seconds.

Turning system misbehavior into opportunities is a real possibility for creators. Drug repositioning is one such area where many new developments came from unintended Black Box Quadrant side effects. Viagra was accidentally developed by a team at Pfizer who was working on a treatment

---

396 Sascha Becker, "Bugs That Were Turned into Features," Medium. *Vollkorn Games,* April 24, 2018.

397 "5 software bugs turned into features," *Bird Eats Bug* (blog), accessed September 28, 2020.

for hypertension and chest pain.[398] Iproniazid, one of the world's first antidepressants, was initially used to treat tuberculosis.[399]

AI RACIAL BIAS

In 2019, *Science Magazine* published an article showing evidence of racial bias in a widely used healthcare algorithm. Researchers estimated the racial bias in the model reduced the number of Black patients identified for necessary extra care by more than half. The issue occurred because the algorithm used health cost as a proxy for health needs. From that, the algorithm concluded Black patients (who were spending less on health on average) were healthier than equally sick white patients.[400]

Racial bias in AI crosses domains. In 2016, ProPublica studied COMPAS (Correctional Offender Management Profiling for Alternative Sanctions), a tool developed by Equivant (formerly Northpointe) that predicts a defendant's risk of committing another crime. ProPublica found the algorithm was "particularly likely to falsely flag Black defendants as future criminals, wrongly labeling them this way at almost twice the rate as White defendants; and White defendants were

---

398 Katherine Ellen Foley, "Viagra's Famously Surprising Origin Story Is Actually a Pretty Common Way to Find New Drugs" *Quartz*, September 10, 2017.

399 Rebecca Kreston, "The Psychic Energizer!: The Serendipitous Discovery of the First Antidepressant," *Discover Magazine*, November 19, 2019.

400 Starre Vartan, "Racial Bias Found in a Major Health Care Risk Algorithm," *Scientific American*, October 24, 2019.

mislabeled as low risk more often than Black defendants."
The tool is widely used to inform decisions for convicts.[401]

Cases of bias in AI are well-documented. A variety of research exists on how bias can creep into AI models along the lines of gender, race, and other features. When machine learning algorithms are learning from past human experiences, they tend to repeat the biases captured in this past data.[402] [403] [404]

E-COMMERCE WASTE

During the COVID-19 pandemic, e-commerce has been a major boon for consumers, retailers, and manufacturers. While storefronts were either closed or in much-reduced capacity, e-commerce allowed for a major part of the consumer economy to keep humming. People could get everything they needed delivered to their doorstep without traveling to where it might not be safe.

Yet, the rise of e-commerce over the years has also led to a sudden and dramatic increase in plastic and cardboard waste. For example, in China alone e-commerce contributed to the usage of 9.4 million tons of packaging material in 2018. This is expected to increase to more than forty-one million tons

401 Julia Angwin and Jeff Larson. "Machine Bias," *ProPublica*, May 23, 2016.
402 Rebecca Heilweil, "Why Algorithms Can Be Racist and Sexist," *Vox*, February 18, 2020.
403 Nicol Turner-Lee, Paul Resnick, and Genie Barton, "Algorithmic Bias Detection and Mitigation: Best Practices and Policies to Reduce Consumer Harms," *Brookings*, October 25, 2019.
404 James Manyika, Jake Silberg, and Brittany Presten, "What Do We Do About the Biases in AI?" *Harvard Business Review*, October 25, 2019.

in 2025.[405] Unintended outputs from the system, coming from single-use plastics and extensive packing material, is leading to a startling environmental impact we have yet to grapple with.

MANAGING THE BLACK BOX QUADRANT

TOOL: HUMAN IN THE LOOP

Machine-learning algorithms are decision-making tools, and we often think of them as substitutes for human decision-making. Yet, they are applied in very different ways than human decision-makers.

Rachel Thomas, co-founder of fast.ai and director at the USF Center for Applied Data Ethics, explains this difference. In the book *97 Things About Ethics Everyone in Data Science Should Know*, where we are both contributing authors, she wrote the ways in which applications of algorithms for decisions dramatically differ from humans:

1. Algorithms are more likely to be implemented with *no recourse process* in place.
2. Algorithms are often used *at scale.*
3. Algorithmics systems are *cheap.*
4. People are more likely to assume algorithms are *objective* or *error-free.*[406]

---

405 David Stanway, "On Singles' Day, Green Groups Warn of China's Surge in Packaging Waste," *Thomson Reuters*, November 11, 2019.

406 Bill Franks, *97 Things about Ethics Everyone in Data Science Should Know: Collective Wisdom from the Experts* (Sebastopol, CA: O'Reilly Media, Inc., 2020).

Because of that, consequences from the Black Box Quadrant can often go undetected, with serious consequences. Consider these examples, shared by Thomas:

- The state of Arkansas implemented software to determine people's healthcare benefits. From this, many people had their benefits reduced with no way to appeal. Tammy Dobbs, a woman with cerebral palsy who needs help to get out of bed, saw her support cut by twenty hours a week. Her benefits were only restored (along with those of other people affected) after a lengthy court case found errors in the software implementation.[407]
- Sarah Wysocki, a fifth-grade teacher in Washington DC with glowing reviews and described by the head of the local PTA as "one of the best teachers I've ever come in contact with," was fired by an algorithm implemented by her public school system along with two hundred other teachers—without recourse. The algorithm determined Wysocki's student's reading and math scores didn't grow as predicted but failed to take into account other factors regarding her performance.[408]

A solution to address these types of problems is to implement a "human in the loop" who can review decisions and suggestions from the algorithms—either pre-decision (as a check) or post-decision (as a recourse). As I researched the topic and interviewed dozens of executives and technologists for this book, the two industries that seemed to consistently have frameworks for reviewing the decisions their

---

407 Ibid.
408 Ibid.

algorithms made were health care and financial services. As with a bank officer who consults with (but does not blindly follow) the recommendations of an algorithm on whether to make a loan before making their final call, implementing a human in the loop at some point of the process (even if only occasionally) is a way of catching potential problems coming from the Black Box Quadrant.

The industries using this often are telling of both the strengths and the limitations of including a human in the loop. Health care and financial services are heavily regulated industries where each individual algorithmic decision is worth a lot in both potential upside and risk. When we are talking about situations where the *volume* of decisions is massive beyond human scale (e.g., massive numbers of social media posts or minutes of streaming video online), including humans in the loop is not always possible. For that, we need to consider other solutions.

TOOL: SYSTEM TRANSPARENCY AND EXPLAINABILITY

The core problems in the Black Box Quadrant are around unmeasured bias and outputs. Given that setup, one of the solutions is to measure them properly.

In terms of identifying unmeasured outputs for system transparency, the solution is to analyze and measure what's *outside* the system more broadly, like when we track potential waste coming from e-commerce delivery (or industrial activity), or when we measure many health indicators to investigate potential side effects of drugs. In at least some ways, the unmeasured outputs problem is a classic externalities problem.[409]

In terms of unmeasured bias, the solution is to measure what's *inside the system* more deeply, understanding how it works and why it makes decisions a certain way. System explainability in machine learning specifically has seen some tremendous developments in recent years, and I invited my friends at Fiddler Labs, the AI explainability company, Anusha Sethuraman (head of product marketing) and Krishna Gade (founder and CEO of Fidder, formerly at Facebook) to cover this here.

***

SYSTEM EXPLAINABILITY AND WHY EXPLAINABLE AI IS THE IDEAL WAY TO BUILD TRUST WITH ARTIFICIAL INTELLIGENCE

By Krishna Gade, founder and CEO of Fiddler, and Anusha Sethuraman, head of marketing at Fiddler

Artificial Intelligence is inherently complex, and though it has become increasingly familiar in everyday lexicon and usage, a great number of questions continue to persist

---

409 Here is the legendary angel investor Naval Ravikant with a succinct explanation of the externalities problem: *"An externality is where there's an additional cost imposed by whatever product is being produced or consumed, that's not accounted for in the price of the product. This can happen for many reasons. Sometimes you can fix it by putting the cost back into the price."*
"Externalities: Calculating the Hidden Costs of Products," *Naval* (blog), January 10, 2020.

around how and why it makes decisions. We believe the key to answering these questions and building trust with AI is increasing the visibility and transparency of AI systems.

To root out and solve problems, you must first be able to understand the how and why behind those problems. It is then you have the power to improve outcomes and increase trust. Explainable AI seeks to answer some of these questions by adding a feedback loop to the predictions being made, enabling users to explain why the model behaved a given way and helping to provide clear and transparent decisions and build trust in outcomes. We believe explainability is the future of business decision making and has the potential to change the way we use AI.

ALGORITHMIC ACCOUNTABILITY

A recent example of algorithmic accountability came from Twitter and Zoom in 2020 which illustrates some of the challenges of implementing AI. A Twitter user who was attempting to share potential racial bias within Zoom's virtual backgrounds then uncovered apparent bias within Twitter's image-cropping algorithm as well. Upon sharing a side-by-side image of himself and his black colleague on Zoom, the user, who is white, noticed the cropped image that showed up on mobile was optimized for his white face. His tweets spurred a spirited conversation, with other users weighing in on their own examples of the tendency toward optimizing for lighter-faced images. This proved out even in the case of dogs, with a yellow lab being favored over a black lab.

Twitter has been transparent about the challenges that come with using AI, as well as the steps the company is taking to mitigate these challenges. This is true not only for image cropping and facial recognition, but spanning cases such as identifying misinformation around politics and the COVID-19 crisis. After this recent instance, Twitter committed to investigating as well as publishing the code for the image cropping feature in question. They further explained they "tested for bias before shipping the model and didn't find evidence of racial or gender bias." Even with rigorous testing on a feature that has been used on the platform since 2017, it is clear it's difficult to solve for every potential issue that comes with using AI.

Twitter is not alone, and the implications of lack of transparency into AI can have an even greater impact when the stakes are higher. For example, the algorithm behind Apple's Goldman Sachs-backed credit card was investigated after complaints about gender discrimination, with the card seemingly offering less credit to women than to men. In their response, similar to Twitter, they said the algorithm had been vetted for potential bias before shipping. Despite best efforts to mitigate bias, the negative impact on women seeking credit could not be avoided. It resulted in a regulatory probe from the New York state government.

The above examples present a clear problem. As complex AI algorithms are applied in more high-stakes and sensitive use cases, there has not been a proportionate increase in the understanding of how and why these models are reaching their outcomes. Complex AI algorithms today are what the industry refers to as black boxes; while they may have high predictive power, their inner workings are usually unknown and unexplainable.

A lot can go wrong with a complex algorithm, such as:

- The data seen in production is very rarely the same as the dataset a model was trained on, resulting in data drift, model decay, and potential bias built into models.
- There can be confusion and doubt about the specific inputs or features causing issues in low-quality predictions and how these features impact predictions.

Issues are often detected after-the-fact, usually when people have already been impacted by them. With black-box models, it is close to impossible to find the root cause of issues when they could exist at so many different points throughout the AI lifecycle. AI explainability is a solution to those problems.

THE REAL-WORLD BENEFITS OF EXPLAINABLE AI

Explainability is the most effective way to ensure AI solutions are transparent, accountable, responsible, and fair across use cases and industries. Here are a few real-world examples of companies leveraging explainability to ensure responsible AI within their businesses.

An AI-Powered Recruiting Company

Hired, an online, AI-powered online job marketplace, uses explainability to increase transparency and mitigate bias on its hiring platform. Hired uses real-time monitoring on how their AI models are working to refine models and identify features contributing to changes in performance using explanations.

The company is able to generate explanations for curators, data scientists, and other stakeholders on the key drivers of specific candidates' assessment to maintain a high-quality matching process. They are also able to provide concrete feedback with candidates to help people improve their profiles and generate explanations to help companies understand why specific candidates were matched with a job.

Financial Services with AI

One of the top five banks in the US uses explainability to validate models before pushing them to production with a goal of instilling an AI-governance framework. This bank uses explainability to understand their models' behavior pre- and post-deployment, and it is able to glean insights which allow its teams to improve model performance over time. Model validators take into account pre-production models with various explainability methods to learn a model's behavior and warn model developers of anything unexpected or spurious.

Model developers employ explainability to quickly understand why performance dips or unexpected predictions occur. These explainability-driven insights can then be utilized in the model iteration feedback loop to help build more robust, better-performing, and ultimately less-biased models.

Finally, and perhaps most critically, explainability provides all stakeholders, ranging from model developers and validators to legal and compliance, the ability to quickly and efficiently understand and assess model behavior throughout the lifecycle. This cross-stakeholder insight in turn contributes to increased protection from regulatory risk.

THE NEXT GENERATION OF AI

In the next ten years, we believe it's increasingly likely explainable AI will be a prerequisite for deploying any AI solution at a business. Without it, AI solutions will lack transparency and trust, and prove risky. We've already seen what has happened with less trustworthy black-box AI models. Explainable AI will enable businesses to build trustworthy, ethical, and responsible AI solutions.

Resources to Find Out More about Explainable AI:

- Learn more about explainable AI, and how to build responsibly using explainability, by visiting Fiddler's website and blog: www.fiddler.ai
- Learn more about explainable AI in industry from this paper by industry experts:
  - Krishna Gade, Sahin Cem Geyik, Krishnaram Kenthapadi, Varun Mithal, and Ankur Taly. Explainable AI in Industry. In Proceedings of the 25th ACM SIGKDD International Conference on Knowledge Discovery & Data Mining (KDD '19). https://doi.org/10.1145/3292500.3332281

Join Explainable AI—XAI group on LinkedIn for the latest resources on XAI.

UNCHARTED ZONE: WHERE COULD UNKNOWN UNKNOWNS COME FROM?

———

Thirty years ago, British computer scientist Sir Tim Berners-Lee created the web as we know it.[410] Today, he thinks it is broken and is trying to fix it.[411] [412]

Berners-Lee's parents were both computer scientists, and from an early age he experimented with electronically controlling model railways. A few years after finishing his BA in physics at The Queen's College in Oxford, he went on to

---

410 "Tim Berners-Lee," People, World Wide Web Consortium, last modified September 18, 2020.

411 Elizabeth Schulze, "The Inventor of the Web Says the Internet Is Broken—but He Has a Plan to Fix It," *CNBC*, November 6, 2018.

412 Tim Berners-Lee, "One Small Step for the Web..." *Medium*, January 2, 2019. https://medium.com/@timberners_lee/one-small-step-for-the-web-87f92217d085.

become a software intern at CERN, the famous European particle physics laboratory. At CERN he noticed scientists were having problems exchanging information across computers. He started developing a way to enable researchers to share and update information among themselves, building upon the TCP/IP protocol (the internet technology proper) created by Vint Cerf and Bob Khan in the 1970s.[413] [414]

By the end of 1990, Berners-Lee had written the first web client and server. People outside of CERN were invited to join this new web community and as it began to grow, Berners-Lee later expressed, "the decision to make the web an open system was necessary for it to be universal. You can't propose that something be a universal space and at the same time keep control of it." When Berners-Lee established the World Wide Web Consortium (W3C) in 1994, the decision to make the web accessible for free without patents and royalties was therefore a conscious one.[415] [416]

In retrospect, the development of the web can be seen as a tool of both good and bad. "The web has created opportunity, given marginalized groups a voice, and made our daily lives easier," Berners-Lee said.[417] "But for all the good we've achieved, the web has evolved into an engine of inequity

---

413   "Tim Berners-Lee," People, World Wide Web Consortium, last modified September 18, 2020.

414   Ibid.

415   Ibid.

416   "Tim Berners-Lee," People, World Wide Web Consortium, last modified September 18, 2020.

417   Tim Berners-Lee, "Where Does the World Wide Web Go from Here?" *Wired*, January 2, 2020.

and division; swayed by powerful forces who use it for their own agendas."[418]

This has encouraged Berners-Lee to fight for rights such as net neutrality, privacy, and openness of the web.[419] In September 2018, he announced he had been working with colleagues at the Decentralized Information Group at MIT to develop Solid, an open-source platform that uses the existing web to enable users to decide which apps can access their data. It's his way to give users back control of what information they share.[420]

Apart from data ownership, Solid intends to provide users with the ability "to avoid vendor lock-in, seamlessly switching between apps and personal data storage servers, without losing any data or social connections," and developers with the ability to "easily innovate by creating new apps or improving current apps, all while reusing existing data that was created by other apps."[421]

Berners-Lee is effectively trying to evolve the web into what he had in mind when first creating it. He says, "the web should be a neutral medium. It's not for the web to try to correct humanity."[422]

418 Tim Berners-Lee, "One Small Step for the Web..." *Medium*, January 2, 2019.
419 "Net Neutrality in Europe: A Statement from Sir Tim Berners-Lee," World Wide Web Foundation, October 26, 2015.
420 K.G. Orphanides, "How Tim Berners-Lee's Inrupt Project Plans to Fix the Web," *Wired*, February 14, 2019.
421 "Home," Solid, accessed October 19, 2020.
422 Billy Perrigo, "Web Founder Tim Berners-Lee on the Future of the Internet," *Time*, March 12, 2019.

The web has changed drastically since it was introduced thirty years ago, and as Berners-Lee says, "it would be defeatist and unimaginative to assume that the web as we know it can't be changed for the better in the next thirty."[423] [424]

DEFINING THE UNCHARTED ZONE QUADRANT

Uncharted Zone unintended consequences are about what extremes can happen when both your users and systems act or misbehave in ways you did not expect.

Four Quadrants of Unintended Consequences
UNCHARTED ZONE

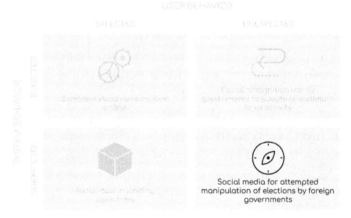

Social media for attempted manipulation of elections by foreign governments

---

423 "Frequently Asked Questions," Frequently asked questions—Tim BL, World Wide Web Foundation accessed 30 July 2020.

424 Alex Hern, "Tim Berners-Lee on 30 Years of the World Wide Web: 'We Can Get the Web We Want'," *The Guardian*, March 12, 2019.

UNKNOWN UNKNOWNS

Uncharted Zone unintended consequences are the thorniest ones by far because they are effectively unknown unknowns, with behaviors from users and systems you did not foresee unfolding over time.

Consequences coming from the Uncharted Zone Quadrant are clearly exemplified by the development of the internet. When it was originally created, the internet was meant for military and academic use. At the time, it was close to impossible to predict the massive humanitarian and commercial applications it would turn out to have many years later, spawning amazing economic and welfare benefits for society. Heck, most of the tools used to keep society running during the COVID-19 shutdowns around the world are only possible with the internet.

But similarly, early internet pioneers could also not see their creation could be used to threaten free elections, invade privacy, hack governments, and cyberbully.

UNCHARTED ZONE QUADRANT IN THE WILD

MIRACLE OF THE COMMONS

"The quasi-entirety of the Internet is built on software created for free by volunteers."

—ANTONIO GARCIA-MARTINEZ, FOUNDER OF ADGROK
AND FORMER PRODUCT MANAGER FOR FACEBOOK

Open-source software is a dominant feature of the tech industry today. But that is hardly what one would have expected in the 1990s and 2000s when proprietary software from tech giants like Microsoft, IBM, and Oracle was the norm.

Today, open-source software's contribution to industry runs into the billions. By 2022, the open-source services industry is expected to be valued at around $33 billion.[425] The majority of the technology industry, including the largest of the industry players, now works with open source. There have also been major investments in such platforms with IBM acquiring RedHat for $32 billion, Microsoft acquiring GitHub for $7.5 billion, and Salesforce acquiring Mulesoft for $6.5 billion.[426] Google's Android operating system, which runs on more than 80 percent of global mobile phones, is open source and any developer can work on it to alter it.[427] Open-source projects like Facebook's PyTorch and Google's Tensorflow are widely used for deep learning.

Because of these companies' efforts to share their developments, many of these technologies have now become industry standards.[428]

425 "10 Early-Stage Open-Source Software Startups to Watch," CB Insights Research, *CB Insights*, June 26, 2020.

426 Rob Marvin, "The Biggest Tech Mergers and Acquisitions of All Time," *PCMag*, July 9, 2019.

427 "Smartphone Market Share—OS," IDC, September 14, 2020.

428 Klint Finley, "How Facebook Has Changed Computing," *Wired*, April 2, 2020.

SOCIAL MEDIA AND POLITICS

Social media went from a way of connecting with classmates in your school to one of the major ways people consume news and other information.

Today, more than half of the US population gets news from social media, and it plays a key role in shaping opinions.[429] This major presence has led to what used to be cute apps used by teens becoming a meaningful force that is shaping elections. For instance, the successes of both Obama and Trump's presidential campaigns have been partially attributed to effective communications in social media.[430] [431] [432] [433] [434] [435] Although some of the stories on the influence of misinformation campaigns are perhaps overblown (e.g., the Cambridge Analytica story), the amount of money political campaigns spend on social media ads stands as evidence of the importance of social media in influencing politics.

429 Elisa Shearer and Elizabeth Grieco, "Americans Are Wary of the Role Social Media Sites Play in Delivering the News," *Pew Research Center's Journalism Project*, August 27, 2020.

430 "How Social Media Is Shaping Political Campaigns," *Knowledge@ Wharton*, August 17, 2020.

431 Valentino Larcinese and Luke Miner, "The Political Impact of the Internet on US Presidential Elections," *STICERD—Economic Organisation and Public Policy Discussion Papers Series*, Suntory and Toyota International Centres for Economics and Related Disciplines, LSE (2017).

432 Jennifer Aaker and Victoria Chang, "Obama and the Power of Social Media and Technology," *Stanford Graduate School of Business*, 2009.

433 Aaron Smith, "The Internet's Role in Campaign 2008," *Pew Research Center*, August 28, 2020.

434 "Facebook Ad Campaign Helped Donald Trump Win Election, Claims Executive," *BBC*, January 8, 2020.

435 Lapowsky, Issie. "This Is How Facebook Actually Won Trump the Presidency," *Wired*, June 3, 2017.

In Q3 2020, for example, political advertisements on Facebook amounted to $264 million.[436]

The combination of foreign influence, misinformation, bots, and filter bubbles will continue to impact elections around the world. Yet, it is hardly fair to expect creators years ago would have predicted such a major impact on society. The ways in which the system developed (e.g., with "fake news" traveling about six times faster than "real news") and people abusing it took consequences from social media into Uncharted Zones.[437] [438]

MANAGING THE UNCHARTED ZONE QUADRANT

TOOL: UNINTENDED CONSEQUENCES ANNUAL REVIEWS

At the onset of a project, it can be very tough to imagine—let alone predict—all the ways unintended consequences could come from it. The only way to keep on top of this is to do regular annual checks to see how your users and systems are behaving (or misbehaving).

We developed a checklist you can use for these annual reviews, with detailed step-by-step insights. You can download it for free at www.greatreboot.com.

---

436 Ari Levy and Salvador Rodriguez, "Why Political Campaigns Are Flooding Facebook with Ad Dollars," *CNBC*, October 9, 2020.

437 Robinson Meyer, "The Grim Conclusions of the Largest-Ever Study of Fake News," *The Atlantic*, March 12, 2018.

438 Peter Dizikes, "Study: On Twitter, False News Travels Faster than True Stories," *MIT News*, March 8, 2018.

TOOL: BLUE SKY ORGANIZATIONS

In 2016, OpenAI was established by founders including Elon Musk, Sam Altman, and Ilya Sutzkever with the mission, "to ensure that artificial general intelligence benefits all of humanity."[439] Among other functions, it has built free software and tools that can help other organizations with training, benchmarking, and experimenting with AI. Ideally, it is working to make sure AI is "human safe."

OpenAI is an example of what I like to think of as a blue-sky organization: a team of people who get together with the explicit goal of building technology responsibly when we are heading toward uncharted zones. These blue-sky organizations tackle potential unintended consequences of tech in society with open minds, often questioning even some basic assumptions of the field.

Examples of blue-sky organizations include Joy Buolamwini's Algorithmic Justice League, which "raises awareness about the impacts of AI, equips advocates with empirical research, builds the voice and choices of the most impacted communities, and galvanizes researchers, policymakers, and industry practitioners to mitigate AI harms and biases."[440] Another example is Innovation4Jobs (I4J), founded by David Nordfors and Vint Cerf and a group I am a part of that supports imagining and creating technologies that create jobs and meaning for people (versus destroying them).[441]

---

439 Kelsey Piper, "Microsoft wants to build artificial general intelligence: an AI better than humans at everything," *Vox*, July 22, 2019.

440 Algorithmic Justice League, accessed November 4, 2020.

441 For more on how Nordfors and Cerf think about this, see their contribution on Part III of this book.

TOOL: DESIGN FICTION FOR BUSINESSES

"Someone once said that a good science-fiction story should be able to predict not the automobile but the traffic jam."
—FREDERIK POHL, FORMER EDITOR
OF *GALAXY SCIENCE FICTION*

It is springtime in Paris and we are attending what many consider the foremost deep tech conference in the world, presented by Hello Tomorrow. NASA is attending, scientists and founders presented, and the topics ranged from next-generation biology to Mars colonization.

When it is time for start-ups to pitch, Julie, the founder of APR (Air Pollution Revealer) comes onto the stage. She explains how her company developed laser scanners to capture how pollution impacted the body of each individual.[442] In the potential use case presented, life insurers could charge premiums from their consumers based on the health or pollution report of an individual.

While the mission of the start-up was highlighted as tackling pollution, the product specifically measured how to penalize individuals for living in pollution. Imagine a case where a country fails to work on a pollution mitigation plan and ultimately the citizens pay the penalty—not only by suffering physically because they live in higher pollution but also by paying higher premiums because they are at-risk individuals.

The start-up was also partnering both with a Tinder-style dating app for people to swipe on "healthy" partners and

---

442 "Home," Air Pollution Revealer, accessed November 18, 2020.

with pharma companies to produce expensive medication that could help reduce body pollution levels.

Luckily, although most of the audience did not realize it at the time, the pitch was totally fake. The event organizers worked with Weave, a consulting strategy company, and Making Tomorrow, a design fiction collective, to infiltrate the event. They had a goal of presenting a design fiction approach and demonstrating strange applications of technology in a plausible way to generate discussions.

"The motivation behind the fake startup pitch was to make the 'audience aware of the possibilities brought by Design Fiction,'" Julie Gauthier, the "CEO" of the fake start-up, said. "Design Fiction enables us to practically approach potential desirables (and non-desirable) futures caused by new technologies." [443]

Martin Lauquin, co-founder of Making Tomorrow said, "... technology (is not often considered as) something that needs to be questioned in order to debate about the potential outcomes of inventions, either good or bad." [444]

Sam Arbesman, scientist in residence at the venture capital firm Lux Capital (and my former colleague at the Kauffman Foundation, a multi-billion-dollar philanthropy), brought to my attention how science fiction-thinking can be used to create better paths for our technologies. Arbesman told

443 "Hello Tomorrow—Design Fiction for Corporate Strategies," Making Tomorrow, March 25, 2019, Vimeo video.
444 "Hello Tomorrow—Design Fiction for Corporate Strategies," Making Tomorrow, March 25, 2019, Vimeo video.

me many of the technologies of today had been imagined before by authors—from Hugo Gernsback predicting television, videophones, and space flight to Arthur C. Clarke's newspad (or tablet), which was predicted in his *2001: A Space Odyssey*.[445] [446]

This tool is admittedly not for every business but it can bear good fruit, especially when we remember some of the amazing tech of today—augmented reality, smartphones, autonomous drones—was science fiction not too long ago. Sci-fi thinking for business decision-making can take at least a few forms:

- *World Building*
  Pigeon Hole Productions founders Trisha Williams and Joseph Unger work with cities and companies to imagine future versions of cities in virtual reality. Williams and Unger had previously helped build worlds for blockbuster video games before striking off in a new direction where they use those same skills in a more important way. Pigeon Hole Productions takes established worlds and uses research and fiction writing to imagine those same places far in the future. One striking example was *Frontera*, which imagines a combined San Diego and Tijuana metropolis in 2038.

  In these world-building exercises, the hosts ask questions like: Does your tech have any role of consequence fifty

445 Matthew Lasar, "The Man Who Foresaw Science Fiction," *Ars Technica*, May 3, 2010.
446 Steve Sande, "Arthur C. Clarke's 2001 Newspad Finally Arrives, Nine Years Late," *Engadget*, February 7, 2020.

years from now? What does the world you helped change look like? Can you imagine how the world functions in utopia (or a dystopia) and how societal changes could impact your tech?

- *Open-Ended Discussions and Workshops*
  Science journalist and author David Ewing Duncan released *Talking to Robots*, a book about twenty-four visions of possible human-robot futures in 2019. To come up with different future robots for each chapter, Duncan discussed different scenarios with other collaborators, including many futurists and thinkers, by asking them, "What robot would you like to meet in the future or are afraid of meeting and why?" The book isn't just about types of robots (a lot of those robots actually exist in the world today), but it also captures how these robots impact humans and their actions and interactions.[447] [448]

---

447 Alice Miller, "*David Ewing Duncan Is Ready for the Robot Revolution*," *Vanity Fair*, July 12, 2019.

448 Adam Frank, "An Imagined Future Speaks In 'Talking to Robots'," *NPR*, July 19, 2019.

FAIRNESS DEBT: THE SHADOW TWIN OF TECHNICAL DEBT

Understand your Fairness Debt and pay it early and often

A version of chapter was previously published as an excerpt in a book where I was one of the contributing authors: 97 Things About Ethics Everyone in Data Science Should Know *by O'Reilly, the foremost technical publisher.*[449]

In software development, the term Technical Debt is used to describe hacky code created on the fly, which does its job short-term but is unwieldy and inefficient to scale in the long-term. It is a familiar concept for developers.

---

449 Bill Franks, *97 Things about Ethics Everyone in Data Science Should Know: Collective Wisdom from the Experts* (Sebastopol, CA: O'Reilly Media, Inc., 2020).

It is time we also become familiar with its shadow twin: Fairness Debt.

Just like its technical counterpart, we incur Fairness Debt when we build systems that work for our current situation and user base today, but also have unintended consequences lurking underneath the surface as you continue to deploy the same solutions tomorrow.

One way to incur Fairness Debt is by optimizing our systems and algorithms for a particular performance metric without adding constraints (e.g., optimizing how much time users spend on an app without regards for other dimensions like their well-being). Data scientists and technologists make these types of optimization choices deliberately and often, even if naively.

But optimization often carries a Fairness Debt when taken to its natural progression. A 2015 Google Ventures post, for example, suggests optimizing for the amount of time users spend watching videos on your app.[450] While at first this is a perfectly rational way to focus engineering efforts, it can get out of control when usage becomes excessive to the detriment of the user. As a friend managing AI products at Amazon said, "It is okay when a company is trying to get a user to go from spending seven to eight minutes a day on their app. It is a whole different game when some users are risking going to between seven and eight hours a day."

---

450 Kerry Rodden, "How to Choose the Right UX Metrics for Your Product," GV Library, *Medium*, December 17, 2015.

At first, Fairness Debts are not paid by the company but by users or society. But once they get big enough, they bite all of us collectively. The backlash against the companies producing smartphones and apps optimized to capture attention—and the real headwinds these businesses are facing from both a user and regulatory standpoint—are evidence debts that can be postponed but not forgiven.

Going beyond "attention optimization," imagine a more sinister situation where you have a Fintech company optimizing only for profitability of the loans getting approved. It is easy to imagine a situation where you end with something like algorithmic redlining—effectively adding a techie twist to the old-school practice of discriminating against people living in whole neighborhoods when they are applying for a loan. Researchers at UC Berkeley have found evidence of that in programs. Their research shows Fintech lenders overcharging Latino and African American mortgage refinance borrowers a combined $765 million yearly, partially due to impermissible discrimination.[451]

But just like Technical Debt, Fairness Debt can be avoided and paid early. We have one such example with Upstart, a consumer-facing online lender.

Imagine, as it happened with Upstart, you are a Fintech founder or technologist waking up to a message from the Consumer Financial Protection Bureau (CFPB) mentioning a review of your fair lending practices only a couple of years

---

451 Robert Bartlett, Adair Morse, Richard Stanton, and Nancy Wallace, "Consumer-Lending Discrimination in the FinTech Era," *NBER Working Paper* no. 25943 (June 2019).

after launching your product.[452] You might have been "moving fast and breaking things," and focused only on improving your tech and growing your business. But you are in a highly regulated industry, and there is growing interest in the unintended consequences of what you do. For instance, Senators Elizabeth Warren and Doug Jones are sending letters asking the Federal Reserve, the Federal Deposit Insurance Corporation (FDIC), and the CFPB about their regulatory agency stance of algorithmic-based lending.[453]

Although they did not call it that, the regulators were rightly seeing the possibility of Fairness Debt occurring. But Upstart took the issues seriously and did not let the debt occur.

Upstart's AI-based models, careful to be fair from the start, have shown fantastic results, so good the CFPB took the unusual step of widely sharing how well they were performing. Upstart was able to approve 23 to 29 percent more applicants than the traditional lending model, with 15 to 17 percent lower interest rates across every tested race, ethnicity, and gender group. In addition, young adults were 32 percent more likely to get approved for loans and people with incomes under $50,000 got approved 13 percent more.[454]

---

452 "Upstart Receives First No-Action Letter Issued by Consumer Financial Protection Bureau," *Upstart* (blog), September 13, 2018; "Fair Lending Report", *Bureau of Consumer Financial Protection*, 2019; Christopher M. D'Angelo, *letter to Consumer Financial Protection Bureau*, September 14, 2017.

453 Elizabeth Warren and Doug Jones, letter to Jerome H. Powell, Joseph M. Otting, Jelena McWilliams and Kathy Kraninger, "Letter to Regulators on Fintech," June 10, 2019.

454 Patrice Alexander Ficklin and Paul Watkins, "An Update on Credit Access and the Bureau's First No-Action Letter," *Consumer Financial Protection Bureau*, August 6, 2019.

Just like Technical Debt, incurring Fairness Debt is a choice, not an inevitability. Pay it off early and often or, even better, do not incur it at all. It is the right choice. AI explainability approaches (which help you understand not only *which* decision an AI is making, but also *why*), like what Upstart used and companies like Fiddler Labs produce, can help with this process. In a world where our technologies and algorithms will be increasingly under scrutiny, companies that are careful about avoiding Fairness Debt will be rewarded later.

Fairness Debt can be intentional or malicious. For the most part it is an accident, and incurred even by very smart, well-intended people.

Managing Unintended Consequences with Scarce Resources

In a different chapter we talk about Fairness Debt (a shadow twin to Technical Debt) and the idea you should avoid incurring it as best as possible and pay it early and often when it does happen. This is a helpful heuristic. Yet, every company—and start-ups especially—are making tough decisions with limited time and resources. Just like with Technical Debt, sometimes the best business move is to incur Fairness Debt and pay it later—as tough as it is to admit this.

An example of a company working through that tough balancing act is Zoom, the video conferencing app. The company experienced triple-digit growth in the first few months of the pandemic and in a short time period grew to become a household name.[455] Yet, it was experiencing serious cyber-security problems throughout this phase of growth—issues identified and extensively explained by Alex Stamos, the former chief security executive for both Yahoo and Facebook who is currently at Stanford University.[456] [457]

From an outsider standpoint, it is plausible to imagine the trade-off Zoom had to make: scale or security. They had a unique opportunity to scale given the pandemic-triggered switch to remote work and made a set of choices that led to some Fairness Debt (and probably some Technical Debt along the way also). But they worked on paying it off, and eventually hired Alex Stamos to help them with the security challenges identified.[458]

It is easy to criticize any incurrence of Fairness Debt from the sidelines but looking at the performance of Zoom's stock price for the relevant period it is hard to argue with the results.

455   Tom Warren, "Zoom Grows to 300 Million Meeting Participants despite Security Backlash," *The Verge*, April 23, 2020.

456   Alex Stamos, "Working on Security and Safety with Zoom," *Medium*, April 8, 2020.

457   "Alex Stamos," Freeman-Spogli Institute, accessed on October 6, 2020.

458   Alex Stamos, "Working on Security and Safety with Zoom," *Medium*, April 8, 2020.

Graph: Zoom Share Price Has Risen More Than 5x Since the Beginning of February

Zoom share price (in $)

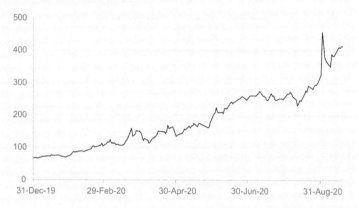

Source: Yahoo! Finance, retrieved September 19, 2020; Great Reboot Project analysis (www.greatreboot.com)

For making choices on how to allocate resources, the spectrum of downstream effects we present in the following chapter called "The (Pretty) Good, the Bad, and the Ugly: Not All Fairness Debt Is Created Equal" is helpful. Some unintended consequences are more damaging than others, and it pays off to prioritize. It is the role of founders and technology creators to walk that fine balance. Unfortunately, there is no one answer, but we hope the toolkit we present here can help you navigate this.

THE (PRETTY) GOOD, THE BAD, AND THE UGLY: NOT ALL FAIRNESS DEBT IS CREATED EQUAL

In a world of ever-growing interdependencies, prioritizing is key. Your time and resources are limited, and not every downstream consequence can be predicted.

A version of this chapter was previously published as an excerpt in a book where I was one of the contributing authors: 97 Things About Ethics Everyone in Data Science Should Know *by O'Reilly, the foremost technical publisher.*[459]

---

459 Bill Franks, *97 Things about Ethics Everyone in Data Science Should Know: Collective Wisdom from the Experts* (Sebastopol, CA: O'Reilly Media, Inc., 2020).

Every day, the systems we build classify the identity and behavior of people non-stop. A credit card transaction is labeled "fraudulent" or not. Political campaigns decide on "likely voters" for their candidate. People constantly claim and are judged on their identity of "not a robot" through CAPTCHAs. Add to this the classification of emails, the face recognition in phones, and targeted ads, and it is easy to imagine thousands of such classification instances per day for even just one person.

For the most part, these classifications are convenient and pretty good for the user and the organizations running them. We mostly forget them, unless they go obviously wrong.

I am a Latino living in the US and I often get ads in Spanish—which would be good targeting, except I am a Brazilian Latino and my native language is Portuguese, not Spanish.

This particular misclassification causes no real harm to me. My online behavior might look similar enough to that of a native Spanish speaker living in the US, and users like me getting mistargeted ads may be nothing more than a "rounding error" by the algorithm. Although it is in no one's interest I get these ads—I am wasting my time, and the company is wasting money—the targeting is probably "good enough."

This "good enough" mindset is at the heart of a lot of prediction applications in data science. As a field, we constantly put people in boxes to make decisions about them, even though we inevitably know predictions will not be perfect. "Pretty good" is fine most of the time and it generally is for ad targeting.

But these automatic classifications can quickly go from pretty good to bad to ugly—either because of scale of deployment or tainted data. As we go to higher-stake fields beyond those they have arguably been perfected for—like social media and online ads—we get into problems.

Take psychometric tests, for example. Companies are increasingly using them to weed out candidates. Some of these companies are reporting good results, with higher performance and lower turnover.[460] The problem is these tests can be "pretty good" but far from great. IQ tests, a popular component of psychometric assessments, are a poor predictor of cognitive performance across many different tasks—though it is certainly correlated to performance in some of them.[461]

When a single company weeds out a candidate who would otherwise perform well, it may not be a big problem by itself. But it can be a big problem when the tests are used at scale, and a job seeker is consistently excluded from jobs in which they would perform well. While the use of these tests by a single private actor may well be justified on an efficiency-for-hiring basis, it should give us pause to see these tests used at scale for both private and public decision making, such as in schools.

Problems with "pretty good" classifications arise from blind spots in the prediction, as well as with tainted data. Somali markets in Seattle were unable to accept food stamps because

---

460 Lauren Weber, "Today's Personality Tests Raise the Bar for Job Seekers," *The Wall Street Journal*, April 15, 2015.

461 Adam Hampshire, Roger R. Highfield, Beth L. Parkin, and Adrian M. Owen, "Fractionating Human Intelligence," *Neuron* 76, no. 6 (2012).

the federal government thought many of their transactions looked fraudulent—with many infrequent, large dollar transactions, one after the other. But this algorithmically suspicious pattern had a perfectly reasonable explanation: it was driven by the fact many families in the community they serve only shopped once a month, often sharing a car to do so. The USDA later reversed the decision of rejecting those food stamps, although only after four months of trouble for the Somali grocery customers.[462] [463]

Similarly, African American voters in Florida have been disproportionately disenfranchised because their names were more often automatically matched to felons' names. This was simply because African Americans have a disproportionate share of common last names (a legacy of original names being stripped due to slavery).[464] Also in Florida, Black crime defendants were more likely to be algorithmically classified as "high risk" for recidivism, and among those defendants who did not reoffend, African Americans were over twice as likely as whites to have been labelled risky.[465]

In all of these cases, there is not necessarily evidence of malicious intent. The results can be explained by a mix of "pretty

462 Florangela Davila, "USDA disqualifies three Somalian markets from accepting federal food stamps," *Seattle Times*, April 10, 2002.

463 D. Parvas, "USDA reverses itself, to Somali grocers' relief," *Seattle Post-Intelligencer*, March 12, 2011.

464 Guy Stuart, "Databases, Felons, and Voting: Errors and Bias in the Florida Felons Exclusion List in the 2000 Presidential Elections," *Harvard University, Faculty Research* Working Papers Series (2002).

465 Sam Corbett-Davies, Emma Pierson, Avi Feller, Sharad Goel, and Aziz Huq, "Algorithmic Decision Making and the Cost of Fairness," ArXiv:1701.08230, June 2017.

good" predictions and data reflecting previous patterns of discrimination—even if the people designing and applying the algorithms had no intention to discriminate.

While the examples I mentioned here have a broad range of technical sophistication, there's no strong reason to believe the most sophisticated technique can get rid of these problems. Even the newest deep learning techniques excel at identifying relatively superficial correlations, not deep patterns or causal paths.[466]

The key problem with the explosion in algorithmic classification is the fact we are invariably designing life around a sleuth of "pretty good" algorithms. "Pretty good" may be a great outcome for ad targeting, but when we deploy them at scale on applications ranging from voter registration to choosing who to hire to loan decisions, the final outcome may well be disastrous.

The path to hell is paved with "pretty good" intentions.

---

466 Gary Marcus, "Deep Learning: A Critical Appraisal," ArXiv:1801.00631, 2018.

THE SIX E'S OF INCLUSION

———

By Frances West, author of *Authentic Inclusion*™ and former chief accessibility officer at IBM.

In this time of extreme challenge created by the global pandemic, the importance of strong, ethical, and inclusive leadership has become more apparent than ever. Technology leaders have an opportunity to redesign and reconnect the world in a more equitable and just way if they intentionally focus on bridging the gap between those leading and the diverse, less privileged stakeholders.

One of the reasons technology leaders bear extra responsibility is because the pandemic has brought out the undeniable fact technology now underpins everything we do in society. We now see more clearly than ever before its impact on how we work, how we learn, how we play, how we socialize, and even how we heal physically and mentally. Online telehealth and teletherapy, for example, became the go-to model for care overnight.

Well before the pandemic, technology had transitioned from driving speed and efficiency in enterprise and government information processing to a human-centered scenario where technology was in the hands of nearly every individual. But with this shift, tech's purpose and principles need to be human centered.

If we agree human-first should be the new thinking and perspective, then it logically follows improving inclusion in technology is a must. We cannot afford and should not allow a digital barrier to be created where some are disenfranchised from advances in technology. All technology should be designed and created with equal access and equal experience in mind, regardless of gender, race, sexual orientation, age, or ability.

Yet in today's workplace, we often do not think about and discuss technology's impact on inclusion. Even when we do, there does not seem to be a holistic way to embed tech inclusion into an organization's operations. That is why I decided to write the book *Authentic Inclusion™ Drives Disruptive Innovation*.[467]

One of the principal ideas of the book is human diversity is at the core of disruptive innovation. True engagement of diversity calls for holistic actions across an institution to

---

467 Frances West, *Authentic Inclusion Drives Disruptive Innovation* (Newton, MA: FrancesWestCo, 2018).

respect an individual's ability to make a difference despite being different.

Today's technology is there to serve humans, and as we invent, develop, and deploy human-impact technologies such as artificial intelligence (AI), it is crucial all human differences are considered proactively and are designed in. In other words, we have to think "human first."

But how do you put the concept of authentic inclusion or human-first into action? Who initiates it and who is accountable? How do you sustain it and scale it so it is not just a one-off reaction to, for example, the COVID-19 crisis, but a transformational action that leads to a fundamental change in the thinking of individuals, the operation of an organization, and the evolution of a society?

In my view, there are six fundamental steps each organization needs to take to operationalize inclusion:

- **Embrace:** For inclusion to be authentic and sustaining, it has to be led from the top. That means the C-suites and the board of directors have to publicly embrace the idea of inclusion as a core value and strategic imperative.
- **Envision:** The leaders of the organization then have to outline the inclusion vision, in the context of the organization's mission and objectives, so there is a clear articulation of the intent.
- **Enact:** To sustain the focus of inclusion, organizational policy and governance, such as hiring or procurement policies, have to uphold the idea of inclusion and provide guidelines for functional or business units to follow.

- **Enlist:** Once there is proper setup from the top of the organization, there then needs to be a programmatic approach to inclusion by enlisting financial resources, individuals, or teams for its implementation.
- **Enable:** Once the organization's vision, policy, financial, and human resources are in place, the next step is to create organizational training and education that span all lines of business, not just HR but in sales, marketing, product design, deployment, customer service, and corporate functions such legal, accounting, research and development.

There is one particular and critical business function worth noting: an organization's information technology accessibility. The simple definition of accessibility is the practice of making your websites, digital content, mobile apps, and any emerging digital technology such as AI and VR usable by as many people as possible. We traditionally think of accessibility as being about people with disabilities. But the practice of accessibility, for example with the use of text-to-speech and captioning technology, also benefits other groups, including those who are aging, who do not speak the native language, or those who are "situationally disabled" due to illness or accident.

Accessibility, in a way, is about extreme personalization and technology made more human.

As previously noted, inclusion involves technology as well as talent. Currently, most startup technologists or enterprise CIOs view accessibility about compliance with government mandates and legislation, such as the Americans with Disabilities Act (ADA). This approach therefore tends to be one of meeting the minimum WCAG (Web Compliance Accessibility Guidelines) standards created by the World Wide Web Consortium.[468]

The reality is technology inclusion is a way for an organization to demonstrate their authentic commitment to inclusion and the technology leaders such as CIOs own the responsibility to ensure all employees, customers, suppliers, and partners can access their digital presence through their website, mobile apps, or any other form of technology.

Once we have the entire organization engaged in the holistic five-step process to operationalize inclusion, the last step is to:

- **Ensure** there is accountability.

There is an expression in business: don't expect if you don't inspect. For diversity and inclusion to have a tangible and sustained impact, we need to have a continuous measurement and feedback process in place to ensure there is progress throughout the entire organization.

Many organizations stop at the embrace level when senior leadership, usually the CEO, makes a pledge publicly about the organization's commitment to diversity and inclusion, but often they do not follow up with a published measurement. If you do not measure progress and communicate internally and externally, there is no transparency or

---

468 "Web Content Accessibility Guidelines (WCAG) Overview," Web Accessibility Initiative (WAI), last updated September 22, 2020.

accountability to change. This is actually one reason why employees and society in general have become skeptical about diversity and inclusion initiatives. This skepticism is more apparent in the tech industry, as there have been significant inclusion issues in major Silicon Valley companies and yet not much transparency in reporting whatever progress has been made.[469]

With the COVID-19 pandemic having a societal impact affecting every individual in a personal way, technology leaders from the startup to enterprise to government have an incredible opportunity to create a new world where we put humans first. They also have the chance to build inclusion into business strategies, technological infrastructure, and organizational processes so we can enable organizations to bring principle, purpose, and profit into a state of harmonious alignment for sustainable talent acquisition, market expansion, and business differentiation.

About Frances West

Frances West is an internationally recognized thought leader, speaker, strategy advisor, and women-in-technology executive known for her work in innovation, technology, and business transformation. Her human-first approach to leadership and focus on digital inclusion come from her journey as a first-generation, non-English speaking immigrant and her career as a technology executive including her roles as IBM's first chief accessibility officer. Frances is an appointed faculty instructor at the University of Massachusetts Medical School and holds

---

469 Sara Harrison, "Five Years of Tech Diversity Reports-and Little Progress," Wired, January 10, 2019.

an honorary doctorate from the University of Massachusetts in Boston in recognition of her work in accessibility, research, and digital inclusion. She is the author of Authentic Inclusion™ Drives Disruptive Innovation *and founder of FrancesWestCo, a global strategy advisory company focused on operationalizing inclusion as a business and technology imperative.*

THREE OPPORTUNITIES FOR ANALOG COMPANIES TRANSITIONING TO DIGITAL

———

By Keyur Desai, Silicon Valley-based data and analytics executive

Everyone, whether they are technologists or teachers, grandparents or children, would likely agree with Marc Andreessen's famous quote stating, "Software is eating the world." Since the internet boom of the mid-1990s, we have all witnessed many aspects of our daily life begin to be substituted by software. Music, movies, and home security are just a few examples on the consumer front.

These digital substitutes have created new forms of value and reduced prices to consume them. I can now buy a single song and string a bunch of singles together to rapidly create my own custom album to listen to instead of buying a single CD. These digital substitutes have created entirely new markets for complements too, such as Wi-Fi-enabled digital music players, Bluetooth headphones, and customized ringtones.

The experience all of us have had with digital services in our personal lives—the convenience, reduced cost, and more personalized ways to consume digital alternatives—has led us to demand the same on the work front. While some progress has occurred over the decades, it is safe to say digitization within our personal lives has progressed far more than digitization within our work lives.

The major reason for this disparity has to do with the fact that the scope of a digital transformation within a corporation is much larger than that within our personal lives. And therefore, the risk of failure of digitizing a company is much higher. For this reason, many executives have seen it safer to invest incrementally in digitization by complementing their existing analog capabilities with digital. Think storefront retailers with a website presence, or hospitals with a website.

Frankly, up until the pandemic many companies spoke of the need to digitally transform but they actually had not seen the threat of digital native competition eliminating them as sufficient to truly accelerate their transformation into a completely digital company. The pandemic, and the higher costs of an analog business model, is what presented an imminent threat to their very existence. As the pandemic unfolded, their consumers and partners had digital substitutes as options, and if they did not become that digital substitute fast they would perish. This dynamic has now put pressure on analog corporations to take the risk of becoming fully digital with new digital business models, not just incrementally improving their analog presence with digital. At the same time, they have a small window in which to make this shift to fully digital, or else digital natives will steal their customers.

This has accelerated the pace at which analog companies must digitize, a pace which, until now, was unseen in the history of computer technology. The chapters of this book on the economics of pandemics and the three waves of the Great Reboot do a wonderful job with a framework tech companies can use for identifying opportunities. But where are the opportunities for analog corporations to fully digitize? We cover those here.

There are three opportunities for analog companies wishing to transition to digital or do a better job of offering digital substitutes:

1. IMPROVE CORE ANALOG OPERATIONS WITH DIGITAL OPERATIONS

Companies which have not made substantial digital investments can start this process by building on analog operations. Another way to think of this option is to simply substitute core analog operations with digital operations. Business leaders can improve core analog business operations in the five following ways:

1. *Improving* Analog Processes

Any process internal to the corporation or externally with customers or suppliers can be improved, like digitizing new account opening processes for banks instead of requiring a paper-based process. (Yes, this still happens!) Or for restaurants: ordering and procuring a meal can be done in person but can be improved upon by allowing digital orders and delivery via their own website or a third party such as Grub-Hub, UberEats, or DoorDash.

2. *Improving* Human Capabilities

This means finding ways to make employees or customers or partners more effective through the use of data, analytics, and digital. For example, creating an end-to-end real-time data and analytics capability that can be used by any member of the company.

3. *Reducing* Risk

Using data, analytics, and digital services to manage risk across all possible corporate risk vectors such as credit, market, operational, reputational, and financial. One example is using artificial intelligence to capture account fraud as it is occurring as opposed to after.

4. *Improving* Competitive Positions

Companies can use digital services to create more effective customer, employee, supplier, and partner experiences, and to also better understand their detailed behaviors. For example, they can get a proactive understanding of competitors and markets by analyzing non-traditional datasets or use personalization to offer a superior customer experience.

5. *Creating* New or Better Products

This means using product telemetry to better understand product usage and environmental factors which promote product usage and to also identify market gaps in turn creating the need for new products. For example, using information about how individual customers behave with the product can in turn inform the company of product improvements and or even new products.

Almost every company has made some level of investments in one or several of these areas pre-pandemic. However post-pandemic, because of the high cost of the analog options and lack of agility in an analog operating model, companies will invest heavily to become mostly digitally operated. Industries will move at different paces. For example, healthcare will eventually digitize care delivery operations with help from 5G wireless, robotics, and artificial intelligence. Even surgeries will be done remotely, and some low-risk ones will eventually be performed autonomously by machine.

During the pandemic, we are seeing what occurs to companies that do not sufficiently invest in all five areas. For example, we are seeing the acceleration of the demise of brick-and-mortar retailers which are unable to attract foot traffic (too expensive when the risk of viral exposure is included in the shopping experience) to compete adequately with digital or hybrid operations like Amazon, Walmart, or Target.

2. COMPLEMENT CORE ANALOG PRODUCTS WITH DIGITAL CAPABILITIES

This is a situation where a company chooses to offer an analog product, but it also enhances the analog product with digital capabilities to make it smart. Think of the Nike shoe as an analog product and Nike smart shoe as the digital complement. The Nike smart shoe can sense terrain type, wearer posture, and more, then adapts lace tension, sole flexibility, and other attributes for better performance of the wearer. The smart shoe therefore enhances an analog shoe by making it smarter. Additionally, two separate companies can be involved in complementing a core analog product with digital, where one company produces the analog and the other a competitive digitally enhanced product. Think Ford analog car versus Tesla self-driving digital car, or a traditional thermostat from Honeywell and a smart thermostat from Nest.

A big opportunity here is to create a data-based business as the digital complement to the analog core business, taking data thrown off by the analog core business and making data-based products from this "data exhaust." If we consider flying in an airplane as the analog and frequent flier program as a digital capability, the frequent flier program enhances flying by making it more rewarding. The data product, which in this case is the frequent flyer program, can become far more valuable than the analog product. In July 2020, United Airlines was worth $9 billion but its United MileagePlus program was worth $21 billion. This program was actually used as collateral to obtain loans during the pandemic.[470] To create data-rich products, companies can:

1. Make raw data from the analog version as the product, such as weather information via weather.com or flight tracking data via Flightradar24.
2. Make derived data the product, such as frequent flier programs or Bloomberg market statistics like P/E ratios.
3. Make insights (descriptive, predictive, or prescriptive) the product, such as Spotify playlists or weather.com's Good Golf Days.
4. Make algorithms as a product, such as Mobileye's AI self-driving algorithm.
5. Data as a pooled data product, such as the Global Data Synchronisation Network (GDSN) information on product information.

3. TRANSFORM THEIR CORE BUSINESS MODEL

This is where companies, with a digital-first approach, are able to radically transform the value proposition to the customer base and offer value which appeals to a much broader set of customers. The value proposition has the potential to generate network effects or data-enabled learning that gracefully makes it beneficial for customers to commit to using the product/service and expand their usage over time. This is also referred to as "user lock-in."

Areas that are ripe for digital transformation are:

---

1. The current technology

Companies have the option to convert their analog product into a digital product, or in other words substitute an analog product with a digital product. The marginal cost of distributing a digital product over the wire is almost zero, and so digitization of a product has additional benefits of creating sizable profits as the business acquires more customers. Take for example an analog product like a movie. It can be converted to be completely digital, and in doing so it allows the company to change the distribution model to a partner-embedded one and reach orders of greater magnitude and more customers than was possible before. The marginal cost of reaching orders of greater magnitude and more customers is almost negligible in creating sizeable profits for a company. Think Netflix streaming versus Netflix's previous DVD model, and the surge in earnings that followed.

2. The product packaging

Some products cannot be digitized, like a shoe or a car or food. But digitization affords the option of allowing customers to customize their product. An example of customizing the product is Nike now allows customers to digitally design and create their own shoe. The interesting thing about enabling customization of the product is now a secondary business to trade the custom products may be created, such as what Nike will now do with applying blockchain to allow custom shoe owners to find and authenticate the original and trade their custom shoe.

Digitization also allows a company to change the product from being made of physical materials to digital materials. Think of a digital keyboard that can be projected anywhere and can be carried in your pocket. The packaging changed to make it portable and usable in many different modes.

3. The go-to-market approach

Companies may also choose to substitute their analog go-to-market approach with a digital go-to-market approach. This is about a company changing to an online sales model either by having physical online stores or embedding their purchases in apps. Retailers have done online sales for years, but many other companies in all industry verticals are beginning to realize they can be disintermediated by smaller companies who can expand their value proposition to the common customer base. For this reason, companies are creating more digital experiences which promote customer intimacy and in turn customer stickiness. One example is Nike with its new direct-to-consumer strategy. Nike will stop selling through partners like Foot Locker and exclusively sell directly. This also affords Nike the opportunity to truly understand its user base, create innovative digital experiences like digital or custom shoes, and develop data-enabled learning, loyalty, and eventually a network effect and "lock-in."

WRITING THE NEXT CHAPTER IN DIGITAL TRANSFORMATION

It has never been more critical for companies to fully invest in their complete digital transformation. Competitive threats are increasing rapidly. Not only is competition coming from traditional competitors within their current industries who are rapidly digitizing, or new digital native competitors who already have digital business models and value propositions, but increasingly competition is emanating from other industries that have historically not posed a threat pre-pandemic. Take for example how delivered groceries became a real substitute for in-person dining or Zoom video meetings became a real substitute for business travel. Industry sector lines are likely to be redrawn. According to McKinsey & Company, entire new ecosystems are likely to emerge in place of many traditional industries by 2025.[471]

The intent of the above framework is to help founders develop a level of prescience toward either what these analog corporations may do to respond to their post-pandemic markets and, in turn, develop a compelling solution for them. Alternatively, the framework can help drive analog corporations which need to know how to respond to the pandemic toward one of these three options with a compelling solution. Either way, never has the pressure for an analog company to transform digitally been greater, and never has the time frame in which to transform been smaller. This dynamic will create a new wave of widespread digital disruption, an era foreseen by Klaus Schwab of *The World Economic Forum* and aptly named the "Fourth Industrial Revolution," a revolution led by digital innovators. If you want to survive, become one fast.

About Keyur Desai

Keyur Desai is a Silicon Valley-based data and analytics executive. He was previously the chief data officer at TD Ameritrade, an innovative online brokerage firm that pioneered

---

471 Venkat Atluri, Miklós Dietz, and Nicolaus Henke, "Competing in a world of sectors without borders," *McKinsey Quarterly,* July 12, 2017.

internet-based trading. With thirty years of expertise in global enterprise data management, data monetization, and analytics, Mr. Desai has consistently maximized the impact of data, analytics, and data products on business results, operational efficiency, enterprise risk, and innovation. Early in his career, Mr. Desai was on the founding team of MicroStrategy, Inc., a pioneer in business intelligence.

GAPS AND ABUNDANCE: REBOOTED INTERNET ACCESS

———

By Martin Cooper (inventor of the mobile phone) and Dane Stangler (senior advisor at the Global Entrepreneurship Network)

The Great Reboot entails a momentous and permanent shift from the analog to the digital economy. Among its many implications, two stand out to us as requiring concerted and even immediate action.

First, for full participation in the post-pandemic economy we need to close the Digital Divide. The Great Reboot is bringing greater economic and social dislocation than we've experienced in recent years. It is forcing adaptation—sometimes painful—by many. No one can guarantee that economic transitions go smoothly, but they can be made somewhat easier if everyone has access to basic tools. One such tool is universal access to affordable wireless broadband.

Second, the digital economy relies heavily on resource inputs such as rare earth minerals and cleaner ways to generate electricity. A critical natural resource often overlooked is the radio frequency spectrum—or simply, the spectrum. Cell phones—smartphones, dumb phones, and everything in between—are already one of the twenty-first century's most essential tools. Reliance on our phones, and whatever they continue to evolve into, will certainly not diminish in the Great Reboot. This means we will continue to depend on the spectrum for our cellular networks, satellites, and a myriad of other things. Yet our current framework for spectrum use must be updated.

THE DIGITAL DIVIDE: A THREAT TO PROSPERITY

The first two months of the COVID-19 pandemic in the United States coincided with the last two months of the 2019–20 school year. Millions of K–12 students finished their classes through virtual learning: synchronous Zoom classes, asynchronous video recordings, and more. For most students, parents, and teachers this was a stopgap with hastily designed curricula and no shortage of technical challenges. In places where broadband and wireless internet access are lacking, schools sought short-term solutions. School buses equipped with Wi-Fi drove around neighborhoods with low penetration rates of home internet. Some schools and districts handed out mobile wireless hotspots.

As the new academic year began in August and September 2020, extended periods of virtual education characterized what school looked like in many parts of the country. The spring stopgap became a permanent state of affairs. The internet access gaps that could be papered over in the spring now posed significant hurdles to student achievement. A picture made the rounds on social media: two schoolchildren hunched over their laptops and books in the parking lot of a Taco Bell. The free Wi-Fi from inside the restaurant was the only way to consistently access the internet at sufficient speeds.

The digital economy, as shown in this book, is marked by unique leverage, speed, and scale. Those are core features driving innovation and prosperity—and they apply to the gaps as well as the gains. Just as a startup software company can scale quickly and outpace its rivals, the gaps between the digital haves and have-nots widen rapidly as effects compound.

Early research on educational changes during the pandemic found significant differences in student experience according to families' broadband access. Access to online educational resources was significantly determined by internet access and speed. Some schools and districts didn't even bother to offer much in the way of virtual options because they knew their student populations wouldn't have adequate access.[472]

---

472 Douglas N. Harris, et al., "How America's Schools Responded to the COVID Crisis," *National Center for Research on Education Access and Choice, Technical Report*, July 13, 2020; Andrew Bacher-Hicks, et al., "Inequality in Household Adaptation to Schooling Shocks: Covid-Induced Online Learning," *National Bureau of Economic Research, Working Paper No. 27555*, July 2020.

Virtual learning has now reached a point of viability and quality that didn't exist even a few years ago. The merging of games and learning, for example, has finally reached a point of effectiveness. While COVID-19 lingers as a threat for a few years (even with a vaccine), students and teachers will grow more comfortable with the incorporation of a virtual component. After the virus has passed, virtual education will remain a much more significant part of learning than before.

Closing the Digital Divide is an urgent short-term priority so we can ensure educational gaps during the pandemic do not grow into permanent "learning chasms."[473] It must also be done with an eye toward the long term so all students can benefit from improved virtual learning.

SPECTRUM: ABUNDANCE NOT SCARCITY

For over a hundred years, the information-carrying capacity of the radio frequency spectrum has doubled every two-and-a-half years. Today, we enjoy ten trillion times more wireless capacity than networks of a century ago.[474] This regular increase is known as the Law of Spectrum Capacity; some have dubbed it Cooper's Law, after one of the authors.

The practical translation of the Law of Spectrum Capacity is we currently enjoy, and have always enjoyed, an abundance of spectrum. This is due to consistent technological tinkering

473 New America Foundation, "Closing the Home Learning and Homework Gap," Event, June 25, 2020.

474 Thomas W. Hazlett, *The Political Spectrum: The Tumultuous Liberation of Wireless Technology, From Herbert Hoover to the Smartphone* (London: Yale University Press), p. 2.

and engineering prowess in increasing spectrum capacity along intensive and extensive margins. Yet our regime of spectrum management is based on an assumption spectrum is scarce.

This assumption hamstrings our ability to fully utilize spectrum at various frequencies. It leads to disputes among businesses, between government agencies, and between the public and private sectors. It limits sharing of spectrum—and it inevitably leads to spectrum underutilization.

The scarcity mindset leads us to assign spectrum rights in a way which means value exists in merely holding spectrum, rather than using it to the greatest extent of public benefit. The dawn of spectrum auctions in the 1990s, replacing comparative hearings, was an improvement (and recently recognized with the Nobel Prize in economics). Yet we continue to lack mechanisms to ensure spectrum is fully utilized for the public interest.

It may not seem like it, but the radio frequency spectrum is a natural resource. It is "owned" by the public and spectrum users are bound to use it for private benefit as well as the public interest. Treating it as scarce shifts value creation to the holding and guarding of spectrum instead of full utilization. This happens despite the Law of Spectrum Capacity holding true for decades.

This abundance of spectrum is good news for the Great Reboot, since so much of the digital economy depends on the spectrum. It's not good news our spectrum management policies take the opposite tack. This is one way—among many, surely—public policy will shape the direction of the Great Reboot and the distribution of its benefits.

DIGITAL INCLUSION AND SPECTRUM ABUNDANCE

These should be among the watchwords of the Great Reboot. It is well within our grasp to close the Digital Divide and realize full digital inclusion. We hope the Great Reboot provides what has been missing: the political will to do so. The increasing prevalence of the digital economy will also underscore the important economic role of the radio frequency spectrum. Recognizing we have an abundance of spectrum—today and forever—should enable entrepreneurs and existing companies to fully realize the promise of the Great Reboot.

Parts of this essay are based on previously published pieces with Medium, The Marconi Society *blog, and* Real Clear Policy.

About Martin Cooper

Martin Cooper is an engineer, inventor, and entrepreneur. He is known as the "father of the cell phone" for creating the world's first cell phone at Motorola and making the first public call on it. He is the author of the forthcoming book Cutting the Cord: The Cell Phone Has Transformed Humanity. *In over nearly three decades at Motorola, Cooper contributed to the development of pagers, two-way radio dispatch systems, quartz crystal manufacture, and more. After leaving Motorola, Cooper became a serial entrepreneur, founding numerous wireless technology companies with his wife Arlene Harris. In 2007,* Time *magazine named Cooper one of the "100 Best Inventors in History."*

About Dane Stangler

Dane Stangler is a fellow at the Bipartisan Policy Center and a senior advisor at the Global Entrepreneurship Network. He was formerly the director of policy innovation at the Progressive Policy Institute, visiting vorzimer professor of entrepreneurship at LIU Post, and the vice president of research and policy at the Kauffman Foundation.

FOUR TAKEAWAYS FOR POLICYMAKERS IN THE REBOOTED ECONOMY

———

By JF Gauthier, founder and CEO at Startup Genome

The decisions government policymakers will make over the coming year will have a significant impact on their economies well into the next two decades, just like the leading innovation policies constructed by Israel and Singapore in the late 1990s made them some of the (unlikely) leaders of the global startup revolution fifteen years later and into today. Governments that focus on shaping the building blocks of an entrepreneurial innovation ecosystem hand in hand with the private sector—so it can soon take the lead—will do even better.

1. ENTREPRENEURIAL INNOVATION POLICY = NEW INDUSTRIAL POLICY

Entrepreneurial and innovation policies must be regarded as the most important topic for your government—by your prime minister, president, regional head of state, and mayor—during the recovery and throughout the next decade as you work to create new jobs and rebuild economies on a durable foundation.

Not only have technology jobs proven to be more resilient than others during the COVID-19 crisis and the Great Recession, but from 2007 to 2011 it created new jobs at an annual rate of 5.9 percent—much faster than any industry—becoming a prized engine of economic recovery.[475] Furthermore, these jobs pay more, are more durable, associated with increased exports, and offer a higher job multiplier.

While Western economies have been growing at a rate of 2 to 3 percent per year, Startup measured the value of entrepreneurial tech and life sciences ecosystems has been growing at an annual rate of about 8 percent, or about four times faster than the rest of our economies.

The COVID-19 crisis has accentuated this disparity in growth rates between technology and traditional sectors because it has directly impacted most traditional sectors while boosting the growth of tech and life sciences sectors.

---

475 JF Gauthier and Arnobio Morelix, "Governments, Don't Let Your Startups and Scaleups Die," Startup Genome, April 2020.

Assuming tech and life sciences sectors account for about 7 percent of the GDP of developed economies, and extrapolating at the above growth rates, by the end of this decade those two sectors will account for almost 11 percent of our GDP and have produced 31 percent of the decade's economic growth. The accelerated pace of digital transformation fostered by the COVID-19 crisis will most likely make us beat these estimates.

Entrepreneurial innovation policies becoming the new "industrial policy" means it must become the foundation of your government's strategy, rooted in the prime minister's (or president's or mayor's) office and central to the work of the Ministries of Finance and of Economics as they build long-term plans in terms of investments, projected economic growth, and job creation as well as make annual budget allocations.

Some governments have realized entrepreneurial innovation ecosystems are the most important engine of their future economy. For instance, in 2019 the late mayor of Seoul committed $1.6 billion over four years to the acceleration of its startup ecosystem for their city of ten million, on top of the billions of dollars committed by its national government.

This provides a good lens against which to assess your government's level of commitment.

2. THE NEW MAP OF INNOVATION

I remember when former Harvard Business School Dean McArthur told me chaos offers the best opportunities for great leaders to outperform and create successful businesses. The COVID-19 crisis is certainly offering the best opportunities since World War II.

People are moving out of cities and top startup ecosystems at an impressive rate, employers are loosening the requirement to live near the HQ or a main office. Combined with the adoption and changing perception of virtual communication platforms, we are witnessing the highest level of labor fluidity ever, especially in top startup ecosystems. This represents a big opportunity for other cities.

Your best chance to take advantage of the current situation is to take bold and swift action, leading the charge within the next twelve months—like Israel and Singapore did in the mid-1990s—rather than following later.

The window of opportunity is relatively small. While tech talent may never be as concentrated as it was in 2019, we can predict the pendulum will swing back, to the advantage of top startup ecosystems.

It is time to invest in making your city an attractive place to live and work remotely and adopt immigration and tax laws enabling an inbound movement of highly paid workers, with their four times job multiplier. Barcelona is a good example of a location which has eased the visa process for foreign tech employees wishing to move and even offered them a tax discount.

3. REBOOTING EDUCATION

For years we have foreseen at one point we would most likely need to make large investments in retraining, reskilling, and upskilling large swaths of our populations because the digital transition of our economy risked happening too fast. This time has come.

Yelp recently published a scary statistic: 60 percent of businesses that closed temporarily due to COVID-19 have now decided to close permanently. Many of these traditional businesses had been struggling and the coronavirus crisis merely accelerated the tipping point. Most of these jobs will not be coming back.

We know the lowest paying jobs have been hurt much more than higher-paying ones. This is because traditional sectors and small businesses—which account for two-thirds of jobs in Europe and about half of them in the US—have both been hit hard.

Rebooting education first means retraining, reskilling, and upskilling adults in their thirties, forties, and fifties must become the focus of your investment in education, and at a scale that rivals the numbers of students attending universities. This will require online and offline education services adapted to older adults who left schools years ago, may not be digitally skilled, and may dislike online methods. The alternative is to support them for years while they do not work and a high, chronic unemployment rate sets in.

While we know many of these businesses—for instance restaurants and bars—will soon be as needed as they were in the past, policymakers unfortunately face two trends which go against swift reopenings.

As the Kauffman Foundation has reported for years, traditional entrepreneurship has gone dramatically down. On top of that, banks no longer play the important role they used to play in terms of financing the creation of small businesses.

Therefore, rebooting education also means supporting entrepreneurial-minded people in traditional sectors in terms of business training, mentoring, and funding so the small businesses that closed permanently can be replaced within a few years.

Thirdly, as entrepreneurial innovation policy becomes central to the economic blueprint of your city or country, large investments in technology-driven entrepreneurship education must also be made.

4. INCLUSION IMPERATIVE

It's time to seriously tackle gender inequalities and reduce inequalities within and among countries with bold action, policies, and programs. Startup Genome has been working arduously to spread the playbooks on how to accelerate the growth of startup ecosystems all over the world. As for having led the global research and worked closely with a hundred governments and startup ecosystem leaders, we know startup ecosystems are not diverse enough. The efforts to make them more diverse have been tepid at best. It doesn't matter what the definition of "minority" means in your country, it is overwhelmingly true across the world.

Unfortunately, the COVID-19 crisis has hurt women and minorities more than others. Again, unless as a government and policymaker you are ready to accept chronic unemployment, this means taking action rapidly.

Experience and studies have shown that without critical mass of their own in a company or an industry, women and minorities cannot expect to succeed in a new job category, company, or industry. Hence the need to create programs tailored to 1) the retraining, reskilling, and upskilling of minorities. 2) entrepreneurship education, mentorship, and support including funding the creation of minority-owned traditional businesses, and 3) tech entrepreneurship and startup support programs, including mentorship and minority incubators and accelerators.

Inclusion in Action

by Arnobio Morelix

The pandemic negatively impacted all kinds of businesses, but it hit minority-owned businesses particularly hard. For policymakers looking to take action to support inclusive ecosystems, it is worthwhile to look at programs that have done this well before. The Latino Business Action Network (LBAN) and the scaling program they do with Stanford University's Latino Entrepreneurship Initiative (SLEI) is best-in-class in this area. I have followed the program for years since my previous roles at the Kauffman Foundation, Startup Genome, and have authored research with SLEI as a contributing data science expert.

I caught up recently with their team to learn how the founders in their program are faring during the pandemic-triggered crisis. Altogether, their program supports over five hundred Latino entrepreneurs owning companies with a combined $3 billion in annual revenue, and over thirty thousand jobs created.

Jerry Porras, professor emeritus at Stanford University Graduate School of Business, co-author of the classic bestseller book *Built to Last*, and part of the board of directors at LBAN, shared several stories about how their network has been supporting entrepreneurs. During the crisis there are two key ways their program was directly impactful for founders, and they serve as insights for policymakers looking to implement inclusion programs in their area. LBAN does a lot more, but these two approaches are particularly relevant during times of crisis.

Networked Problem-Solving. "I have 100,000 masks I need to get to the East Coast. Can anybody help?" "I have applied for an emergency stimulus package loan at the bank but have not heard from anybody in a couple of weeks. Does anybody have suggestions of what to do?"

These are examples of problems founders in the LBAN network shared with one another for help, relying on the network to problem-solve together. They found answers for these, and more, with impressive results. For example, SLEI alumni were more likely to access stimulus loans in the United States than other Latino-owned businesses (over four times more likely), and non-minority owned businesses (nearly three times more likely).

Knowing You Are Not Alone. Entrepreneurship is overwhelmingly a lonely journey. Cohort programs like LBAN provide entrepreneurs with an opportunity to support each other emotionally and psychologically by creating facilitated meeting opportunities for founders (which happened to be online in times of social distancing). This is particularly helpful in a time of crisis.

* * *

Policymakers who elevate these issues to the top of the agenda for their prime ministers, presidents, governors, and mayors and build momentum for action across these sets of policies will find themselves reaping the benefits in a matter of a few years. Your starting point doesn't matter. Proactivity and action across driving forces of economic growth and policies that keep unemployment at bay will reap the highest return on government investments.

About JF Gauthier

Silicon Valley serial entrepreneur and founder and CEO of Startup Genome. He is the world's leading voice in innovation ecosystem development, having advised more than one hundred governments and private-public partnerships across thirty-five countries. He has founded five businesses and led others across two continents and three sectors (tech, life sciences and cleantech), achieving two exits plus one at scaleup stage. He is also an active angel investor and previously worked in corporate innovation, advising IBM, Cisco, Agilent/HP, J&J, and Abbott for the firm of Kim Clark (former dean of Harvard Business School) alongside Clayton Christensen and other thought leaders.

REBOOTED: RECAP

REBOOTED CHAPTER BY CHAPTER SUMMARIES

Rebooted: An Uncommon Guide to Radical Success and
Fairness in the New World of Life, Death, and Tech
By Arnobio Morelix

WELCOME TO THE GREAT REBOOT

In the introduction to this book, I present how the COVID-19 pandemic placed incredible strain on the global economy and accelerated the adoption of powerful technologies for both companies and governments. In fact, changes many of us expected to unfold over ten years basically happened in ten weeks. We rebooted our world. Like rebooting a computer with a new operating system, these changes will lead our society to function in fundamentally different ways. I conclude this chapter by outlining the idea this book can help anticipate in terms of what is to come in the decades ahead. It's a guide for sailing in a sea of change at the complex intersection of society, the economy, and technology in a world we do not fully understand.

PART II. CIRCLES OF IMPACT

CHAPTER 1. ECONOMICS OF PANDEMICS

The two economies we are living in—analog and digital—work closely together but are ultimately different. While interwoven, thinking of them as two economies (even if just as an analogy) helps us understand the shift we are going through in the Great Reboot. The analog economy is slowing down while the digital economy is accelerating, and there is an expectation companies and countries at the right side of the Digital Divide will come out drastically ahead of their peers. The shift from analog to digital is why asking whether the recovery will be V-shaped, L-shaped, or whatever other shape is the wrong question. What is important is the composition of the economy will be dramatically different after the recovery. Additionally, research says the aftereffects of pandemics have lasted for forty years historically, but we don't know if that will be the case after COVID-19. The defining characteristic of companies that will succeed in the decades after the Great Reboot is not their size or age, but rather digital proficiency and speed proficiency.

CHAPTER 2. THREE WAVES OF THE GREAT REBOOT

The pandemic-triggered economic crisis will affect different industries, in different ways, at different times. There will ultimately be three waves of the Great Reboot. In the First Wave, we saw "Shock and Substitutes" where many goods and services became cost-prohibitive, so major substitutions occurred and caused societal shocks. In the Second Wave comes "The Rise of Complements" where complements of digital movement of people and goods starkly rise in demand and value, such as the internet and cell phone infrastructure. In the Third Wave, we will see "A Fragile Return" to normalcy that defined the pre-COVID-19 times, including people flocking back to restaurants, live entertainment, global travel, and the in-person office will likely lead to a "Roaring 2020s." But there will also be changes in preferences such as remote work and digital services that will lead to massive job losses. At the end of the three waves, we will then establish the "No Normal," where unpredictability reigns supreme in our society.

CHAPTER 3. FOUR CIRCLES OF IMPACT OF THE GREAT REBOOT

Much like an immune system, society is vulnerable to different shocks. So, the COVID-19 pandemic has not created many new trends but more or less exposed fragilities already in place. These big societal changes make up the Great Reboot, and we need to carefully look at the impact in four circles: home, work, city, and world. The next four chapters explore these places and impacts in detail.

CHAPTER 4. HOME: THE LONELIER FUTURE OF OUR SOCIAL LIVES

In our home lives, many people all over the globe are having less in-person interactions, leading to a loneliness epidemic. The emotional distance we are experiencing grows primarily from two I's: isolation and intermediation. This new period of isolation, defined by a sparsity of person-to-person inter-action, has led to less face-to-face interactions and less par-ticipating in churches, clubs, and the like, which provided social support. As for intermediation having an impact, this is shown through human interactions being done indi-rectly through machines instead of through humans. By 2030, accelerated by the shifts triggered in the COVID-19 crisis, digital interfaces will mostly dominate human social interaction. All of this new isolation and intermediation can potentially lead people to the Holy Trinity of Despair: loneliness, economic exclusion, and online engagement in extreme communities. A lack of community and economic inclusion can lead more people to go radical and join polit-ically extreme groups.

CHAPTER 5. WORK: THE CHAOTIC TRANSITION TO THE FUTURE OF JOBS

In our work lives, expect more rapid transitions. The three most common jobs in the United States employ ten million people and most of them will soon be gone due to automation. These trends were already ongoing but expect many of these jobs to go away in less than a year. This is but one aspect of how work changes. The long-term impact of the Great Reboot on jobs has three main drivers: automation, new jobs divide, and an "unbundling" of the firm. AI and digital apps will replace many jobs, but if you are able to acquire a job where you manage the AI or digital interfaces you can still have a career. On top of automation and high-skill jobs, there's also the rise of the "gig economy" with work becoming more flexible and less fixed on working for one company.

CHAPTER 6. CITY: THE RESHUFFLED MAP OF INNOVATION

In the past few decades, large cities have had an amazing run. Especially in the US, crime declined dramatically, downtowns were renewed, and innovation ecosystems thrived in these places. But their time dominating the conversation may be coming to an end with the Great Reboot, as the hyper-reliance on big cities as the focus of innovation, economic activity, and growth is showing serious cracks. Smaller cities are seeing large population growth because they are more affordable in terms of housing and other living costs and large city infrastructures are failing. The limitations of the "big city" model of economic development already existed, but the COVID-19 pandemic exposed them further. We can also expect remote work to remain an important part of post-pandemic life and ultimately scatter teams so they are not completely centered around big cities. The metropolitan giants will remain because they have unique features but expect them to take a hit in the long-term.

CHAPTER 7. WORLD: THE SHIFTING DYNAMICS OF HYPER-LOCAL AND HYPER-GLOBAL

While COVID-19 created a major public health crisis, it also created a crisis for global supply chains. The movement of goods and people became severely restricted, and some products were particularly sensitive to pandemic-related shocks. These shocks won't be totally temporary, with an ongoing pushback against globalization from nationalist movements around the world. Looking forward, we expect to see more local-first supply chains, less global travel for businesses, and rising localism movements that will see countries (and in some cases states within countries) isolate themselves.

PART III. NEW OPERATING SYSTEM TOOLKIT

TECH BUTTERFLY EFFECT AND TOOLS FOR THE NO NORMAL

The butterfly effect—the notion small events can trigger massive shifts a world away—is increasingly being seen in technology. A technologist making changes to a small piece of software can set off a figurative tsunami elsewhere. Tech is unique for these kinds of event chains because of three key drivers: leverage, speed, and scale. When it comes to leverage, the modern tech industry is remarkable because a relatively small level of inputs—people, capital, locations—can have an outsized impact. For speed, tech businesses and products can grow so much faster than other industries such as companies like Facebook, which went from a college dorm room to a nearly trillion-dollar company in roughly a decade. Tech's scale has led it to reach the highest industry concentration among the top ten largest companies on record. All of these things have led tech to become more relevant than ever during the Great Reboot.

FOUR QUADRANTS OF UNINTENDED CONSEQUENCES IN TECHNOLOGY

Powerful technologies, created by intelligent people, often end up as something even they could not predict in the beginning. To help mitigate this, we need to build tools that allow people to think through the unintended consequences or downstream effects of these technologies so we can make better decisions as a society. To help in this process of thinking through consequences (a.k.a. "anti-epiphanies"), we created the framework of the Four Quadrants of Unintended Consequences. The two dimensions in the quadrants' framework are user behavior (expected and unexpected) and system behavior (expected and unexpected). From these we derive four quadrants: Flywheel, Hijack, Black Box, and Uncharted Zone.

FLYWHEEL: WHAT HAPPENS IF YOU SUCCEED WILDLY?

Unintended consequences in the Flywheel Quadrant are about the extremes that can happen when your system and your users work precisely as you designed. One of the most interesting examples of this is casinos implementing rewards programs which incentivize gaming more have been later associated with gambling disorders and addictions. The rewards programs simply worked *too well*.

HIJACK: WHO IS THE WORST (AND BEST) POSSIBLE USER?

Consequences in the Hijack Quadrant are about the extremes that can happen when your system works exactly as you designed it, but your users apply the technology in ways other than originally anticipated. One example of Hijack is facial recognition technology, which was originally designed for straightforward applications such as the security of personal devices like laptops and smartphones. However, security agencies around the world have been deploying this technology and coupling it with their huge databases to crack down on democratic or lawful activities.

BLACK BOX: WHAT ARE THE HIDDEN BIASES AND OUTPUTS?

Consequences in the Black Box Quadrant are about what extremes can happen when your users act mostly as you expected but your system misbehaves and yields uneven results. For example, a standard lending algorithm could be biased against certain groups by race or gender if the model is not properly trained.

UNCHARTED ZONE: WHERE COULD UNKNOWN UNKNOWNS COME FROM?

These consequences are about what extremes can happen when both your users and systems act or misbehave in ways you never expected. These are the thorniest consequences by far because they are effectively unknown unknowns. For example, the internet was created for academic use and there was virtually no way to know many years later it would mostly be for totally different users and use cases.

FAIRNESS DEBT: THE SHADOW TWIN OF TECHNICAL DEBT

In this chapter, I outline the concept of Fairness Debt. Just like its technical counterpart, we incur Fairness Debt when we build systems that work for our current situation, but also have unintended consequences lurking underneath the surface. One of the biggest ways to incur Fairness Debt is by optimizing our systems and algorithms for a particular metric without adding constraints. Fairness Debts are not paid by the company but by users or society at first. But once they get big enough, they bite all of us collectively. One example is financial firms building algorithms designed to optimize for profitability but then eventually those programs discriminate against certain borrowers in the process. You need to understand your Fairness Debt and pay it early and often.

THE (PRETTY) GOOD, THE BAD, AND THE UGLY: NOT ALL FAIRNESS DEBT IS CREATED EQUAL

This "good enough" mindset is at the heart of a lot of prediction applications in data science. As a field, we constantly put people in boxes to make decisions about them, even though we inevitably know predictions will not be perfect. The key problem with algorithmic classification is we are invariably designing life around "pretty good" algorithms. "Pretty good" may be a great outcome for ad targeting, but when we deploy them at scale on applications ranging from voter registration to choosing who to hire to loan decisions, the final outcome may well be disastrous.

THE SIX E'S OF INCLUSION *BY FRANCES WEST*

In the coronavirus era, the importance of ethical and inclusive leadership has become more apparent than ever. Technology leaders have an opportunity to redesign and reconnect the world in a more equitable and just way if they intentionally focus on bridging the gap between those leading and the diverse, less privileged stakeholders. There are six fundamental steps each organization needs to take to operationalize inclusion: embrace, envision, enact, enlist, enable, and ensure.

THREE OPPORTUNITIES FOR ANALOG COMPANIES TRANSITIONING TO DIGITAL *BY KEYUR DESAI*

Since the internet boom of the mid-1990s, we have all witnessed many aspects of our daily life begin to be substituted by software. Digital substitutes have created new forms of value and reduced prices to consume them. As the pandemic impacts us today, analog companies have three clear opportunities to transition to digital or do a better job of offering digital substitutes. These include improving core analog operations with digital help, complementing core analog products, and transforming core businesses models.

GAPS AND ABUNDANCE: REBOOTED INTERNET ACCESS *BY MARTIN COOPER AND DANE STANGLER*

The Great Reboot entails a momentous shift from the analog to the digital economy. Among its many implications, two stand out to us as requiring immediate action. First, for full participation in the post-pandemic economy we need to close the Digital Divide with tools such as affordable wireless broadband. Second, our current framework for radio frequency spectrum use must be updated so it can be better utilized in the public interest.

FOUR TAKEAWAYS FOR POLICYMAKERS IN THE REBOOTED ECONOMY *BY JF GAUTHIER*

The decisions government policymakers will make over the coming year will have a significant impact on their economies well into the next two decades, just like the leading innovation policies architected by Israel and Singapore in the late 1990s made them some of the (unlikely) leaders of the global startup revolution fifteen years later and still today. These decisions include promoting entrepreneurial innovation policies, attracting tech talent to your region in the next twelve months, rebooting education, and tackling gender and racial inequalities.

ACKNOWLEDGMENTS

First of all, I want to thank my wife, Catherine. Thank you so much for all your love and support.

Some people say writing a book is like having a baby. As someone who had an infant at home while writing, I will not make that comparison. It is nonetheless a serious challenge that would not have been possible without the tremendous work of the *Rebooted* team: Lubin Arora and Sean Ludwig. Lubin is a longtime collaborator, with consulting and research experience at places like Startup Genome, McKinsey & Company, and Bain & Company, and worked with me on research, writing, and project management. Sean (formerly a communications director at Tech:NYC, and reporter for *VentureBeat*) is a talented technology and business writer and editor who worked with me on writing, editing, and strategy. I am also grateful to Raymond Lægreid, who supported me on some of the early research for this book.

I would like to thank the fantastic team at New Degree Press who helped me through the journey of getting the dream realized: Natalie Bailey, Cass Lauer, Jen Wichman, and Abbey Murphy (my editors); Gjorgji Pejkovski, Mateusz Cichosz, and Max Yenin (the book designers); and Brian Bies and Eric Koester from the broader publishing team.

I am very grateful for all the external contributors who trusted me to share their knowledge in this book: Cosmin Georghe, Vint Cerf, David Nordfors, Krishna Gade, Anusha Sethuraman, Frances West, Keyur Desai, Martin Cooper, Dane Stangler, and JF Gauthier.

Rebooted could not have happened without the collective wisdom of entrepreneurs and experts who took the time to share their experiences with me in various ways: Ade Mabogunje, Alberto Todeschini, Alicia Robb, Anand Rao, Ben Lorica, Bharath Kadaba, Bill Franks, Bjoern L. Herrmann, Carolina Barcenas, Collin Cunningham, David Rigby, David Talby, Elizabeth Frame Ellison, Fabrice Cavarretta, Felipe Matos, Francisco José Tavira Sánchez, Gary Bolles, Gaurav Deshpande, Jason Maynard, Jean-Phil Nsengimana, Jordan Bell-Masterson, Ken Stanley, Kurt Muehmel, Labhesh Patel, Lais de Oliveira, Lea Cademenos, Manasi Joshi, Marianna Presotto, Marina Gorbis, Martin Spier, Matheus Goya, Nicolas Goeldel, Nitzan Hermon, Nora Silver, Norris Krueger, P. Srikar Reddy, Ruben Nieuwenhuis, Sam Arbesman, Sri Ambati, Stephen Hardy, Ted Zoller, Torsten Kolind, Triveni Gandhi, Uma Rani Amara, Usman Ahmed, and Victor Hwang. Plus, thank you to the hundreds of partners, clients, and professional colleagues I have had the chance to talk with and learn from this year.

I have read extensively to write this book, and a handful of experts especially influenced my thinking. We have not talked directly about the topics in this book, but I would like to express my gratitude to you: Antonio Garcia Martinez, Chris Arnade, Nassim Taleb, Paul Kedrosky, and Tyler Cowen.

My thank you to the fantastic beta readers and supporters of this project: Abhishek Sharan, Alexander Hirschfeld, Alexandra Paz-Cox, Alexandra Wojciak, Alexis Taylor, Alice Armitage, Andrew Lefeber, Andrew Stoll, Annie Roos, Antonio Chillaron, Antonio Resende, Aqeel Zaman, Arif Zaman, Benedito Pacífico Da Rocha, Benjamin Tumbleson, Bernardo Medeiros, C.J. Penkert, Camila Mendes Froede, Cecilia Wessinger, Chad Renando, Chris Cusack, Dave Parker, Ed Roos, Eduardo Carlos Tavares, Edvaldo Araujo Rabelo, Eilat Levitan, Eutiquio "Tiq" Chapa, Evan Engstrom, Fabian Vandenreydt, Fernando Antonio de Almeida, Feysel Rahmeto, Fiddler Labs, Francisco Francinaldo Rafael De Olive, Gabe Downey, Gabriel Queiroz, Gary Schoeniger, Giancarlo Lupatini, Giselle Procopio Maia, Ilya Tabakh, Jake Carr, Jason Dormido, Jeremie Gluckman-Picard, John Coler, John Eddy, Jones Madruga, José Benedito De Sá, José Domingos Adriano, Jose Francisco Florencio Neto, Jose Romero, Josemar Andrade Alves, Julia Elmer, Julie Heath, Jussara França Lima, Kellie St.John-Sweeting, Kelly Powers, Larry Flanagan, Liz Grace, Lu Gonzalez, Maria Delfina, Maso Bove, Matthias Ivantsits, Megan Sartori, Melinda Holloran, Michael Freeman, Nicholas Alexander, Nick Butel, Nick Callais, Norris Krueger, Osvaldo Pacífico, Paul Williams, Pauline Wang, PC Sims, Pedro G Dos Santos, Peter Rinn, Phillip Yates, Phyllis Cobbs, Rafael Demarco, Rocco Sannelli and the team at Dataiku, Ron And Louise Ronnau, Sangeeta Badal, Sara Roos, Stephen Hardy, Suzanne Downey, Thea Stauffenecker,

Tilman Wiewinner, Torsten Kolind, Victor Luiz Da Silva, Vivian Escorsin, Wally Meyer, and anonymous.

This book concludes an important decade for me. As I think about the journey that took me here, my heart flows with gratitude toward the tremendous organizations and teams I have had the joy to be a part of. I am grateful to my colleagues at Startup Genome: JF Gauthier, Marc Penzel, Rahul Chatterjee, Stephan Kuester, Tricia Whitlock, Pranav Arya, Farshad Fahimi, Sama Siddiqui, Dushyant Sharma, Niranjan Anand, Utkarsh Jain, Adam Bregu, Patricia Russ, Akshat Agarwal, and more. At *Inc. Magazine*, I would like to specially thank Marli Guzzetta, Eric Schurenberg, and Scott Omelianuk. Thank you to everyone at the Global Entrepreneurship Network: Christopher Schroeder, Cristina Fernandez, Dane Stangler, Jonathan Ortmans, Jeff Hoffman, Kizito Okechukwu, Mark Marich, and Peter Komives. Thank you to Maria Maso and Juliana Garaizar at the Business Angel Minority Association. Muito obrigado y muchas gracias to the team at Stanford University and the Latino Business Action Network (currently and formerly): Deborah Whitman, Eutiquio "Tiq" Chapa, Inara Tareque, Jerry Porras, Mark Madrid, Marlene Orozco, Paul Oyer, and Philip Pompas. At the Kauffman Foundation (currently and formerly, directly and indirectly), thank you to the people who have made my time there a very formative experience: Alex Krause, Amisha Miller, Andy Stoll, Barb Pruitt, Chris Jackson, Chris Newton, Derek Ozkal, Emily Fetsch, Evan Absher, Jason Wiens, Joshua Russell-Fritch, Keith Mays, Lacey Graverson, Larry Jacob, Mette Kramer, Michelle St. Clair, Philip Gaskin, Robert Fairlie, Tammy Flores, Wendy Guilles, and more. At Sebrae, a special thanks to Marden Marcio Magalhaes, Julio Agostini, and Fabio Veras.

Thank you to the schools that have educated me: UC Berkeley, University of Kansas, Escola do Sebrae, Asian School of Business, Universidade Federal de Minas Gerais, Sao Miguel Arcanjo, Colegio Logosofico.

Thank you to the long-time friends and mentors who read early drafts and generously shared their expertise: Dane Stangler (who gave me tremendous opportunities even when he did not need to—and taught me to write acknowledgments!); EJ Reedy (who taught me about how kindness and work go well together); Romario Vieira de Melo (who taught me to keep moving); Vanuza (who took the extra time to teach me to read and write as a kid when other teachers wouldn't); and Yasuyuki Motoyama (who taught me about rigor in thinking), Sandra, Courtney, Gilmara, and Wellington (who taught me about the depths of mind and heart). My friends journeying with me through life: Arthur Mota, Brandon Ballweg, Caroline Schaffrath Demarco, Colin Tomkins-Bergh, Francisco Florencio, Leonardo Rangel, Mateus Batista Sacola, Paulo Arantes, Rafael Demarco. Muito obrigado.

(A few people are a part of many of these groups, but I avoided mentioning the same person multiple times. You know who you are. Thank you!)

Most importantly, I would like to thank my family, who has done so much for me. My wife, Catherine Morelix, for her unfailing love and support. My baby son, Manoel, for the giggles of happiness when I most needed them. My Dad,

Arnobio Moreira Felix, for showing me the joy of books. My Mom, Gilda Rocha Alves, for teaching me the joy of adventure. My brothers—Felipe, Igor, and Theo Morelix—for their loving camaraderie. Meus avos: Gino de Sa Alves, Terezinha Rocha Alves, Manoel Felix de Sousa, e Zelia Moreira de Sousa—muito obrigado por seu amor e sabedoria. My godmothers: Adley and Ariadne Felix, for their blessings. My father and mother-in-law—Jeannie and Michael Butel, as well as Nick Butel (my brother-in-law)—for their ever-present support. To my whole family: aunts, uncles, cousins and more—I love you and I miss you. Escrevo isto aqui com muitas saudades.

To you, reader, my most sincere thank you. All the best to you on your own reboot.

Muito obrigado. Abraços,
Arnobio

ABOUT THE AUTHOR, ARNOBIO MORELIX

———

Arnobio Morelix is a Silicon Valley-based leader working at the intersection of technology, economics, and policy. His work has been featured widely in national and global media, including the *New York Times*, the *Economist*, the *Wall Street Journal*, and the BBC, among others. Arnobio has authored research and analysis with Stanford University, *The World Economic Forum*, the Inter-American Development Bank, the Kauffman Foundation, and others. A frequent public speaker and presenter at South by Southwest, Facebook, and the Federal Reserve Bank, Arnobio has advised and worked with CEOs and founders, plus current and former government ministers.

Arnobio is the chief data scientist at *Inc. Magazine.* He also serves as senior advisor at the Global Entrepreneurship Network and advisory board member at the Business Angel Minority Association.

Follow him on LinkedIn (linkedin.com/in/arnobiomorelix) and Twitter (@amorelix), as well as www.greatreboot.com.

APPENDIX

WELCOME TO THE GREAT REBOOT

Arthur AI. "Home." Accessed November 20, 2020. https://www. arthur.ai/.

Bartash, Jeffry. "Jobless Claims Jump Another 4.4 Million—26 Million Americans Have Lost Their Jobs to the Coronavirus." *MarketWatch*, April 23, 2020. https://www.marketwatch.com/story/jobless-claims-jump-another-44-million-25-million-americans-have-lost-their-jobs-to-the-coronavirus-2020-04-23.

Bergh, Colin Tomkins. "A Reflection of Entrepreneurs in Pop Culture: The Celebritization of Entrepreneurs." *The Ewing Marion Kauffman Foundation*, February 26, 2015. https://www.kauffman.org/currents/the-celebritization-of-entrepreneurs/.

Chiappetta, Marco. "Uber Eats Demand Soars Due to COVID-19 Crisis." *Forbes Magazine*, March 25, 2020. https://www.forbes.com/sites/marcochiappetta/2020/03/25/uber-eats-demand-soars-due-to-covid-19-crisis/#54dae08b580c.

"Coronavirus: US Passes Six Million Covid-19 Cases." *BBC News,* August 31, 2020. https://www.bbc.co.uk/news/world-53976793.

"Coronavirus: Worst Economic Crisis since 1930s Depression, IMF Says." *BBC News,* April 9, 2020. https://www.bbc.co.uk/news/ business-52236936.

"COVID-19 Leads to Massive Labour Income Losses Worldwide." *International Labour Organization,* September 23, 2020. https://www.ilo.org/global/about-the-ilo/newsroom/news/ WCMS_755875/lang--en/index.htm.

Evans, Dein Alex. "How Zoom Became So Popular during Social Distancing." *CNBC,* April 4, 2020. https://www.cnbc. com/2020/04/03/how-zoom-rose-to-the-top-during-the-coro-navirus-pandemic.html.

Frank, Bills. *97 Things about Ethics Everyone in Data Science Should Know: Collective Wisdom from the Experts.* Newton, MA: O'Reilly Media, Inc., 2020.

Furceri, Davide, Prakash Loungani, Jonathan D. Ostry, and Pietro Pizzuto. "COVID-19 Will Raise Inequality If Past Pandemics Are a Guide." *VOX, CEPR Policy Portal,* May 8, 2020. https:// voxeu.org/article/covid-19-will-raise-inequality-if-past-pan-demics-are-guide.

"George Floyd: Huge Protests against Racism Held across US." *BBC News,* June 7, 2020. https://www.bbc.co.uk/news/world-us-can-ada-52951093.

Ghaffary, Shirin. "How to Avoid a Dystopian Future of Facial Recognition in Law Enforcement." *Vox*, December 10, 2019. https://www.vox.com/recode/2019/12/10/20996085/ai-facial-recognition-police-law-enforcement-regulation.

Ghosh, Iman. "What Is Big Tech Contributing to Help Fight COVID-19?" *Visual Capitalist*, April 14, 2020. https://www.visualcapitalist.com/big-tech-covid-19/.

Guzman, Joseph. "More than 100,000 Small Businesses Have Permanently Closed Due to Coronavirus, Study Estimates." *TheHill*, May 13, 2020. https://thehill.com/changing-america/well-being/longevity/497519-more-than-100000-small-businesses-have-permanently.

Hempel, Jessi. "LinkedIn Top Startups 2020: The 50 US Companies on the Rise." *LinkedIn*, September 22, 2020. https://www.linkedin.com/pulse/linkedin-top-startups-2020-50-us-companies-rise-jessi-hempel/?published=t.

Hill, Kashmir. "The Secretive Company That Might End Privacy as We Know It." *The New York Times*, January 18, 2020. https://www.nytimes.com/2020/01/18/technology/clearview-privacy-facial-recognition.html.

"How The COVID-19 Pandemic Is Deepening Economic Inequality in the US" *NPR*, August 16, 2020. https://www.npr.org/2020/08/16/902977077/how-the-covid-19-pandemic-is-deepening-economic-inequality-in-the-u-s?t=1601330530305.

Johnson, Khari. "Pymetrics open-sources Audit AI, an algorithm bias detection tool." Venture Beat, May 31, 2018. https://venturebeat.com/2018/05/31/pymetrics-open-sources-audit-ai-an-algorithm-bias-detection-tool/.

Levitz, Eric. "Mark Zuckerberg Should Run for President as Nominee of the 'Innovation Party,' Argues Brilliant Political Journalist." *Intelligencer*, April 26, 2016. https://nymag.com/intelligencer/2016/04/mark-zuckerberg-for-president.html.

Lohr, Steve. "Remember the MOOCs? After Near-Death, They're Booming." *The New York Times*, May 26, 2020. https://www.nytimes.com/2020/05/26/technology/moocs-online-learning.html.

Lunden, Ingrid. "Lattice, a People Management Platform, Picks up $45M at a $400M Valuation." *TechCrunch*, July 14, 2020. https://techcrunch.com/2020/07/14/lattice-a-people-management-platform-picks-up-45m-at-a-400m-valuation/.

Malara, Neha. "Dell Beats Revenue Estimates as Remote Working Lifts Workstation Demand." *Thomson Reuters*, May 28, 2020. https://fr.reuters.com/article/us-dell-tech-results-idUKKBN2343H0.

Manighetti, Elena and Ryan Osbourne. "The Route." *Sailing Kittiwake* (blog). Accessed June 25, 2020. http://sailingkittiwake.com/the-route/.

Morelix, Arnobio. "The Post-Pandemic Economy: The Great Reboot." Inc.com. Inc., April 28, 2020. https://www.inc.com/arnobio-morelix/the-post-pandemic-economy-great-reboot.html.

"Ninth Case of Fast-Moving Coronavirus Confirmed in US" *Thomson Reuters*, February 3, 2020. https://uk.reuters.com/article/uk-china-health-usa-california-idUKKBN1ZX01P.

Ohlheiser, Abby. "Analysis | A Year Ago, You Probably Thought Mark Zuckerberg Was Running for President." *The Washington Post*, April 10, 2018. https://www.washingtonpost.com/news/the-intersect/wp/2018/04/10/a-year-ago-you-probably-thought-mark-zuckerberg-was-running-for-president/.

Ohlheiser, Abby. "Analysis | Even Mark Zuckerberg Can't Stop the Meme That He Is Running for President." *The Washington Post*, August 3, 2017. https://www.washingtonpost.com/news/the-intersect/wp/2017/08/03/even-mark-zuckerberg-cant-stop-the-meme-that-he-is-running-for-president/.

"Reuters Launches 'The Great Reboot,' a Section Dedicated to the Future of the Workplace." Thomson Reuters, September 29, 2020. https://www.reuters.com/article/rpb-thegreatreboot/reuters-launches-the-great-reboot-a-section-dedicated-to-the-future-of-the-workplace-idUSKBN26K2BX.

Roger, Marshall. "Social Media, Addiction, and Democracy." *Deccan Herald*, September 24, 2020. https://www.deccanherald.com/opinion/panorama/social-media-addiction-and-democracy-892611.html.

Shah, Dhawal. "By the Numbers: MOOCs During the Pandemic." *The Report by Class Central*, August 31, 2020. https://www.classcentral.com/report/mooc-stats-pandemic/.

Sherwood, Jessica. "'Nobody Told Us about the Coronavirus Pandemic'." *BBC News*, April 21, 2020. https://www.bbc.com/news/uk-52332899.

Stangler, Dane. "The Economic Future Just Happened." *The Ewing Marion Kauffman Foundation*, June 9, 2009. https://www.kauffman.org/entrepreneurship/reports/the-economic-future-just-happened/.

Taylor, Derrick Bryson. "A Timeline of the Coronavirus Pandemic." *The New York Times*, February 13, 2020. https://www.nytimes.com/article/coronavirus-timeline.html.

"Tom Hanks Delivers Powerful Graduation Speech to Class of 2020: 'You've Been Chosen'." NBC Bay Area, May 4, 2020. https://www.nbcbayarea.com/entertainment/entertainment-news/tom-hanks-delivers-powerful-graduation-speech-to-class-of-2020-youve-been-chosen/2283865/.

Vacher, Frédéric. "3D Printing Communities Rise to Meet Covid-19 Challenges." *STATNews*, August 8, 2020. https://www.statnews.com/2020/08/10/collective-intelligence-collaboration-3d-printing-challenge-covid-19/.

VandeHei, Jim. "Bring on a Third-Party Candidate." *The Wall Street Journal*, April 25, 2016. http://www.wsj.com/articles/bring-on-a-third-party-candidate-1461624062.

Vincent, James. "Twitter Taught Microsoft's AI Chatbot to Be a Racist Asshole in Less than a Day." *The Verge*, March 24, 2016. https://www.theverge.com/2016/3/24/11297050/tay-microsoft-chatbot-racist.

Wilhelm, Alex. "Hopin Raises $40M Series A as Its Virtual Events Business Accelerates." *TechCrunch*, June 25, 2020. https://techcrunch.com/2020/06/25/hopin-raises-40m-series-a-as-its-virtual-events-business-accelerates/.

Wilson, Matthew. "14 Successful Companies That Started during US Recessions." *Business Insider*, April 20, 2020. https://www.businessinsider.com/successful-companies-started-during-past-us-recessions-2020-4?r=US&IR=T.

Witkowski, Wallace. "Adobe Stock Rises as Coronavirus Work-from-Home Shift Boosts Subscription Revenue." *MarketWatch*, June 11, 2020. https://www.marketwatch.com/story/adobe-stock-rises-as-subscription-revenue-tops-street-view-2020-06-11.

Wolff, Edward. "Household Wealth Trends in the United States, 1962 to 2016: Has Middle Class Wealth Recovered?" *NBER Working Paper Series*, No. 24085 (2017). https://doi.org/10.3386/w24085.

PART I. TWO ECONOMIES

CHAPTER 1. ECONOMICS OF PANDEMICS

Accardi, Nicolette. "GameStop to Close up to 450 Stores Worldwide." *NJ.com*, September 16, 2020. https://www.nj.com/business/2020/09/gamestop-to-close-up-to-450-stores-worldwide.html.

Agrawal, Ajay, Joshua Gans, and Avi Goldfarb. "The Simple Economics of Machine Intelligence." *Harvard Business Review*,

February 17, 2017. https://hbr.org/2016/11/the-simple-econom-ics-of-machine-intelligence.

Ali, Fareeha. "Ecommerce Trends amid Coronavirus Pandemic in Charts." *Digital Commerce 360*, August 26, 2020. https://www.digitalcommerce360.com/2020/08/25/ecom-merce-during-coronavirus-pandemic-in-charts/.

Bardwell, Thomas. "23 Million Gamers on Global Pandemic Lock-down Shatter Steam Records." *CCN.com*, September 23, 2020. https://www.ccn.com/23-million-gamers-on-global-pandemic-lockdown-shatter-steam-records/.

Black, Thomas. "FedEx Surges as E-Commerce Demand Sends Profit Climbing." *Bloomberg News*, September 15, 2020.

Chapman, Cate. "Economy Contracts at Record Pace." *LinkedIn*, August 1, 2020. https://www.linkedin.com/feed/news/econo-my-contracts-at-record-pace-5252138/.

Chin, Kimberly. "Peloton Posts First-Ever Profit as Pandemic Speeds Sales." *The Wall Street Journal*, September 10, 2020. https://www.wsj.com/articles/peloton-posts-first-ever-profit-as-pandemic-speeds-sales-11599776415?mod=business_lead_pos6.

Cowen, Tyler. "The Speed Premium in an Exponentially Growing Pandemic World." *Marginal Revolution* (blog), March 24, 2020. https://marginalrevolution.com/marginalrevolution/2020/03/the-speed-premium-in-an-exponentially-growing-pandemic-world.html.

Dmitrieva, Katia. "US Jobs Report May. 2020: Unemployment Rate Falls to 13.3%." *Bloomberg News*, June 5, 2020. https://www.bloomberg.com/news/articles/2020-06-05/u-s-jobless-rate-unexpectedly-fell-in-may-as-hiring-rebounded.

Doorn, Philip van. "After 150 Days of the COVID-19 Pandemic, Here Are the Best- and Worst-Performing Stocks." *Market-Watch*, August 11, 2020. https://www.marketwatch.com/story/after-150-days-of-the-covid-19-pandemic-here-are-the-best--and-worst-performing-stocks-2020-08-10.

Hanbury, Mary. "Fast-Fashion Giant Boohoo Reports Blockbuster Sales Growth during the Lockdown and Acquires Oasis and Warehouse." *Business Insider*, June 17, 2020. https://www.businessinsider.com/boohoo-sales-surge-during-pandemic-acquires-oasis-and-warehouse-2020-6.

Hartogs, Jessica. "Peloton Can't Keep up with Demand." *LinkedIn*, September 15, 2020. https://www.linkedin.com/feed/news/peloton-cant-keep-up-with-demand-5282354/.

Jiang, Irene. "Restaurants Rehired Nearly 1.4 Million Workers in May. Here's Why That Number May Be Less Impressive than It Sounds." *Business Insider*, June 8, 2020. https://www.businessinsider.com/restaurants-rehired-workers-in-may-but-gains-may-not-last-2020-6?r=US&IR=T.

Jordà, Òscar, Sanjay Singh, and Alan Taylor. "Longer-Run Economic Consequences of Pandemics." *Federal Reserve Bank of San Francisco* Working Paper, (September 2020). https://doi.org/10.3386/w26934.

Kalogeropoulos, Demitri. "Stitch Fix Isn't Nearly Done Growing." *The Motley Fool*, September 27, 2020. https://www.fool.com/investing/2020/09/27/stitch-fix-isnt-nearly-done-growing/.

Kumar, Lakshay. "Gaming Becomes Top Activity Online During Coronavirus Lockdown." *TheQuint*, March 21, 2020. https://www.thequint.com/tech-and-auto/tech-news/gaming-becomes-top-activity-amid-coronavirus-lockdown.

LibGuides. "Video-on-Demand Research Guide: Industry Classification—NAICS and SIC." Last updated Sep 29, 2020. https://libguides.du.edu/c.php?g=558882&p=3843760.

Link, Jeff. "Will We Ever Want to Use Touchscreens Again?" *Built In*, last updated June 24, 2020. https://builtin.com/design-ux/future-touchless.

Martinez, Peter. "Gold's Gym Files for Bankruptcy after Blow from Coronavirus Pandemic." *CBS Interactive*, September 2, 2020. https://www.cbsnews.com/news/golds-gym-files-bankruptcy-chapter-11-coronavirus-pandemic/.

Morelix, Arnobio. "The Post-Pandemic Economy: The Great Reboot." *Inc.com*, April 28, 2020. https://www.inc.com/arnobio-morelix/the-post-pandemic-economy-great-reboot.html.

North American Industry Classification System. Suitland, MD: United States Census Bureau, 2017. https://www.census.gov/eos/www/naics/2017NAICS/2017_NAICS_Manual.pdf.

Raymond, Adam K. "Household-Name Companies That Have Filed for Bankruptcy Because of Coronavirus." *Intelligencer*,

August 3, 2020. https://nymag.com/intelligencer/2020/08/major-companies-filing-for-bankruptcy-due-to-coronavirus.html.

Reddy, Srikar, and Arnobio Morelix, "Companies Now Face an Urgent Choice: Go Digital, or Go Bust." World Economic Forum, October 19, 2020. https://www.weforum.org/agenda/2020/10/digital-transformation-or-bust/.

Scaggs. Alexandra, "Big Tech Smashes Expectations." *LinkedIn*, August 24, 2020. https://www.linkedin.com/feed/news/big-tech-smashes-expectations-4903028/.

Siegel, Robert and Ryan Kissick. "Stripe: Increasing the GDP of the Internet." Faculty & Research. *Stanford Graduate School of Business*, 2016. https://www.gsb.stanford.edu/faculty-research/case-studies/stripe-increasing-gdp-internet.

Statistics Canada. "51—Information and cultural industries—Sector." North American Industry Classification System (NAICS) Canada 2012. March 23, 2018. https://www23.statcan.gc.ca/imdb/p3VD.pl?Function=getVD&TVD=118464&CVD=118465&CPV=51&CST=01012012&CLV=1&MLV=5.

Steam Database. "Steam—Lifetime concurrent players on Steam chart." Accessed October 5, 2020. https://steamdb.info/app/753/graphs/.

Thomas, Lauren. "Retailers Are Reporting Record Online Sales during the Pandemic. But It Won't Last Forever." *CNBC*, August 30, 2020. https://www.cnbc.com/2020/08/30/corona-

virus-retailers-report-record-online-sales-during-pandemic.
html.

US Bureau of Labor Statistics. "Charts of the largest occupations
in each area, May 2019." *Occupational Employment Statistics.*
Accessed August 25, 2020. https://www.bls.gov/oes/current/
area_emp_chart/area_emp_chart.htm.

US Bureau of Labor Statistics. "Unemployment Rate." *Current
Employment Statistics,* Accessed September 28, 2020. https://
data.bls.gov/timeseries/LNS14000000.

Valinsky, Jordan. "24 Hour Fitness Files for Bankruptcy and
Closes 100 Gyms." *CNN,* June 15, 2020. https://www.cnn.
com/2020/06/15/investing/24-hour-fitness-bankruptcy/index.
html.

Westin, David. "Verizon CEO Hans Vestberg: Gaming Traffic Up
75% Since Virus (Video)." Bloomberg News, March 18, 2020.
https://www.bloomberg.com/news/videos/2020-03-18/verizon-
ceo-says-gaming-traffic-up-75-since-virus-video.

CHAPTER 2. THREE WAVES OF THE GREAT REBOOT

Ali, Fareeha. "Ecommerce Trends amid Coronavirus Pandemic in Charts." *Digital Commerce 360,* August 26, 2020.
https://www.digitalcommerce360.com/2020/08/25/ecom-
merce-during-coronavirus-pandemic-in-charts/.

Arbesman, Samuel. *Overcomplicated: Technology at the Limits of
Comprehension.* New York: Portfolio/Penguin, 2017.

Automattic. "Work with Us." September 30, 2020. https://automattic.com/work-with-us/.

"Ball Fever—Berlin Celebrates the 'Golden Twenties'—Arts.21." *Deutsche Welle*, January 6, 2008. https://www.dw.com/en/ball-fever-berlin-celebrates-the-golden-twenties-arts21-05012008/av-3040934.

Ceurvels, Matteo. "Latin America Ecommerce 2020." *eMarketer*, June 17, 2020. https://www.emarketer.com/content/latin-america-ecommerce-2020.

Cramer-Flood, Ethan. "China Ecommerce 2020." *eMarketer*, June 10, 2020. https://www.emarketer.com/content/china-ecommerce-2020.

Cramer-Flood, Ethan. "Global Ecommerce 2020." *eMarketer*, June 22, 2020. https://www.emarketer.com/content/global-ecommerce-2020.

Folha de S.Paulo. "O inesquecível carnaval de 1919." May 27, 2020. https://www1.folha.uol.com.br/webstories/entretenimento/2020/06/o-inesquecivel-carnaval-de-1919/.

Franck, Thomas. "Hardest-Hit Industries: Nearly Half the Leisure and Hospitality Jobs Were Lost in April." *CNBC*, May 8, 2020. https://www.cnbc.com/2020/05/08/these-industries-suffered-the-biggest-job-losses-in-april-2020.html.

Gilbertson, Dawn. "Same Old Vegas? Here's What Coronavirus Has and Hasn't Changed about Sin City." *USA Today*, June 10, 2020. https://eu.usatoday.com/story/travel/airline-news/2020/06/07/

las-vegas-open-visitors-need-know-free-parking-masks-casinos/5309192002/.

Kochhar, Rakesh, and Amanda Barroso. "Young Workers Likely to Be Hard Hit as COVID-19 Strikes a Blow to Restaurants and Other Service Sector Jobs." *Pew Research Center*, August 26, 2020. https://www.pewresearch.org/fact-tank/2020/03/27/young-workers-likely-to-be-hard-hit-as-covid-19-strikes-a-blow-to-restaurants-and-other-service-sector-jobs/.

"Many in US Won't Return to Gym or Dining out, New Poll Shows." *Los Angeles Times*, May 23, 2020. https://www.latimes.com/world-nation/story/2020-05-23/coronavirus-reopening-poll-return-gym-dining-out-restaurants.

Matthews, Dylan, and Byrd Pinkerton. "He Co-Founded Skype. Now He's Spending His Fortune on Stopping Dangerous AI." *Vox*, June 19, 2019. https://www.vox.com/future-perfect/2019/6/19/18632586/jaan-tallinn-skype-kazaa-artificial-intelligence-risk-threat.

Morelix, Arnobio. "The Impact of COVID-19 on Global Startup Ecosystems." *Startup Genome*, April 01, 2020. https://startupgenome.com/blog/impact-of-covid19-on-global-startup-ecosystems.

Morelix, Arnobio. "The Post-Pandemic Economy: The Great Reboot." *Inc.com*, April 28, 2020. https://www.inc.com/arnobio-morelix/the-post-pandemic-economy-great-reboot.html.

Morelix, Arnobio. "What the Lower Unemployment Rate Really Means for the Economy." *Inc.com*, June 9, 2020. https://www.

inc.com/arnobio-morelix/unemployment-figures-fastest-re-
cession-jobs.html.

National Bureau of Economic Research. "US Business Cycle
Expansions and Contractions." Accessed September 28, 2020.
https://www.nber.org/cycles/cyclesmain.html.

Nikos-Rose, Karen. "Coronavirus Economic Effects Might Last
Decades, UC Davis Research Suggests." *UC Davis*, May 20,
2020. https://www.ucdavis.edu/coronavirus/news/corona-
virus-economic-effects-might-last-decades-uc-davis-re-
search-suggests/.

Russon, Mary-Ann. "Coronavirus: How Africa's Supply Chains
Are Evolving." *BBC News*, June 25, 2020. https://www.bbc.
co.uk/news/business-53100287.

Staff. "Paris Années Folles." *ParisVoice*, March 19, 2017. http://paris-
voice.com/paris-annees-folles/.

Stangler, Dane. "The Economic Future Just Happened." *The Ewing
Marion Kauffman Foundation*, June 9, 2009. https://www.
kauffman.org/entrepreneurship/reports/the-economic-fu-
ture-just-happened/.

Statt, Nick. "Facebook Teases a Vision of Remote Work Using
Augmented and Virtual Reality." *The Verge*, May 21, 2020.
https://www.theverge.com/2020/5/21/21266945/facebook-ar-
vr-remote-work-oculus-passthrough-future-tech.

Taleb, Nassim N., Daniel G. Goldstein, and Mark W. Spitznagel.
"The Six Mistakes Executives Make in Risk Management." *Har-*

vard Business Review, August 1, 2014. https://hbr.org/2009/10/the-six-mistakes-executives-make-in-risk-management.

US Bureau of Labor Statistics. "Unemployment Rate" *Current Employment Statistics*. Accessed September 28, 2020. https://www.bls.gov/charts/employment-situation/civilian-unemployment-rate.htm.

US Census Bureau, "2Q 2020 E-commerce, Quarterly Data." Accessed November 1, 2020.

"What Is Curbside Pick Up?" *Parcel Pending* (blog), September 6, 2019. https://www.parcelpending.com/blog/what-is-curbside-pick-up/.

PART II. CIRCLES OF IMPACT

CHAPTER 3. FOUR CIRCLES OF IMPACT OF THE GREAT REBOOT

Reddy, Srikar, and Arnobio Morelix, "Companies Now Face an Urgent Choice: Go Digital, or Go Bust." World Economic Forum, October 19, 2020. https://www.weforum.org/agenda/2020/10/digital-transformation-or-bust/.

CHAPTER 4. HOME: THE LONELIER FUTURE OF OUR SOCIAL LIVES

Arnade, Chris. *Dignity: Seeking Respect in Back Row America*. New York: Sentinel, 2019.

Ballard, Jamie. "Amid COVID-19, Millennials Are (Still) the Loneliest Generation." *YouGov*, May 1, 2020. https://today.yougov.

com/topics/relationships/articles-reports/2020/05/01/loneli-
ness-mental-health-coronavirus-poll-data.

Bennhold, Katrin. "Equality and the End of Marrying Up."
The New York Times, June 12, 2012. https://www.nytimes.
com/2012/06/13/world/europe/13iht-letter13.html.

Booth, Robert. "Robots to Be Used in UK Care Homes to Help
Reduce Loneliness." *The Guardian*, September 7, 2020. https://
www.theguardian.com/society/2020/sep/07/robots-used-uk-
care-homes-help-reduce-loneliness.

Brand, Michael. "Why Our Service Organizations Are Dying (and
6 Ways to Fix Them)." *LinkedIn*,June 21, 2016. https://www.
linkedin.com/pulse/why-our-service-organizations-dying-
6-ways-fix-them-michael.

Dal Bo, Ernesto, F Finan, O Folke, T Persson, and J Rickne. "Economic and Social Outsiders but Political Insiders: Sweden's
Radical Right" *Unpublished manuscript*, Department of Political Science, UC Berkeley, March 2020.

Flores, Taya. "Fraternal, Service Groups Battle Declining Membership." *Journal and Courier*, October 11, 2014. https://eu.jconline.
com/story/news/2014/10/11/fraternal-service-groups-battle-de-
clining-membership/16874977/.

Gardels, Nathan. "Jared Diamond: Why Nations Fail or Succeed
When Facing a Crisis." *Berggruen Institute*, July 31, 2020.
https://www.berggruen.org/the-worldpost/articles/jared-di-
amond-why-nations-fail-or-succeed-when-facing-a-crisis/.

Gates, Bill. "How to Handle a National Crisis." *gatesnotes.com*, May 20, 2019. https://www.gatesnotes.com/Books/Upheaval.

Glenn, Heidi. "America's 'Complacent Class': How Self-Segregation Is Leading to Stagnation." *NPR*, March 2, 2017. https://www.npr.org/2017/03/02/517915510/americas-complacent-class-how-self-segregation-is-leading-to-stagnation.

Global Web Index, 2019 Social Media User Trends Report. London: Global Web Index, 2019.

Gurri, Martin. *The Revolt of the Public and the Crisis of Authority in the New Millennium*. San Francisco: Stripe Press, 2018.

Haidt, J., and J. Twenge. "Social media use and mental health: A review." *Unpublished manuscript*, New York University, 2019.

Hedegaard, Holly, Curtin SC, Warner M. "Suicide mortality in the United States, 1999-2017," *NCHS Data Brief* 2018.

Jones, Jeffrey M. "US Church Membership Down Sharply in Past Two Decades." *Gallup*, October 6, 2020. https://news.gallup.com/poll/248837/church-membership-down-sharply-past-two-decades.aspx.

Rosenfeld, Michael J., Reuben J. Thomas, and Sonia Hausen. "Disintermediating Your Friends: How Online Dating in the United States Displaces Other Ways of Meeting." *Proceedings of the National Academy of Sciences* 116, no. 36: 17753–58, (2009). https://doi.org/10.1073/pnas.1908630116.

Sher, Leo. "The Impact of the COVID-19 Pandemic on Suicide Rates." *QJM: An International Journal of Medicine* 113, no. 10, pp. 707–712, (2020). https://doi.org/10.1093/qjmed/hcaa202.

SoftBank Robotics. "Pepper the Humanoid and Programmable Robot: SoftBank Robotics." Accessed September 19, 2020. https://www.softbankrobotics.com/emea/en/pepper.

"The Rise of Japan's 'Super Solo' Culture." *BBC Worklife*, January 15, 2020. https://www.bbc.com/worklife/article/20200113-the-rise-of-japans-super-solo-culture.

Twenge, Jean M., Brian H. Spitzberg, and W. Keith Campbell. "Less in-Person Social Interaction with Peers among US Adolescents in the 21st Century and Links to Loneliness." *Journal of Social and Personal Relationships 36*, no. 6 (2019): 1892–1913. https://doi.org/10.1177/0265407519836170.

Ueda, Peter, Catherine H. Mercer, Cyrus Ghaznavi, and Debby Herbenick. "Trends in Frequency of Sexual Activity and Number of Sexual Partners Among Adults Aged 18 to 44 Years in the US, 2000-2018." *JAMA Network Open 3*, no. 6 (2020). https://doi.org/10.1001/jamanetworkopen.2020.3833.

Walker, Peter. "May Appoints Minister to Tackle Loneliness Issues Raised by Jo Cox." *The Guardian*, January 16, 2018. https://www.theguardian.com/society/2018/jan/16/may-appoints-minister-tackle-loneliness-issues-raised-jo-cox.

Zarroli, Jim. "'Deaths of Despair' Examines the Steady Erosion of US Working-Class Life." *NPR*, March 18, 2020. https://www.

npr.org/2020/03/18/817687042/deaths-of-despair-examines-the-steady-erosion-of-u-s-working-class-life.

CHAPTER 5. WORK: THE CHAOTIC TRANSITION TO THE FUTURE OF WORK

Arntz, Melanie, Terry Gregory, and Ulrich Zierahn. "Revisiting the Risk of Automation." *Economics Letters* 159 (2017). https://doi.org/10.1016/j.econlet.2017.07.001.

Autor, David, and Anna Salomons. "Is Automation Labor-Displacing? Productivity Growth, Employment, and the Labor Share." *National Bureau of Economic Research* (July 2018). https://doi.org/10.3386/w24871.

Baker, S.R., N. Bloom, S.J. Davis, and S.J. Terry. "COVID-Induced Economic Uncertainty (No. 26983)" *National Bureau of Economic Research* (2020).

Coase, R.H. The Nature of the Firm. *Economica* 4, no. 16 (1937).

"Coase's Theory of the Firm." *The Economist*, July 29, 2017. https://www.economist.com/schools-brief/2017/07/29/coases-theory-of-the-firm.

Cowen, Tyler. "Industrial Revolution Comparisons Aren't Comforting." *Bloomberg.com*, Feb 16, 2017. https://www.bloomberg.com/opinion/articles/2017-02-16/industrial-revolution-comparisons-aren-t-comforting.

Crook, Rebecca. "In Pictures: Six Trendsetting Checkout-Free Stores from around the Globe." *Retail Week*, August 13, 2020.

https://www.retail-week.com/tech/in-pictures-six-trendsetting-checkout-free-stores-from-around-the-globe/7035501. article.

Dawson, Ross. "How to Prepare for the Future of Work—Human-Machine Collaboration, Humanisation, Education." *Ross Dawson*, November 6, 2016. https://rossdawson.com/how-to-prepare-for-the-future-of-work-human-machine-collaboration-humanisation-education/.

Frey, Carl Benedikt, and Michael A. Osborne. "The Future of Employment: How Susceptible Are Jobs to Computerisation?" *Technological Forecasting and Social Change* 114 (2017): 254–80. https://doi.org/10.1016/j.techfore.2016.08.019.

"Gartner CFO Survey Reveals 74% Intend to Shift Some Employees to Remote Work Permanently." *Gartner*, April 3, 2020. https://www.gartner.com/en/newsroom/press-releases/2020-04-03-gartner-cfo-surey-reveals-74-percent-of-organizations-to-shift-some-employees-to-remote-work-permanently2.

Global Workplace Analytics. "Work from Home Experience Survey Results." Global Workplace Analytics, August 25, 2020. https://globalworkplaceanalytics.com/global-work-from-home-experience-survey.

Google. "France." COVID-19 Community Mobility Report, November 15, 2020. https://www.gstatic.com/covid19/mobility/2020-11-15_FR_Mobility_Report_en.pdf.

Google. "Germany." COVID-19 Community Mobility Report, November 15, 2020. https://www.gstatic.com/covid19/mobility/2020-11-15_DE_Mobility_Report_en-GB.pdf.

Google. "India." COVID-19 Community Mobility Report, November 15, 2020. https://www.gstatic.com/covid19/mobility/2020-11-15_IN_Mobility_Report_en-GB.pdf.

Google. "New Zealand." COVID-19 Community Mobility Report, November 6, 2020. https://www.gstatic.com/covid19/mobility/2020 11-06_NZ_Mobility_Report_en-GB.pdf.

Google. "Taiwan." COVID-19 Community Mobility Report, November 6, 2020. https://www.gstatic.com/covid19/mobility/2020-11-06_TW_Mobility_Report_en.pdf.

Google. "United Kingdom." COVID-19 Community Mobility Report, November 15, 2020. https://www.gstatic.com/covid19/mobility/2020-11-15_GB_Mobility_Report_en-GB.pdf.

Google. "United States." COVID-19 Community Mobility Report, November 15, 2020. https://www.gstatic.com/covid19/mobility/2020-11-15_US_Mobility_Report_en.pdf.

Hagel III, John, and Marc Singer. "Unbundling the Corporation." *Harvard Business Review*, August 1, 2014. https://hbr.org/1999/03/unbundling-the-corporation.

Hasija, Sameer, V. "Paddy" Padmanabhan and Prashant Rampal. "Will the Pandemic Push Knowledge Work into the Gig Economy?" *Harvard Business Review*, August 17, 2020. https://hbr.

org/2020/06/will-the-pandemic-push-knowledge-work-into-the-gig-economy.

Hernández-Morales, Aitor, Kalina Oroschakoff, and Jacopo Barigazzi. "The Death of the City." *POLITICO*, August 3, 2020. https://www.politico.eu/article/the-death-of-the-city-coronavirus-towns-cities-retail-transport-pollution-economic-crisis/.

Kelso, Alicia. "Self-Order Kiosks Are Finally Having a Moment in the Fast Food Space." *Forbes Magazine*, July 30, 2019. https://www.forbes.com/sites/aliciakelso/2019/07/30/self-order-kiosks-are-finally-having-a-moment-in-the-fast-food-space/?sh=7dc-dc49b4275.

Khalili, Joel. "Remote Workers Rejoice—Facebook's New Enterprise Virtual Reality Platform Is Here." *TechRadar*, May 22, 2020. https://www.techradar.com/uk/news/remote-workers-rejoice-facebooks-new-enterprise-virtual-reality-platform-is-here.

Kosner, Anthony Wing. "Google Cabs and Uber Bots Will Challenge Jobs 'Below the API'." *Forbes Magazine*, February 4, 2015. https://www.forbes.com/sites/anthonykosner/2015/02/04/google-cabs-and-uber-bots-will-challenge-jobs-below-the-api/?sh=3ef66f1169cc.

Maddison, Angus. *The World Economy, Volumes 1 and 2*. Paris: OECD, 2006.

Manyika, James, Susan Lund, Michael Chui, Jacques Bughin, Jonathan Woetzel, Parul Batra, Ryan Ko, and Saurabh Sanghvi. "Jobs Lost, Jobs Gained: What the Future of Work Will Mean for Jobs, Skills, and Wages." McKinsey & Company, May 11, 2019. https://www.mckinsey.com/featured-insights/future-of-work/jobs-lost-jobs-gained-what-the-future-of-work-will-mean-for-jobs-skills-and-wages.

Marx, Karl, and Friedrich Engels. *The Communist Manifesto*. London: Penguin, 1985.

Maxim, Robert, and Mark Muro. "Automation and AI Will Disrupt the American Labor Force. Here's How We Can Protect Workers." *Brookings* (blog), February 25, 2019. https://www.brookings.edu/blog/the-avenue/2019/02/25/automation-and-ai-will-disrupt-the-american-labor-force-heres-how-we-can-protect-workers/.

Morelix, Arnobio. "What the Lower Unemployment Rate Really Means for the Economy." *Inc.com*, June 9, 2020. https://www.inc.com/arnobio-morelix/unemployment-figures-fastest-recession-jobs.html.

Nordfors, David and Vint Cerf. The People Centered Economy: The New Ecosystem for Work. IIIJ Foundation, 2018.

"Quick-Service Restaurants Rush to Introduce Self-Ordering Kiosks." *Retail Technology Review*, February 19, 2020. https://www.retailtechnologyreview.com/articles/2020/02/19/quick-service-restaurants-rush-to-introduce-self-ordering-kiosks/.

Rao, Venkatesh. "The Premium Mediocre Life of Maya Millennial." *ribbonfarm* (blog), September 10, 2017. https://www.ribbonfarm.com/2017/08/17/the-premium-mediocre-life-of-maya-millennial/.

"Robot Automation Will 'Take 800 Million Jobs by 2030'—Report."
BBC News, November 29, 2017. https://www.bbc.co.uk/news/
world-us-canada-42170100.

Sparshott, Jeffrey. "The Robots Are Coming for Your Paycheck."
The Wall Street Journal, February 17, 2015. https://blogs.wsj.
com/economics/2015/02/17/the-robots-are-coming-for-your-
paycheck/.

Stern, Fritz, and Tim Tilton. "The Political Theory of Swedish
Social Democracy." *Foreign Affairs* 70, no. 3 (1991). https://doi.
org/10.2307/20044862.

Summers, J., Hao-Yuan Cheng, Hsien-Ho Lin, Lucy Telfar Bar-
nard, Amanda Kvalsvig, Nick Wilson, and Michael G Baker.
"Potential lessons from the Taiwan and New Zealand health
responses to the COVID-19 pandemic." *The Lancet Regional
Health—Western Pacific*. (2020). https://doi.org/10.1016/j.lan-
wpc.2020.100044.

"The Executive's Guide to Returning to the Workplace Post
COVID 19." *Gartner*, Accessed November 20, 2020. https://
www.gartner.com/en/insights/an-executive-guide-to-return-
ing-to-the-workplace.

US Bureau of Labor Statistics. "Table 6. Employed persons working at home, workplace, and time spent working at each location by full- and part-time status and sex, jobholding status,
and educational attainment, 2019 annual averages." Current
Employment Statistics. Accessed October 28, 2020.

United States Bureau of Labor Statistics, "Civilian unemployment rate." The Employment Situation, accessed 24 July 2020.

United States Bureau of Labor Statistics. "Civilian labor force participation rate." The Employment Situation, accessed 24 July 2020 https://www.bls.gov/charts/employment-situation/civilian-labor-force-participation-rate.htm.

Waters, Richard. "Google Chief Warns of IT Threat." *Financial Times*, January 23, 2014. https://www.ft.com/content/206bb2e2-847f-11e3-b72e-00144feab7de.

"Why One Man Left Silicon Valley and Set up a Survival Camp." *BBC News*, August 5, 2017. https://www.bbc.com/news/av/world-us-canada-40814714.

World Inequality Database. "Wealth Inequality—Top 1% Share." Accessed 30 September 2020.

CHAPTER 6. CITY: THE RESHUFFLED MAP OF INNOVATION

Austin Chamber of Commerce. "Population Overview." Accessed November 20, 2020. https://www.austinchamber.com/economic-development/austin-profile/population/overview.

Florida, Richard, and Benjamin Schneider. "The Global Housing Crisis." *Bloomberg News*, April 11, 2018. https://www.bloomberg.com/news/articles/2018-04-11/the-housing-crisis-extends-far-beyond-superstar-cities.

Florida, Richard. "Understanding the Great Crime Decline in US Cities." *Bloomberg*, January 16, 2018. https://www.bloomberg.

com/news/articles/2018-01-16/understanding-the-great-crime-decline-in-u-s-cities.

Google. "Taiwan." COVID-19 Community Mobility Report, November 15, 2020. https://www.gstatic.com/covid19/mobility/2020-11-06_TW_Mobility_Report_en.pdf.

Google. "United Kingdom." COVID-19 Community Mobility Report, November 15, 2020. https://www.gstatic.com/covid19/mobility/2020-11-06_NZ_Mobility_Report_en-GB.pdf.

Graham, Paul. "How to Be Silicon Valley." *paulgraham.com*, May 2006. http://www.paulgraham.com/siliconvalley.html.

Hernández-Morales, Aitor, Kalina Oroschakoff, and Jacopo Barigazzi. "The Death of the City." POLITICO, August 3, 2020. https://www.politico.eu/article/the-death-of-the-city-coronavirus-towns-cities-retail-transport-pollution-economic-crisis/.

Kesler, Charles. "California's Biggest Cities Confront a 'Defecation Crisis'." *The Wall Street Journal*, August 16, 2019.

Kotkin, Joel. "The Coronavirus Is Changing the Future of Home, Work, and Life." *The Daily Beast*, April 11, 2020. https://www.thedailybeast.com/the-coronavirus-is-changing-the-future-of-home-work-and-life.

LinkedIn Workforce Report. "New York City." LinkedIn, November 2020.

LinkedIn Workforce Report. "San Francisco." LinkedIn, November 2020. https://www.linkedin.com/jobs/blog/linkedin-workforce-report-november-2020-san-francisco-ca

Lonsdale, Joe. "California, Love It and Leave It." *The Wall Street Journal*, November 15, 2020. https://www.wsj.com/articles/california-love-it-and-leave-it-11605472619.

Markoff, John. "Silicon Valley May Have Lost Its Way." *The New York Times*, September 28, 1992. https://www.nytimes.com/1992/09/28/business/silicon-valley-may-have-lost-its-way.html.

Martínez, Antonio García (@antoniogm). "Atherton, Woodside, Portola Valley..." Twitter, 16 July 2020. twitter.com/antoniogm/status/1283628371600003073.

Martínez, Antonio García. Chaos Monkeys: Obscene Fortune and Random Failure in Silicon Valley. New York: HarperCollins-Publishers, 2016.

Martínez, Antonio García (@antoniogm). "Ever the Contrarian, I've Decided to Move to the City Everyone Is Fleeing, and Take Residence in One of Those Old SF Edwardians Held Together by Paint and Prop 13. I Have No Doubt This Is a Terrible Idea." Twitter, November 15, 2020. https://twitter.com/antoniogm/status/1327851848196182017.

Martínez, Antonio García (@antoniogm). "'If the Startup IPOs, I Might Buy a House' Is a Thing Real People in the SF Bay Area Say." Twitter, 16 July 2020. twitter.com/antoniogm/status/1283623456488042498.

Morelix, Arnobio, Victor Hwang, and Inara Tareque. "Zero Barriers: Three Mega Trends Shaping the Future of Entrepreneurship." Ewing Marion Kauffman Foundation (2017). https://doi.org/10.2139/ssrn.2919020.

MYMOVE. "Coronavirus Moving Study Shows More Than 15.9 Million People Moved During COVID-19." October 12, 2020. https://www.mymove.com/moving/covid-19/coronavirus-moving-trends/.

Novet, Jordan. "San Francisco Housing Has Cooled as Some Flee the City, but Demand Is Still There." *CNBC*, September 27, 2020. https://www.cnbc.com/2020/09/27/san-francisco-housing-suburbs-red-hot-but-city-still-in-demand.html.

Patino, Marie. "New Data Shows Just How Much Americans Moved Temporarily During Covid." *Bloomberg News*, October 12, 2020. https://www.bloomberg.com/news/articles/2020-10-12/new-data-shows-short-term-moves-spiked-during-covid.

PwC. "PwC MoneyTree Report Q3 2020." Accessed November 20, 2020. https://www.pwc.com/us/en/industries/technology/moneytree.html.

Redfin. "Austin Housing Market." Accessed November 18, 2020. https://www.redfin.com/city/30818/TX/Austin.

Redfin. "Manhattan Housing Market." Accessed November 18, 2020. https://www.redfin.com/city/35948/NY/Manhattan/housing-market.

Redfin. "New York Housing Market." Accessed November 18, 2020. https://www.redfin.com/city/30749/NY/New-York/housing-market.

Redfin. "San Francisco Housing Market." Accessed November 18, 2020. https://www.redfin.com/city/17151/CA/San-Francisco/housing-market.

Steckelberg, Aaron, and Carolyn Y. Johnson. "These Are the Top Coronavirus Vaccines to Watch." *The Washington Post*, November 23, 2020. https://www.washingtonpost.com/graphics/2020/health/covid-vaccine-update-coronavirus/?itid=sn_coronavirus_5/.

Thompson, Derek. "Get Ready for the Great Urban Comeback." *The Atlantic*, September 4, 2020. https://www.theatlantic.com/magazine/archive/2020/10/how-disaster-shaped-the-modern-city/615484/.

Wood, Shawn Paul. "Silicon Valley Has Some of America's Slowest Internet Connections." *Adweek*, November 6, 2014. https://www.adweek.com/digital/silicon-valley-has-terrible-reception/.

"Zillow 2020 Urban-Suburban Market Report." Zillow Research, October 2, 2020. https://www.zillow.com/research/2020-urb-suburb-market-report-27712/.

CHAPTER 7. WORLD: THE SHIFTING DYNAMICS OF HYPER-LOCAL AND HYPER-GLOBAL

"A Conversation with Nassim Nicholas Taleb." *The Washington Post*, March 15, 2009. https://www.washingtonpost.com/wp-dyn/content/article/2009/03/12/AR2009031202181_pf.html.

Altman, Steven A. "Will Covid-19 Have a Lasting Impact on Globalization?" *Harvard Business Review*, August 17, 2020. https://hbr.org/2020/05/will-covid-19-have-a-lasting-impact-on-globalization.

Apuzzo, Matt, and David D. Kirkpatrick. "Covid-19 Changed How the World Does Science, Together." *The New York Times*, April 1, 2020. https://www.nytimes.com/2020/04/01/world/europe/coronavirus-science-research-cooperation.html.

Gelles, David. "The Husband-and-Wife Team Behind the Leading Vaccine to Solve Covid-19." *The New York Times*, November 10, 2020. https://www.nytimes.com/2020/11/10/business/biontech-covid-vaccine.html.

Goldman Sachs. "Insights—How COVID-19 Is Shaping the Global M&A Outlook." June 16, 2020. https://www.goldmansachs.com/insights/pages/from_briefings_16-june-2020.html.

Higgins-Dunn, Noah. "Bill Gates Says More than 50% of Business Travel Will Disappear in Post-Coronavirus World." *CNBC*, November 18, 2020. https://www.cnbc.com/2020/11/17/coronavirus-bill-gates-says-more-than-50percent-of-business-travel-will-disappear-long-term.html.

Honan, Katie. "New York City Seeks Rain Ponchos as Surgical Gowns Dwindle." *The Wall Street Journal*, April 13, 2020. https://www.wsj.com/articles/new-york-city-seeks-rain-ponchos-as-surgical-gowns-dwindle-11586821702.

Korin, Netta. "Using Blockchain to Monitor the COVID-19 Vaccine Supply Chain." *World Economic Forum*, November 20, 2020. https://www.weforum.org/agenda/2020/11/using-blockchain-to-monitor-covid-19-vaccine-supply-chain/.

Kuipers, Jacob A. "Covid-19 Accelerated Nationalist Trends in Cross-Border M&A." *M&A Review*, September 17, 2020. https://ma-review.com/covid-19-accelerated-nationalist-trends-in-cross-border-ma/.

Lee, Yen Nee. "5 Charts Show Which Travel Sectors Were Worst Hit by the Coronavirus." *CNBC*, May 6, 2020. https://www.cnbc.com/2020/05/06/coronavirus-pandemics-impact-on-travel-tourism-in-5-charts.html.

Mack, Eric. "How SpaceX Starlink Broadband Will Envelop Earth and Transform the Sky." *CNET*, November 22, 2020. https://www.cnet.com/features/how-spacex-starlink-broadband-service-will-envelop-earth-transform-the-sky/.

Morelix, Arnobio. "What the Lower Unemployment Rate Really Means for the Economy." *Inc.com*, June 9, 2020. https://www.inc.com/arnobio-morelix/unemployment-figures-fastest-recession-jobs.html.

Porter Jr., Gerald, and Edward Ludlow. "Hand Sanitizer Will Be Hard to Find for a Long Time." *Bloomberg.com*, April 8, 2020.

https://www.bloomberg.com/news/articles/2020-04-08/hand-sanitizer-is-going-to-be-hard-to-find-for-a-long-long-time.

Price, Michael. "As COVID-19 Forces Conferences Online, Scientists Discover Upsides of Virtual Format." *Science*, April 30, 2020. https://www.sciencemag.org/careers/2020/04/covid-19-forces-conferences-online-scientists-discover-upsides-virtual-format.

Riquier, Andrea. "Another COVID-19 Victim: Globalization." *MarketWatch*, September 28, 2020. https://www.marketwatch.com/story/another-covid-19-victim-globalization-11601303609.

Russon, Mary-Ann. "Coronavirus: How Africa's Supply Chains Are Evolving." *BBC News*, June 25, 2020. https://www.bbc.co.uk/news/business-53100287.

Silver, Laura, Shannon Schumacher, and Mara Mordecai. "In the US and UK, Globalization Leaves Some Feeling 'Left Behind' or 'Swept Up'." *Pew Research Center*, November 10, 2020. https://www.pewresearch.org/2020/10/05/in-u-s-and-uk-globalization-leaves-some-feeling-left-behind-or-swept-up/.

Thomson, Cameron and Marcin Jakubowski. "Toward an Open Source Civilization: Innovations Case Narrative: Open Source Ecology." *Innovations: Technology, Governance, Globalization*. 2012. https://doi.org/10.1162/INOV_a_00139.

Tung, Liam. "SpaceX's Starlink in Action: Internet Satellites Keep Emergency Workers Online amid Wildfires." *ZDNet*, September 30, 2020. https://www.zdnet.com/article/

spacexs-starlink-in-action-internet-satellites-keep-emergen-
cy-workers-online-amid-wildfires/.

Vacher, Frédéric. "3D Printing Communities Rise to Meet Covid-
19 Challenges." *STAT News*, August 8, 2020. https://www.
statnews.com/2020/08/10/collective-intelligence-collabora-
tion-3d-printing-challenge-covid-19/.

Wan, William. "America Is Running Short on Masks, Gowns and
Gloves. Again." *The Washington Post*, July 9, 2020. https://www.
washingtonpost.com/health/2020/07/08/ppe-shortage-masks-
gloves-gowns/.

World Health Organization. "Public Statement for Collaboration
on COVID-19 Vaccine Development." Press Release. Last
updated April 16, 2020. https://www.who.int/news/item/13-
04-2020-public-statement-for-collaboration-on-covid-19-vac-
cine-development.

WTO. "Trade Set to Plunge as COVID-19 Pandemic Upends Global
Economy." Press Release, April 8, 2020. https://www.wto.org/
english/news_e/pres20_e/pr855_e.htm.

PART III. NEW OPERATING SYSTEM TOOLKIT

TECH BUTTERFLY EFFECT AND TOOLS FOR THE NO NORMAL

Andersson, Hilary. "Social Media Apps Are 'Deliberately' Addictive to Users." *BBC News*, July 3, 2018. https://www.bbc.co.uk/
news/technology-44640959.

Bellis, Mary. "Biography of Mark Zuckerberg, Creator of Facebook." *ThoughtCo*, June 19, 2019. https://www.thoughtco.com/mark-zuckerberg-biography-1991135.

Carter, Shawn M. "More Signs Point to Mark Zuckerberg Possibly Running for President in 2020." *CNBC*, August 15, 2017. https://www.cnbc.com/2017/08/15/mark-zuckerberg-could-be-running-for-president-in-2020.html.

Clifford, Matt (@matthewclifford). "The century's best advert for: (a) science (b) startups (c) immigration." Twitter, November 9, 2020. https://twitter.com/matthewclifford/status/1325799713111764992.

Desjardins, Jeff. "Mark Zuckerberg Turned $1 Million into $1 Billion in Just One Year—Here's How Long It Took Other Billionaires to Do the Same." *Business Insider*, April 5, 2018. https://www.businessinsider.com/how-long-it-takes-millionaires-to-become-billionaires-2018-4?IR=T.

Desjardins, Jeff. "Timeline: The March to a Billion Users [Chart]." *Visual Capitalist*, March 11, 2019. https://www.visualcapitalist.com/timeline-the-march-to-a-billion-users/.

"Facebook Buys Instagram Photo Sharing Network for $1bn." *BBC News*, April 10, 2012. https://www.bbc.co.uk/news/technology-17658264.

Franzese, Derek. "Facebook Interview." 17 May 2010. https://www.youtube.com/watch?v=--APdD6vejI.

Gelles, David. "The Husband-and-Wife Team Behind the Leading Vaccine to Solve Covid-19." *New York Times*, November 10, 2020. https://www.nytimes.com/2020/11/10/business/biontech-covid-vaccine.html.

Geron, Tomio. "Facebook Prices Third-Largest IPO Ever, Valued At $104 Billion." *Forbes Magazine*, May 18, 2012. https://www.forbes.com/sites/tomiogeron/2012/05/17/facebook-prices-ipo-at-38-per-share/#67c30bfd728a.

"Hunted—India's Lynch Files." *TheQuint*, Accessed July 22, 2020. https://www.thequint.com/quintlab/lynching-in-india/.

Levy, Miranda. "Beware the Health Dangers of 'Doomscrolling'." *The Telegraph*, September 24, 2020. https://www.telegraph.co.uk/health-fitness/body/beware-health-dangers-doomscrolling/.

Lorenz, E.N. "Predictability: does the flap of a butterfly's wings in Brazil set off a tornado in Texas?" Presented at 139th Annual Meeting of the American Association for the Advancement of Science, 29 Dec 1972.

Mingis, April Montgomery and Ken. "The Evolution of Apple's IPhone." *ComputerWorld*, September 10, 2019. https://www.computerworld.com/article/2604020/the-evolution-of-apples-iphone.html.

Morelix, Arnobio, Victor Hwang, and Inara Tareque. "Zero Barriers: Three Mega Trends Shaping the Future of Entrepreneurship." *Ewing Marion Kauffman Foundation* (2017). https://doi.org/10.2139/ssrn.2919020.

Pham, Sherisse. "The Company That Owns TikTok Now Has One Billion Users and Many Are Outside China." *CNN*, June 20, 2019. https://edition.cnn.com/2019/06/20/tech/tiktok-byted-ance-users/index.html.

Rao, Leena. "Peter Thiel: We Would Be A Lot More Careful About Funding Facebook Today. But..." *TechCrunch*, September 27, 2010. https://techcrunch.com/2010/09/27/peter-thiel-we-would-be-a-lot-more-careful-about-funding-facebook-today-but/.

Raskin, Aza. "No More More Pages?" *Humanized* (blog), April 25, 2006. https://web.archive.org/web/20120606053221/http://humanized.com/weblog/2006/04/25/no_more_more_pages/

Startup Genome. "State of the Global Startup Economy." Accessed September 30, 2020. https://startupgenome.com/article/state-of-the-global-startup-economy.

Stone, Brad. "Microsoft Buys Stake in Facebook." *The New York Times*, October 25, 2007. https://www.nytimes.com/2007/10/25/technology/25facebook.html.

Suttie, Jill. "How to Overcome Your Brain's Fixation on Bad Things." *Greater Good Magazine*, January 13, 2020. https://greatergood.berkeley.edu/article/item/how_to_overcome_your_brains_fixation_on_bad_things.

Transcript courtesy of Bloomberg Government. "Transcript of Mark Zuckerberg's Senate Hearing." *The Washington Post*, April 8, 2019. https://www.washingtonpost.com/news/the-switch/wp/2018/04/10/transcript-of-mark-zuckerbergs-sen-ate-hearing/.

Watercutter, Angela. "Doomscrolling Is Slowly Eroding Your Mental Health." *Wired*, June 25, 2020. https://www.wired.com/story/stop-doomscrolling.

WhatsApp. "Labeling Forwarded Messages." *WhatsApp* (blog). Last modified July 10, 2018. https://blog.whatsapp.com/labeling-forwarded-messages.

"WhatsApp Now Lets You Share and Forward a Message to Multiple Chats (with Frequent Chats on Top)." *Android Police*, August 11, 2016. https://www.androidpolice.com/2016/08/11/whatsapp-now-lets-forward-share-message-multiple-chats-easily-displays/.

World Bank Data. "Fixed Telephone Subscriptions (per 100 People)." Accessed August 30, 2020. https://data.worldbank.org/indicator/IT.MLT.MAIN.P2.

FOUR QUADRANTS OF UNINTENDED CONSEQUENCES IN TECHNOLOGY

Andreessen, Marc and Katie Hauna. "From the Internet's Past to the Future of Crypto." *16z Podcast on SoundCloud*. Accessed October 8, 2020. https://soundcloud.com/a16z/nternet-past-crypto-future-crypto-regulatory-summit.

Blystone, Dan. "The Story of Instagram: The Rise of the # 1 Photo-Sharing Application." *Investopedia*, August 29, 2020. https://www.investopedia.com/articles/investing/102615/story-instagram-rise-1-photoosharing-app.asp.

Breland, Ali. "Tech Talent Balks at Government Work." *The-Hill,* October 24, 2018. https://thehill.com/policy/technology/412854-tech-talent-balks-at-government-work.

Digital Magazine. "A Brief History of Slack." June 7, 2017. https://www.borndigital.com/2015/09/25/a-brief-history-of-slack-2015-09-25.

Environmental Protection Agency. "DDT Regulatory History: A Brief Survey (to 1975)." September 14, 2016. https://archive.epa.gov/epa/aboutepa/ddt-regulatory-history-brief-survey-1975.html.

Fulcrum Digital. "The Importance of Ethics in Technology Innovation." March 17, 2020. https://fulcrumdigital.com/the-importance-of-ethics-in-technology-innovation/.

High, Peter. "The Father of the Internet, Vint Cerf, Continues to Influence Its Growth." *Forbes Magazine,* March 26, 2018. https://www.forbes.com/sites/peterhigh/2018/03/26/the-father-of-the-internet-vint-cerf-continues-to-influence-its-growth/.

Hunt, Melissa G., Rachel Marx, Courtney Lipson, and Jordyn Young. "No More FOMO: Limiting Social Media Decreases Loneliness and Depression." *Journal of Social and Clinical Psychology* 37, no. 10 (2018). https://doi.org/10.1521/jscp.2018.37.10.751.

Locke, John. *The Works of John Locke in Nine Volumes.* London: Rivington, 1824 12th ed. August 10, 2020.

Matney, Lucas. "Zoom's Paid Usage Skyrockets as Remote Work Takes Over." *TechCrunch*, June 2, 2020. https://techcrunch.com/2020/06/02/zooms-paid-usage-skyrockets-as-remote-work-takes-over/?guccounter=1.

Merton, Robert K. "The Unanticipated Consequences of Purposive Social Action." *American Sociological Review* 1, no. 6 (1936). https://doi.org/10.2307/2084615.

Nice, Chuck. "Transcript of 'A Funny Look at the Unintended Consequences of Technology.'" *TED*, April 2017. https://www.ted.com/talks/chuck_nice_a_funny_look_at_the_unintended_consequences_of_technology/transcript?language=en.

O'Brien, Chris. "Slack IPO Starts Trading at $38.50 for $23 Billion Valuation." *VentureBeat*, June 20, 2019. https://venturebeat.com/2019/06/20/slack-ipo-starts-trading-at-38-50-for-23-billion-valuation/.

O'Connell, Brian. "History of Snapchat: Timeline and Facts." *TheStreet*, February 28, 2020. https://www.thestreet.com/technology/history-of-snapchat.

Scott, Andrew C. "When Did We Discover Fire? Here's What Experts Actually Know." *Time*, June 1, 2018. https://time.com/5295907/discover-fire/.

Smith, Adam. *The Theory of Moral Sentiments*. Edinburgh, 1761.

Stamos, Alex. "Working on Security and Safety with Zoom." *Medium*, April 8, 2020. https://medium.com/@alexstamos/working-on-security-and-safety-with-zoom-2f61f197cb34.

Tam, Donna. "Flickr Founder Plans to Kill Company e-Mails with Slack." *CNET*, August 14, 2013. https://www.cnet.com/news/flickr-founder-plans-to-kill-company-e-mails-with-slack/.

"The Internet's Original Sin." *Dark Reading* (blog), March 6, 2007. https://www.darkreading.com/risk-management/the-internets-original-sin/d/d-id/1052613.

Winter, Jessica. "Here's Why Instagram Is Even More Depressing than Facebook." *Slate Magazine*, July 23, 2013. https://slate.com/technology/2013/07/instagram-and-self-esteem-why-the-photo-sharing-network-is-even-more-depressing-than-facebook.html.

Wolverton, Troy. "The Internet's 'Father' Says It Was Born with Two Big Flaws." *Business Insider*, January 20, 2019. https://www.businessinsider.com/google-vint-cerf-explains-why-early-internet-lacked-security-and-room-2019-1?r=US&IR=T.

FLYWHEEL: WHAT HAPPENS IF YOU SUCCEED WILDLY?

Amazon Developer Services and Technologies. "What Is Automatic Speech Recognition?" Alexa Skills Kit. Accessed October 12, 2020. https://developer.amazon.com/en-US/alexa/alexa-skills-kit/asr.

Amazon Web Services. "Amazon Web Services (AWS)—Cloud Computing Services." Accessed October 8, 2020. https://pages.awscloud.com/EMEA-Data-Flywheel.html?nc1=f_ls.

Andersson, Hilary. "Social Media Apps Are 'Deliberately' Addictive to Users." *BBC News*, July 3, 2018. https://www.bbc.com/news/technology-44640959.

Beilfuss, Lisa. "The Latest Trend in Mobile Gaming: Stock-Trading Apps." *The Wall Street Journal*, January 22, 2019. https://www.wsj.com/articles/the-latest-trend-in-mobile-gaming-stock-trading-apps-11548158400.

Binkley, Christina. "Casino Chain Mines Data on Gamblers, And Strikes Pay Dirt with Low-Rollers." *The Wall Street Journal*, May 4, 2000. https://www.wsj.com/articles/SB957397104215402276.

"Casino Operator Overhauls Player Club Program." *Las Vegas Sun*, April 4, 2000. https://lasvegassun.com/news/2000/apr/04/casino-operator-overhauls-player-club-program/.

CB Insights. "The Data Flywheel: How Enlightened Self-Interest Drives Data Network Effects." CB Insights Research. *CB Insights*, October 16, 2019. https://www.cbinsights.com/research/team-blog/data-network-effects/.

Collins, James C. *Good to Great*. New York: Harper Business, 2001.

Davies, Rob. "Gambling Firms Criticised for 'Enticing' Loss-Making Customers." *The Guardian*, November 10, 2019. https://www.theguardian.com/society/2019/nov/10/gambling-firms-under-scrutiny-for-enticing-loss-making-customers.

Davies, Rob. "Problem Gamblers Much More Likely to Attempt Suicide—Study." *The Guardian*, July 19, 2019. https://www.

theguardian.com/society/2019/jul/19/problem-gamblers-much-more-likely-to-attempt-suicide-study.

Davies, Rob. "Report Shows Betting Industry's Reliance on Problem Gamblers." *The Guardian*, January 2, 2020. https://www.theguardian.com/society/2020/jan/02/gambling-report-shows-industrys-reliance-on-loss-making-customers.

Halligan, Brian. "Replacing the Sales Funnel with the Sales Flywheel." *Harvard Business Review*, November 20, 2018. https://hbr.org/2018/11/replacing-the-sales-funnel-with-the-sales-flywheel.

Harvard University. "B. F. Skinner." Department of Psychology. Accessed October 12, 2020. https://psychology.fas.harvard.edu/people/b-f-skinner.

Heaven, Will Douglas. "Video Game Addiction Is Now Being Recognized-What Happens next?" *MIT Technology Review*, June 17, 2020. https://www.technologyreview.com/2019/11/25/128/video-game-addiction-is-now-being-recognizedwhat-happens-next/.

Henderson, Richard, Robin Wigglesworth, and Eric Platt. "The Lockdown Death of a 20-Year-Old Day Trader: Free to Read." *Financial Times*, July 2, 2020. https://www.ft.com/content/45d0a047-360f-4abf-86ee-108f436015a1.

Husain, Az. "Casino Analytics Is Entering A New Renaissance." *Raving*, October 3, 2018. https://betravingknows.com/articles/data-analytics/2018/casino-analytics-is-entering-a-new-renaissance/.

ICRG. "Original Donors." Accessed October 12, 2020. https://www.icrg.org/about-ncrg/history/original-donors.

Johnson, Sharon. "5 Whys: What You Need to Know to Pass Your Six Sigma Certification Exam." *Six Sigma Study Guide*, August 26, 2019. https://sixsigmastudyguide.com/5-whys/.

Lal, Rajiv, and Patricia Carrolo. "Harrah's Entertainment Inc." *Harvard Business School Case 502-011*, October 2001. https://www.hbs.edu/faculty/Pages/item.aspx?num=28566.

Levy, Steven. "How Amazon Rebuilt Itself Around Artificial Intelligence." *Wired*, January 2, 2020. https://www.wired.com/story/amazon-artificial-intelligence-flywheel/.

"Problem Gamblers Much More Likely to Attempt Suicide—Study." *The Guardian*, July 19, 2019. https://www.theguardian.com/society/2019/jul/19/problem-gamblers-much-more-likely-to-attempt-suicide-study.

Robinhood. "Upgrading to Gold." Accessed October 8, 2020. https://robinhood.com/us/en/support/articles/upgrading-to-gold/.

Rodden, Kerry. "How to Choose the Right UX Metrics for Your Product." Medium. *GV Library*, December 17, 2015. https://library.gv.com/how-to-choose-the-right-ux-metrics-for-your-product-5f46359ab5be.

Rosengren, John. "How Casinos Enable Gambling Addicts." *The Atlantic*, November 15, 2016. https://www.theatlantic.com/magazine/archive/2016/12/losing-it-all/505814/.

Schüll Natasha Dow. *Addiction by Design Machine Gambling in Las Vegas*. Princeton, New Jersey: Princeton University Press, 2014.

Serrat, Olivier. "The Five Whys Technique." *Knowledge Solutions*, (2017). https://doi.org/10.1007/978-981-10-0983-9_32.

Staff and Wire. "Harrah's Entertainment Inc. Changes Name to Caesars Entertainment Corp." *Las Vegas Sun*, November 23, 2010. https://lasvegassun.com/news/2010/nov/23/us-harrahs-name-change/.

Terry, Jon. "The 5 Whys of Lean: Planview LeanKit." *Planview*, January 21, 2020. https://www.planview.com/resources/guide/lean-principles-101/5-whys-of-lean/.

Thompson, Andrew. "Slot Machines Perfected Addictive Gaming. Now, Tech Wants Their Tricks." *The Verge*, May 6, 2015. https://www.theverge.com/2015/5/6/8544303/casino-slot-machine-gambling-addiction-psychology-mobile-games.

Tom Knowles, West Coast Technology Reporter. "I'm so Sorry, Says Inventor of Endless Online Scrolling." *The Times*, April 27, 2019. https://www.thetimes.co.uk/article/i-m-so-sorry-says-inventor-of-endless-online-scrolling-9lrv59mdk.

Tsang, Edward, and Thom Fruehwirth. *Foundations of Constraint Satisfaction*. Norderstedt, Germany: Books on Demand, 1996.

Walker, Rob. "How Robinhood Convinced Millennials to Trade Their Way Through a Pandemic." Medium. *Marker*, June 15, 2020. https://marker.medium.com/how-robinhood-convinced-millennials-to-trade-their-way-through-a-pandemic-1a1db97c7e08.

Watercutter, Angela. "Doomscrolling Is Slowly Eroding Your Mental Health." *Wired*, January 2, 2020. https://www.wired.com/story/stop-doomscrolling.

Wohl, Michael J. A. "Loyalty Programmes in the Gambling Industry: Potentials for Harm and Possibilities for Harm-Minimization." *International Gambling Studies* (2018). https://doi.org/10.1080/14459795.2018.1480649.

Wursthorn, Michael, and Euirim Choi. "Does Robinhood Make It Too Easy to Trade? From Free Stocks to Confetti." *The Wall Street Journal*, August 20, 2020. https://www.wsj.com/articles/confetti-free-stocks-does-robinhoods-design-make-trading-too-easy-11597915801.

HIJACK: WHO IS THE WORST (AND BEST) POSSIBLE USER?

Adler, David. "Silk Road: The Dark Side of Cryptocurrency." *Fordham Journal of Corporate and Financial Law*, February 21, 2018. https://news.law.fordham.edu/jcfl/2018/02/21/silk-road-the-dark-side-of-cryptocurrency/.

Amazon AWS. "Amazon Rekognition." Accessed October 29, 2020. https://aws.amazon.com/rekognition/.

App Annie State of Mobile 2020 Report. San Francisco, CA: App Annie, 2020. https://www.appannie.com/en/go/state-of-mobile-2020/.

"Apple's App Store Launches with More than 500 Apps." *AppleInsider*, July 10, 2008. https://appleinsider.com/articles/08/07/10/apples_app_store_launches_with_more_than_500_apps.

Beschizza, Rob. "A Brief History of IPhone Hacking." *Wired*, June 4, 2017. https://www.wired.com/2007/10/a-brief-history/.

Bradsher, Keith. "In Hong Kong's Crackdown on Protests, Face Mask Ban May Be the Start." *The New York Times*, October 6, 2019. https://www.nytimes.com/2019/10/06/world/asia/hong-kong-protests-face-mask-ban.html.

Burtsell, Richard. "Advocatus Diaboli." *The Catholic Encyclopedia. Vol. 1.* New York: Robert Appleton Company, 1907. http://www.newadvent.org/cathen/01168b.htm.

Cohen, Peter. "Apple Updates ITunes for the IPhone." *PCWorld*, June 29, 2007. https://www.pcworld.com/article/133590/article.html.

Denham, Elizabeth. "Blog: Live Facial Recognition Technology—Police Forces Need to Slow down and Justify Its Use." *ICO* (blog), October 31, 2019. https://ico.org.uk/about-the-ico/news-and-events/news-and-blogs/2019/10/live-facial-recognition-technology-police-forces-need-to-slow-down-and-justify-its-use/.

Dredge, Stuart. "Steve Jobs Resisted Third-Party Apps on IPhone, Biography Reveals." *The Guardian*, October 24, 2011. https://www.theguardian.com/technology/appsblog/2011/oct/24/steve-jobs-apps-iphone.

Gardiner, Sian. "IPhone in Numbers." *The Telegraph*, September 6, 2014. https://www.telegraph.co.uk/technology/apple/11074752/ iPhone-in-numbers.html.

Google Books. "Google Books Ngram Viewer." Accessed October 29, 2020. https://books.google.com/ngrams/ graph?content=red+teaming&year_start=1800&year_end= 2019&corpus=26&smoothing=3&case_insensitive=true&- direct_url=t4;,red teaming;,co;,so;;red teaming;,co;;Red Teaming;,co;;Red teaming;,co.

Hao, Karen. "The Two-Year Fight to Stop Amazon from Selling Face Recognition to the Police." *MIT Technology Review*, June 15, 2020. https://www.technologyreview.com/2020/06/12/1003482/ amazon-stopped-selling-police-face-recognition-fight/.

IBM. "IBM CEO's Letter to Congress on Racial Justice Reform." *THINKPolicy*(blog), July 2, 2020. https://www.ibm.com/blogs/ policy/facial-recognition-sunset-racial-justice-reforms/.

ICO Investigation into How the Police Use Facial Recognition Technology in Public Places. Wilmslow, UK: Information Commissioner's Office, 31 October 2019. https://ico.org.uk/media/ about-the-ico/documents/2616185/live-frt-law-enforcement- report-20191031.pdf.

Kuo, Lily. "China's Great Firewall Descends on Hong Kong Internet Users." *The Guardian*, July 8, 2020. https://www.theguardian. com/world/2020/jul/08/china-great-firewall-descends-hong- kong-internet-users.

Raviv, Shaun. "The Secret History of Facial Recognition." *Wired*, January 21, 2020. https://www.wired.com/story/secret-history-facial-recognition/.

"Schelling Point: Cooperating Without Communicating." *Naval*, December 29, 2019. https://nav.al/schelling-point.

Schelling, Thomas C. *The Strategy of Conflict*. Cambridge, Massachusetts: Harvard University Press, 1994.

Schmidt, Blake. "Hong Kong Police Already Have AI Tech That Can Recognize Faces." *Bloomberg News*, October 22, 2019. https://www.bloomberg.com/news/articles/2019-10-22/hong-kong-police-already-have-ai-tech-that-can-recognize-faces.

Silva, Matthew De. "Hong Kong Protestors Revive Mesh Networks to Preempt Internet Shutdown." *Quartz*, September 3, 2019. https://qz.com/1701045/hong-kong-protestors-use-bridgefy-to-preempt-internet-shutdown/.

Snell, Jason. "Apple Opens ITunes App Store." *Macworld*, July 10, 2008. https://www.macworld.com/article/1134380/app_store.html.

Stephens, Roya and Adarsh Mahesh. *State of the App Economy—6th Edition*. Washington, DC: The App Association, 2018. https://www.ftc.gov/system/files/documents/public_comments/2018/08/ftc-2018-0048-d-0121-155298.pdf.

"The Best Marketing Campaigns of All Time (And What Made Them So Successful)." *Alston & Clayden*, March 22, 2018. https://alstonclayden.ae/marketing-campaigns-time/.

Wakefield, Jane. "Hong Kong Protesters Using Bluetooth Bridgefy App." *BBC News*, September 3, 2019. https://www.bbc.co.uk/news/technology-49565587.

Walker, Rob. "Why Every CEO Needs to Think Like a Hacker, a Stalker, or a White Supremacist." Medium. *Marker*, September 9, 2019. https://marker.medium.com/why-every-ceo-needs-to-think-like-a-hacker-a-stalker-or-a-white-supremacist-8ef03fd6bf33.

Zenko, Mika. *Red Team: How to Succeed by Thinking like the Enemy*. New York: Basic Books, 2015.

BLACK BOX: WHAT ARE THE HIDDEN BIASES AND OUTPUTS?

"5 software bugs turned into features." *Bird Eats Bug* (blog). Accessed September 28, 2020. https://birdeatsbug.com/5-bugs-that-became-features.

Angwin, Julia, Jeff Larson. "Machine Bias." *ProPublica*, May 23, 2016. https://www.propublica.org/article/machine-bias-risk-assessments-in-criminal-sentencing.

Becker, Sascha. "Bugs That Were Turned into Features." *Medium*. Vollkorn Games, April 24, 2018. https://medium.com/vollkorn-games/bugs-that-were-turned-into-features-a0f435dc32b9.

"Externalities: Calculating the Hidden Costs of Products." Naval (blog), January 10, 2020. https://nav.al/externalities.

Foley, Katherine Ellen. "Viagra's Famously Surprising Origin Story Is Actually a Pretty Common Way to Find New Drugs." *Quartz*, September 10, 2017. https://qz.com/1070732/viagras-famously-surprising-origin-story-is-actually-a-pretty-common-way-to-find-new-drugs/.

Franks, Bill. *97 Things about Ethics Everyone in Data Science Should Know: Collective Wisdom from the Experts*. Sebastopol, CA: O'Reilly Media, Inc., 2020.

Heilweil, Rebecca. "Why Algorithms Can Be Racist and Sexist." *Vox*, February 18, 2020. https://www.vox.com/recode/2020/2/18/21121286/algorithms-bias-discrimination-facial-recognition-transparency.

Kreston, Rebecca. "The Psychic Energizer!: The Serendipitous Discovery of the First Antidepressant." *Discover Magazine*, November 19, 2019. https://www.discovermagazine.com/health/the-psychic-energizer-the-serendipitous-discovery-of-the-first-antidepressant.

Latour, Bruno, *Pandora's Hope*. Cambridge, MA: Harvard University Press, 1999.

Manyika, James, Jake Silberg, and Brittany Presten. "What Do We Do About the Biases in AI?" *Harvard Business Review*, October 25, 2019. https://hbr.org/2019/10/what-do-we-do-about-the-biases-in-ai.

"Microsoft 'Deeply Sorry' for Racist and Sexist Tweets by AI Chatbot." *The Guardian*, March 26, 2016. https://www.theguardian.

com/technology/2016/mar/26/microsoft-deeply-sorry-for-of-
fensive-tweets-by-ai-chatbot.

Stanway, David. "On Singles' Day, Green Groups Warn of China's
Surge in Packaging Waste." *Thomson Reuters*, November 11,
2019. https://www.reuters.com/article/us-singles-day-pollu-
tion-idUSKBN1XL0A4.

Turner-Lee, Nicol, Paul Resnick, and Genie Barton. "Algorithmic
Bias Detection and Mitigation: Best Practices and Policies
to Reduce Consumer Harms." *Brookings*, October 25, 2019.
https://www.brookings.edu/research/algorithmic-bias-de-
tection-and-mitigation-best-practices-and-policies-to-re-
duce-consumer-harms/.

Vartan, Starre. "Racial Bias Found in a Major Health Care Risk
Algorithm." *Scientific American*, October 24, 2019. https://www.
scientificamerican.com/article/racial-bias-found-in-a-major-
health-care-risk-algorithm/.

Vincent, James. "Twitter Taught Microsoft's AI Chatbot to Be
a Racist Asshole in Less than a Day." *The Verge*, March 24,
2016. https://www.theverge.com/2016/3/24/11297050/tay-mic-
rosoft-chatbot-racist.

UNCHARTED ZONE: WHERE COULD UNKNOWN UNKNOWNS COME FROM?

Aaker, Jennifer, Victoria Chang. "Obama and the Power of Social
Media and Technology." *Stanford Graduate School of Business*, 2009. https://www.gsb.stanford.edu/faculty-research/
case-studies/obama-power-social-media-technology.

Air Pollution Revealer. "Home." Accessed November 18, 2020. http://www.airpollution-revealer.com/ Algorithmic Justice League. Accessed November 4, 2020. https://www.ajl.org/.

Berners-Lee, Tim. "One Small Step for the Web..." *Medium*, January 2, 2019. https://medium.com/@timberners_lee/one-small-step-for-the-web-87f92217d085.

Berners-Lee, Tim. "Where Does the World Wide Web Go from Here?" *Wired*, January 2, 2020. https://www.wired.com/story/tim-berners-lee-world-wide-web-anniversary/.

CB Insights. "10 Early-Stage Open-Source Software Startups to Watch." *CB Insights Research*, June 26, 2020. https://www.cbinsights.com/research/open-source-startups-expert-intelligence/.

Dizikes, Peter. "Study: On Twitter, False News Travels Faster than True Stories." *MIT News*, March 8, 2018. https://news.mit.edu/2018/study-twitter-false-news-travels-faster-true-stories-0308.

"Facebook Ad Campaign Helped Donald Trump Win Election, Claims Executive." *BBC News*, January 8, 2020. https://www.bbc.com/news/technology-51034641.

Finley, Klint. "How Facebook Has Changed Computing." *Wired*, April 2, 2020. https://www.wired.com/story/how-facebook-has-changed-computing/.

Frank, Adam. "An Imagined Future Speaks In 'Talking to Robots'." *NPR*, July 19, 2019. https://www.npr.org/2019/07/19/743416668/an-imagined-future-speaks-in-talking-to-robots?t=1605650324214.

Knowledge@Wharton. "How Social Media Is Shaping Political Campaigns." August 17, 2020. https://knowledge.wharton.upenn.edu/article/how-social-media-is-shaping-political-campaigns/.

Lapowsky, Issie. "This Is How Facebook Actually Won Trump the Presidency." *Wired*, June 3, 2017. https://www.wired.com/2016/11/facebook-won-trump-election-not-just-fake-news/.

Larcinese, Valentino and Luke Miner. "The Political Impact of the Internet on US Presidential Elections." *STICERD—Economic Organisation and Public Policy Discussion Papers Series*, Suntory and Toyota International Centres for Economics and Related Disciplines, LSE (2017). https://sticerd.lse.ac.uk/dps/eopp/eopp63.pdf.

Lasar, Matthew. "The Man Who Foresaw Science Fiction." *Ars Technica*, May 3, 2010. https://arstechnica.com/tech-policy/2010/05/ralph-124c-41-a-century-later/.

Levy, Ari, and Salvador Rodriguez. "Why Political Campaigns Are Flooding Facebook with Ad Dollars." *CNBC*, October 9, 2020. https://www.cnbc.com/2020/10/08/trump-biden-pacs-spend-big-on-facebook-as-election-nears.html.

Making Tomorrow. "Hello Tomorrow—Design Fiction for Corporate Strategies." March 25, 2019. Vimeo video. https://vimeo.com/326333140?mc_cid=d40cb87416&mc_eid=4736becbdd.

Marvin, Rob. "The Biggest Tech Mergers and Acquisitions of All Time." *PCMag UK*, July 9, 2019. https://uk.pcmag.com/facebook/117931/the-biggest-tech-mergers-and-acquisitions-of-all-time?p=1.

Meyer, Robinson. "The Grim Conclusions of the Largest-Ever Study of Fake News." *The Atlantic*, March 12, 2018. https://www.theatlantic.com/technology/archive/2018/03/largest-study-ever-fake-news-mit-twitter/555104/.

Miller, Alice. "David Ewing Duncan Is Ready for the Robot Revolution." *Vanity Fair*, July 12, 2019. https://www.vanityfair.com/style/2019/07/david-ewing-duncan-talking-to-robots-interview.

Orphanides, K.G. "How Tim Berners-Lee's Inrupt Project Plans to Fix the Web." *Wired*, February 14, 2019. https://www.wired.co.uk/article/inrupt-tim-berners-lee.

Perrigo, Billy. "Web Founder Tim Berners-Lee on the Future of the Internet." *Time*, March 12, 2019. https://time.com/5549635/tim-berners-lee-interview-web/.

Piper, Kelsey. "Microsoft wants to build artificial general intelligence: an AI better than humans at everything." *Vox*, July 22, 2019. https://www.vox.com/2019/7/22/20704184/microsoft-open-ai-billion-investment-artificial-intelligence.

Sande, Steve. "Arthur C. Clarke's 2001 Newspad Finally Arrives, Nine Years Late." *Engadget*, February 7, 2020. https://www.engadget.com/2010-01-28-arthur-c-clarkes-2001-newspad-finally-arrives-nine-years-late.html.

Schulze, Elizabeth. "The Inventor of the Web Says the Internet Is Broken—but He Has a Plan to Fix It." *CNBC*, November 6, 2018. https://www.cnbc.com/2018/11/05/inventor-of-the-web-says-the-internet-is-at-a-tipping-point-and-reveals-a-new-plan-to-fix-it.html.

Shearer, Elisa, and Elizabeth Grieco. "Americans Are Wary of the Role Social Media Sites Play in Delivering the News." *Pew Research Center's Journalism Project*, August 27, 2020. https://www.journalism.org/2019/10/02/americans-are-wary-of-the-role-social-media-sites-play-in-delivering-the-news/.

"Smartphone Market Share—OS." IDC, September 14, 2020. https://www.idc.com/promo/smartphone-market-share/os.

Smith, Aaron. "The Internet's Role in Campaign 2008." *Pew Research Center*, August 28, 2020. https://www.pewresearch.org/internet/2009/04/15/the-internets-role-in-campaign-2008/.

Solid. "Home." Accessed October 19, 2020. https://solidproject.org/.

World Wide Web Consortium. "Tim Berners-Lee." People. Last modified September 18, 2020. https://www.w3.org/People/Berners-Lee/.

World Wide Web Foundation. "History of the Web." The Web. Accessed November 4, 2020. https://webfoundation.org/about/vision/history-of-the-web/.

World Wide Web Foundation. "Net Neutrality in Europe: A Statement from Sir Tim Berners-Lee." October 26, 2015. https://

webfoundation.org/2015/10/net-neutrality-in-europe-a-state-ment-from-sir-tim-berners-lee/.

FAIRNESS DEBT: THE SHADOW TWIN OF TECHNICAL DEBT

Bartlett, Robert, Adair Morse, Richard Stanton, and Nancy Wallace. "Consumer-Lending Discrimination in the FinTech Era." *NBER Working Paper* No. 25943 (June2019). https://doi.org/10.3386/w25943.

Bureau of Consumer Financial Protection. "Fair Lending Report." 2019. https://files.consumerfinance.gov/f/documents/201909_cfpb_corrected-2018-fair-lending_report.pdf.

Christopher M. D'Angelo. *Letter to Consumer Financial Protection Bureau*, September 14, 2017. https://files.consumerfinance.gov/f/documents/201709_cfpb_upstart-no-action-letter.pdf

Ficklin, Patrice Alexander and Paul Watkins. "An Update on Credit Access and the Bureau's First No-Action Letter." *Consumer Financial Protection Bureau*, August 6, 2019. https://www.consumerfinance.gov/about-us/blog/update-credit-access-and-no-action-letter/.

Freeman-Spogli Institute. "Alex Stamos." Accessed on October 6, 2020. https://cisac.fsi.stanford.edu/people/alex-stamos-0.

Rodden, Kerry. "How to Choose the Right UX Metrics for Your Product." GV Library. *Medium*, December 17, 2015. https://library.gv.com/how-to-choose-the-right-ux-metrics-for-your-product-5f46359ab5be.

Stamos, Alex. "Working on Security and Safety with Zoom." *Medium*, April 8, 2020. https://medium.com/@alexstamos/working-on-security-and-safety-with-zoom-2f61f197cb34.

"Upstart Receives First No-Action Letter Issued by Consumer Financial Protection Bureau." *Upstart* (blog), September 13, 2018. https://www.upstart.com/blog/upstart-receives-first-no-action-letter-issued-consumer-financial-protection-bureau.

Warren, Elizabeth, and Doug Jones. Letter to Jerome H. Powell, Joseph M. Otting, Jelena McWilliams and Kathy Kraninger. "Letter to Regulators on Fintech." June 10, 2019. http://faculty.haas.berkeley.edu/morse/media/2019.6.10%20Letter%20to%20Regulators%20on%20Fintech%20FINAL1.pdf.

Warren, Tom. "Zoom Grows to 300 Million Meeting Participants despite Security Backlash." *The Verge*, April 23, 2020. https://www.theverge.com/2020/4/23/21232401/zoom-300-million-users-growth-coronavirus-pandemic-security-privacy-concerns-response.

THE (PRETTY) GOOD, THE BAD, AND THE UGLY: NOT ALL FAIRNESS DEBT IS CREATED EQUAL

Corbett-Davies, Sam, Emma Pierson, Avi Feller, Sharad Goel, and Aziz Huq. "Algorithmic Decision Making and the Cost of Fairness." *Proceedings of the 23rd ACM SIGKDD International Conference on Knowledge Discovery and Data Mining* (2017). https://doi.org/10.1145/3097983.3098095.

Davila, Florangela. "USDA disqualifies three Somalian markets from accepting federal food stamps." *The Seattle Times,*

April 10, 2002. https://archive.seattletimes.com/archive/?-
date=20020410&slug=somalis10m.

Hampshire, Adam, Roger R. Highfield, Beth L. Parkin, and Adrian
M. Owen. "Fractionating Human Intelligence." *Neuron* 76, no.
6 (2012). https://doi.org/10.1016/j.neuron.2012.06.022.

Marcus, Gary. "Deep Learning: A Critical Appraisal." ArX-
iv:1801.00631 (2018). https://arxiv.org/abs/1801.00631

Parvaz, D. "USDA Reverses Itself, to Somali Grocers' Relief." *Seattle Post-Intelligencer*, March 12, 2011. https://www.seattlepi.
com/news/article/USDA-reverses-itself-to-Somali-grocers-re-
lief-1091449.php.

Stuart, Guy. "Databases, Felons, and Voting: Errors and Bias in
the Florida Felons Exclusion List in the 2000 Presidential Elections." *SSRN Electronic Journal* (2002). https://doi.org/10.2139/
ssrn.336540.

Weber, Lauren. "Today's Personality Tests Raise the Bar for Job
Seekers." *The Wall Street Journal*, April 15, 2015. https://www.
wsj.com/articles/a-personality-test-could-stand-in-the-way-
of-your-next-job-1429065001.

THE SIX ES OF INCLUSION

Harrison, Sara. "Five Years of Tech Diversity Reports-and Little
Progress." *Wired*, January 10, 2019. https://www.wired.com/
story/five-years-tech-diversity-reports-little-progress/.

Web Accessibility Initiative (WAI). "Web Content Accessibility Guidelines (WCAG) Overview." Last updated September, 22 2020. https://www.w3.org/WAI/standards-guidelines/wcag/.

West, Frances. *Authentic Inclusion Drives Disruptive Innovation.* Newton, MA: FrancesWestCo, 2018.

THREE OPPORTUNITIES FOR ANALOG COMPANIES TRANSITIONING TO DIGITAL

Atluri, Venkat, Miklós Dietz, and Nicolaus Henke, "Competing in a world of sectors without borders." *McKinsey Quarterly*, July 12, 2017.https://www.mckinsey.com/business-functions/mckinsey-analytics/our-insights/competing-in-a-world-of-sectors-without-borders.

Laney, Douglas B. "Your Company's Data May Be Worth More Than Your Company." *Forbes*, July 2020. https://www.forbes.com/sites/douglaslaney/2020/07/22/your-companys-data-may-be-worth-more-than-your-company/?sh=768665a4634c.

GAPS AND ABUNDANCE: REBOOTED INTERNET ACCESS

Bacher-Hicks, Andrew, Joshua Goodman and Christine Mulhern. "Inequality in Household Adaptation to Schooling Shocks: Covid-Induced Online Learning." *National Bureau of Economic Research, Working Paper No. 27555* (July 2020). http://www.nber.org/papers/w27555.

Harris, Douglas N., Lihan Liu, Daniel Oliver, Cathy Balfe, Sara Slaughter, and Nicholas Mattei. "How America's Schools Responded to the COVID Crisis." *National Center for Research on Education Access and Choice, Technical Report,* July 13, 2020. https://educationresearchalliancenola.org/files/publications/20200713-Technical-Report-Harris-et-al-How-Americas-Schools-Responded-to-the-COVID-Crisis.pdf.

New America Foundation. "Closing the Home Learning and Homework Gap." Event, June 25, 2020. https://www.newamerica.org/oti/events/closing-home-learning-and-homework-gap/.

W. Hazlett, Thomas. *The Political Spectrum: The Tumultuous Liberation of Wireless Technology, From Herbert Hoover to the Smartphone.* London: Yale University Press, 2017, p. 2.

FOUR TAKEAWAYS FOR POLICYMAKERS IN THE REBOOTED ECONOMY

Gauthier, JF, and Arnobio Morelix. "Governments, Don't Let your Startups and Scaleups Die." *Startup Genome,* April 2020. https://startupgenome.com/reports/well_designed_funding_policy_crisis.

CPSIA information can be obtained
at www.ICGtesting.com
Printed in the USA
FSHW020303240221
78886FS

9 781636 763132